OUTRAGEOUS HERO
The B.T. Collins Story

OUTRAGEOUS HERO

The B.T. Collins Story

By

MAUREEN COLLINS BAKER

BRYCE HILL PUBLISHING
SUNNYVALE, CALIFORNIA

OUTRAGEOUS HERO
The B.T. Collins Story

Published in the United States
by
Bryce Hill Publishing
P.O. Box 2133
Sunnyvale, CA 94087-0133
www.brycehillpublishing.com

Cover & Book Design by
Arrow Graphics, Inc.
info@arrow1.com
Printed in the United States of America

Library of Congress Cataloging-in-Publication Data

Baker, Maureen Collins
Outrageous Hero: The B.T. Collins Story / Maureen Collins Baker
p. cm.
Library of Congress Control Number: 2008922772
ISBN 978-0-9798697-4-7

1. Baker, Maureen C.
2. B.T. Collins 3. Politician—California—Memoir.

First Edition

For those gentle heroes he left behind,
who willed him their tomorrows;
for the "Annies" who kept him alive
to make the world a better place;
and for my hero,
my sister Marialis
without whom "Outrageous Hero"
would never have seen the light of day.

CONTENTS

PROLOGUE

I had always planned to write about my brother, B.T. Collins. We were alike in ways that created a strong and sentimental bond between us. Progeny of parents who had survived the Depression and weathered a world war, we had been raised to honor the principles of their generation. I cared passionately about his causes. I shared his outrage and his despair over honor lost and values trashed. I cried when he couldn't, both my tears and those he was too disciplined to shed.

I wanted him to see how proud I was of all he had become. I wanted to celebrate his accomplishments in print, to show how he had turned personal misfortune into an incredibly successful life.

Then he died.

But it is not too late to tell his story, one that began as a tribute to the man he was and became a tale of how heroes are made.

He started out a kid, a skinny red-haired kid who threw a rolled-up newspaper on your lawn and drove his parents and the girls, (even when they were no longer "girls"), crazy. He was just a kid who went to war, and went again, and returned physically half, but mentally, a man times two . . . and more; the boy next door who grew up to be the kind of American we used to be proud to be and now have too often forgotten.

He was not a household word, although he was well on his way to becoming one. He never could keep his mouth shut, a trait that earned him slots on all the major news networks and in many of the world's best-known newspapers and magazines. The antics of government since his death would have provided ample fodder for his verbal cannons.

B.T. stood simply for Brien Thomas (our mother was an O'Brien), not "Big Time," as he would have had us believe. He was a Vietnam veteran, California's living legend born in New York. He was a Republican widely admired by Democrats, a conservative who played pied piper to those he laughingly called "whining, hand-wringing liberals," a one-armed, one legged warrior who made anti-war activists stop in their tracks and re-examine their positions. If you had met him, you would have remembered him. If you knew him or only knew of him, you would have formed a strong opinion. He was not for the faint of heart. He never bored. No one was blasé about B.T. Collins.

When he died, people spoke of "knowing him," even some who had never actually met him. Many, even those who spoke less kindly of him when he was alive, called him a "hero." His comments on these late-in-the-day fans would have been absolutely brutal. Never a hero in his own eyes, he particularly disapproved of the term when attached to his military service. The loss of his arm and leg, to his mind, was an accident of combat, not an act of courage, ("I throw grenades like a girl."), an event for which he held himself ultimately responsible, although he had been decorated on more than one occasion for his actions under fire.

"Outrageous" was the adjective with which he could more easily identify. And he was that: a near-blasphemous public persona, honed to his own standards of perfect imperfection.

In an age when so few have the courage of their convictions, he flaunted his. In an era when words are minced and sentences parsed, he played with neither terms nor tenses. In major ways and small ways, his words became deeds.

He offered to donate his organs, what few he had left.

He gave blood and made you give yours.

He strode past a parade of protesters, minus an arm and a leg, and registered for the draft.

He listened, he read, he acted, he led; not by plebiscite or in acquiescence to polls, but based on what he honestly believed.

B.T. Collins made you cheer. You rose to your feet when he finished speaking, and you stood a little taller when he walked by. He made you laugh when you wanted to cry. He made you cry when you had never cried before, at least in a public place, over something sentimental like courage or country. He could make you feel so good . . . or so bad, (if he wanted your money).

He was the quintessential con man. But he wasn't selling snake oil or the Brooklyn Bridge. The products he pushed were rules to live by.

He survived disfigurement and pain with humor and uncommon courage. He rose each day and thumped across the bedroom to the bathroom where he stood one-legged to brush his teeth and shave. He painstakingly dressed himself, although an on-site Sears' repairman one morning had to zip his fly. He dragged a length of wood around all day and never mentioned it; he slipped on a leather holster that ended in a metal hook, shook your right hand with his left, and made believe it didn't matter.

He returned to college among the physically whole and the politically disenchanted after failing twice as a student himself. Wearing his fatigue jacket with its First Air Cavalry patch, he walked into classrooms filled with bearded, bead-wearing, anti-war classmates, who had burned flags and draft cards while his friends lay dying . . . and he never hit anyone.

He stood by his troops. And over the years there were multiple battlefields and troops of every size, age, and color. He called us to task, yanking our increasingly complacent American chains. He got our goat and refused, absolutely refused, to let it go.

"Old soldiers" may "just fade away." B.T. Collins wasn't into fading. Old warriors leave tracks . . . on your heart and mind, soul and psyche. They amputate. When they finally go, they take part of you with them.

B.T. Collins was an *old* warrior. He just died young.

That he was not without fault, he let you know within minutes of meeting him. He drank: too much, and for too long a time. He refused to apply himself academically. He broke more hearts than Valentino and Casanova combined. He was committed to causes and country, but never, forever, to the women he loved who loved him. Women were drawn to him . . . flies to risky honey . . . in embarrassing numbers. *He* wasn't embarrassed, but the family found the sheer quantity of his conquests, shall we say, "disconcerting."

"Did he never marry?" the unknowing have asked, sympathetically.

"No time," he would have replied.

"No guts," the actual answer. His capacity for loving far outdistanced his ability to live up to its obligations. "Marrying me would be like getting warts," he joked. "Find someone healthier, more reliable," he advised.

The real message: "choose someone worthy of you; someone who won't come up short."

Yet, once a relationship ended, he wouldn't let go. Christmas would come and there'd be flying lessons, or the offer to pay for a daughter's college tuition, or dog food for a new puppy. Small, and some not so small, kindnesses that said, "It's my fault, not yours."

Impossible to live with; impossible to live without, "He was," a nun once said, "the orneriest son-of-a-bitch I ever loved." No one could make you so angry and still leave you laughing. His good deeds were legion, his politically incorrect behavior and loud mouth legendary. Eloquent, crass, straightforward, yet inalterably complex, he pushed and pulled within the confines of a single moment. He could make you blush with embarrassment and flush with pride on the same occasion. Polarized, he saw every issue as black and white, but threw out all the rules for a comrade-in-arms, the unprotected, the abused. He told the truth . . . always, and for the politically cynical, this was a temptation too sweet to resist. He became a total anomaly for those who understand service only in proportion to what's in it for them.

Resolutely in control, he still cried like a baby at the touch of a single name engraved in a great granite wall. The only way to know him, really know him, was to be able to cut through the enormous load of bullshit and blarney of which he was the undisputed master. Those who failed to do this; those who bought his line, had more than had the wool pulled over their eyes . . . they'd missed the very essence of the man, and the experience of a lifetime.

As a biographer, I make no claim to impartiality, although I have traveled the country, watched miles of videotape, and conducted over 300 interviews before completing my brother's story. I have written to let you know B.T. Collins. I have written to honor heroes, and to preserve our memory of his kind of American. I have written out of love for my brother *and* for my country.

Once we were once a nation of Patrick Henrys and Nathan Hales, of "Give me liberty or give me death," of regrets that we had "*but one life* to give to our country." We were both our own and our brother's keepers. It wasn't necessary to defend defending our country and what it stands for. Lately, telling the truth or taking a stand represents risks not lightly undertaken. Concern for the common good too often pales in the glare of personal gain.

My brother believed we are better than that.

And I'm thinking. We could use another B.T. Collins or two, or three, or a million or more.

I

THE WAKE

---·•◆•·---

"Why are you crying," his mother asked gently.
"A little girl pushed me," he managed between sobs.
"So, what did you do?" his mother responded.
"I told her, 'You are a very rude little girl.'"

B.T. Collins, age 4

He hollered, "Grenade!" just before it went off. Then his body followed the blast, soaring in seeming slow motion into the sweat-soaked air. It returned to earth, hitting the hardened ground with jarring force, a human body bag of bones and sinew torn asunder. He sat still in a scarlet pool of his own making; the jungle's brittle grasses turned brown-red beneath him. The heat made waves in the surrounding light, but he was cold . . . so cold. He cried out in anguish to the blur of human forms nearby.

For one ever so brief moment, he thought, *so this is what it all comes down to.* And he knew that he was dying.

My brother, B.T. Collins, did not die that day in Vietnam. On the contrary, he was reborn. June 20, 1967 became his "life-day;" one he would celebrate for the next 26 years. All that he subsequently became, he believed, dated from that moment in the Mekong. His age matched the time he had left. And he would squeeze more living into those few years than most people manage in 100.

He'd made a promise to the dead to live in their stead. It was a promise kept. To use his own phrase, "The world would be different because he was there." The payback for having been saved began.

In the end, he died without permission. It hadn't been discussed. While he understood responsibility to his country, he forgot that *being loved* carried its load as well. He went, thoughtlessly, without saying goodbye. He had told us he would live forever. Beneath the hurt of those he left behind, there was a gnawing, understandable anger. How could he do such a thing? How dare he so invade us, body and soul, then take off without so much as a by-your-leave?

There had been warnings, of course, but those close to him were too terrified to pay attention. A diabetic with a heart condition, he had pushed himself beyond all reasonable limits. He began to walk a line so tight, so close to the edge, that dying young was inevitable. It was a predictable outcome for which we were, nevertheless, ill prepared.

While no one is invincible, he had so long pretended to be, that people had been conned into believing that lie, as they had so many others. He didn't really want to get married. He didn't mind not having an arm and a leg. He never worried. Asking him to slow down was asking the impossible, for B.T. Collins was in a hurry. There was so much yet to be done and so little time, so little time. Less, it turned out, than even he had imagined.

He had a massive coronary on his way to a luncheon at which the Chairman of the Joint Chiefs of Staff was speaking. To friends waiting for him at an annual Saint Patrick's Day celebration, he joked, "I'll be a little late; Colin Powell wants to have his picture taken with me."

Begged by his staff to cut back on his schedule, he was going to do one last bit before resting; voice his support for the retention of California's threatened McClellan Air Force Base. He reached the inn where the General was speaking, only to collapse outside the dining room door. A friend watched him stand very tall, shoulders square, mixed image of the ramrod soldier he once had been and the care-worn warrior he had become, those inimitable blue eyes fixed on some distant yonder. Then he sighed and was done.

My brother had always responded to personal health crises with sarcasm. Once, while being transferred on a gurney in a hospital elevator, he announced to those sharing the space, gesturing with the hook that replaced his right arm, "You come into this place with a heart attack, and look what happens to you." Beneath the sheets lay the obvious outline of a missing right leg. The non-patients were understandably disconcerted.

On this last occasion, however, he was still—minus insults, rolling eyes, and smart remarks—his already pale complexion gone blue-gray.

The news went out like a shot. In those days, everything B.T. Collins said or did was recorded somewhere. Crowds gathered at Sacramento's Sutter General and later, at Mercy Hospital. They lined the halls of the emergency wing; they stood rows deep in the waiting rooms and on the sidewalks outside. An eight-hour vigil began.

"We came because we had to," Senator Leroy Greene explained, "because we wanted to, because we needed to." Ironically, B.T. had promised Greene on the latter's 70th birthday that he didn't need to worry because he wouldn't run against the senator until he died.

Mercy Hospital administrator, Sister Kathleen Horgan, commented she had never seen so many people so upset over a single patient. But she understood. They were a pair these two, he so tall and she so tiny: co-conspirators in a series of charitable causes. Pictures of them showed her tilting her head way back just for eye contact when they spoke, he the redheaded Irishman from New York and she, the nun, with the brogue straight from Dublin. For years, he had irreverently referred to her and to her fellow sisters as "those bimbos in blue." Yet, she knew the man beneath the mouth and prayed for his immortal soul, for which he claimed to care not a wit.

A family friend found our sister on the golf course. *It must be serious this time*, Marialis thought. *They've come to get me*. They drove immediately from Sunnyvale to Sacramento, California's heavy traffic holding them back. Arriving, she saw the press and crowds in front of the hospital and she was afraid. A member of our brother's inner circle pushed through the cameras to meet her.

Brien was as loud as Marialis was quiet, as brusque as she was gentle. Yet, each kept a sensitive side well hidden. They were the family redheads, growing up a pair, only 13 months apart. His often improper and roundly unbelievable behavior embarrassed her. But now he was quiet. Reaching his room, she heard only the wheeze of multiple machines and the hush of his dying. Bruised and bloated from hours of heroic efforts to keep him alive, he was, she told me, scarcely recognizable. He had fought the good battle and lost.

On the south side of Chicago, the phone rang in my university office. The news was bad, very bad. Racing home along the city's Lake Shore Drive I prayed out loud, crying in the car, pounding the steering wheel, "Please, God, please," I begged. My home phone rang at intervals the rest of the afternoon. At 8:00 that evening, it was over. Although a team of doctors had worked furiously to save him, Brien Thomas (B.T.) Collins, California Assemblyman, Vietnam veteran, everybody's best friend, and my brother, died on March 19, 1993. He was 52 years old.

To lose a younger brother leaves a hole. To lose a B.T. Collins left an abyss. It was as if our world cracked open, and we all fell in. The man was an event. He consumed any space he entered with sheer size, noise, and ideology. After spending time with him, you staggered forth thinking, *I need a drink, a therapist, my mother. My God! Who is this guy anyway?*

He was the family black sheep, who caused us all considerable angst. We winced at his colorful vocabulary. We worried when he drank. When he partied his way out of the University of Pennsylvania, my mother cried. Mother *never* cried.

Nevertheless, we were proud of his celebrity status. It was fun to slide into a seat on an airline, open the newspaper offered and see his face or read his comments. I got a kick out of telling friends to "watch *ABC* tonight," or "pick up the latest issue of *People* Magazine." Most important to the family after Vietnam, he was alive. And, Mother added, "not in jail."

But now he was gone. All gone. Forever.

The day following his death, B.T.'s fellow Vietnam veteran, Andy Anderson, met me at the Sacramento airport, holding a sign that read, "The Older Sister." B.T. loved introducing me as such, volunteering my age, inflated by several years, because I looked so much younger than he. Reaching the house I knew so well, I entered as a stranger. The rooms were packed with friends who were answering phones, taking messages, making lists. My brother kept friends, family, and volunteers apart. It was a combat thing that soldiers understand—something about not putting all your love in one basket, a subtle form of insurance against losing everyone who matters in a single swoop.

How many of us in that house had put all our eggs in his basket? I wondered. I came close. He had always been there for me, and I counted on him to continue.

Marialis, came forward. There was neither the space nor the time to speak privately. And there was nothing to say . . . nothing. This time he'd really *done it*, and no amount of whispered Hail Mary's or silent pleas to God Almighty would bring him back. We hugged. I thought maybe if I could feel her arms around me, it hadn't really happened.

We joined his inner circle outside by the pool. His friends were planning a massive final salute. Numb, we simply nodded in acquiescence to every suggestion made. I had not yet grasped to what extent B.T. was important. It seemed odd that others were planning my brother's funeral.

There was to be a private wake, a mass at Sacramento's Sacred Heart Cathedral, and a public memorial. An old-fashioned Irish wake would follow, with music and dancing, and food and entertainment. The funeral director was confounded by the fact that B.T., *cum casket*, would be present at all the functions planned. No way, we were going to let him miss his own party!

The mass was a given, although B.T. had made much of the fact that he didn't believe in God. It had been a long time since he had been to church for anything other than a wedding or a funeral. A local nun, not Sister Kathleen, had actually used his well-advertised lack of faith to raise money for charity. The raffle prize was B.T.'s attendance at mass with the sister in question. In the end, a considerable sum was collected in anticipation of his presence in a house of worship.

B.T.'s beliefs aside, this mass was also in deference to my mother and father's memory, not to mention the saving of his immortal soul to which he laid no claim. Our parents had found B.T.'s declarations of atheism and or agnosticism incomprehensible . . . something he would simply get over. But he had an ironclad rule about never recanting anything. His public proclamation of godlessness was more likely due to an attempt to annoy rather than to any deep thoughts about dogma which he certainly entertained.

One local Catholic was outraged. "In celebrating the mass, the Bishop would clearly be in violation of church law." B.T., whom she described in a letter to the editor as, "a notorious apostate who had not repented was not to be provided with ecclesiastical rights."

Apostate!

He would have loved that! He probably would have changed publicly from agnostic to apostate as he had changed from atheist to agnostic, his only exception to his famous inflexibility. "Nobody," he declared, "asked my religion when I went to Vietnam."

Those who knew him realized he did protest too much. Old B.T. only voiced the inner doubts of many Christians, Jews, Buddhists, whomever. When the winds come and the crops fail and the bullets rain, where is God? When the innocent and unprotected lie dying, murdered, suffering, where in the hell is God?

The standard Catholic reply that this could all be laid at the feet of man's inhumanity to man just didn't wash with him.

The open-by-invitation-only wake on the first night was jammed. Over 500 came that evening, from every phase of B.T.'s life. There were childhood friends: Steven Galef, about whom my father used to tease, "Why can't you be like that nice Jewish kid?"; Dick Ehrlich, the subject of an article B.T. had written for the *Wall Street Journal*; and Bob Simpson, whose young son was one of B.T.'s many godchildren. There were veterans: John Philp who had traded pain and insults with B.T. in an Army hospital; Henry Cook and Ruben Garcia who had been with him in the Special Forces; and Joe Forgione, Dave Porreca, and Dean Parker who had served with B.T. in Vietnam in the First Air Cavalry. Politicians and fellow hell raisers like former Reagan presidential adviser Ed Rollins were in abundance. B.T. had rudely managed to die on Rollins' birthday.

B.T.'s closed coffin was covered with my father's flag. When our father retired as principal of the Midland School in Rye, New York, the faculty presented it to him in honor of his well-known love of country. The evening's emcee was the President of Santa Clara University, Reverend Paul Locatelli. B.T. had finished his undergraduate and law degrees at this Jesuit institution.

I was touched by the fact that this priest was unable to maintain his composure, supposedly routine in one who presides over death and dying. It was a tough night. Denial hung heavy on the air, yet the deceased repeatedly supplied the desperately needed comic relief.

Messages had been sent from the famous and near famous who were not able to attend. Among them was a letter from Jerry Brown's father, former Governor, Edmund "Pat" Brown. He said that he counted B.T. among those who in times of crisis surmount incalculable odds, that our nation had lost a real hero, the state of California, a dedicated public servant, and the people, a champion.

I wondered, as the letter was read, how many of those present remembered the six-page article in a 1981 Sunday *Los Angeles Times*, in which B.T., stalked by a reporter, during a bout of late night drinking, had complained about the younger Brown. Everything from the Governor's failure to wash his hair, drive a better car, and tune into the people had been divulged. Brown Senior had been among the first to call for my brother's resignation. Yet, later private correspondence revealed Governor Pat Brown's forgiveness and fondness for B.T. Over the years, B.T. had written the former Governor often, signing his letters affectionately, "Your second son."

Condolences came from former San Francisco Mayor George Christopher. The Mayor warned that recovering from B.T.'s death might take longer than we imagined. Tula, his wife of 55 years, had died suddenly two years before, and he missed her more, rather than less, each day. Six months after her death, he recalled, B.T. had driven to San Francisco to meet him for lunch. On that occasion, he described B.T. as, "Not his usual fun loving self, but, rather, the epitome of consoling silence."

When Christopher visited his wife's grave later that day, he found a huge bouquet of roses at the foot of the stone. The accompanying card read simply, *Tula, the old man really misses you! B.T.*

The roses were symbolic. Years before, Mayor Christopher had invited Khrushchev to visit him in San Francisco. He greeted the Russian leader with an armload of roses. The roses, he explained, were for the "boss." He then presented them to Mrs. Khrushchev.

The eulogies began with B.T.'s long-time right arm, confidante, and chief of staff, Nora Romero. She was the general and B.T. merely the company commander. Without her, the family literally would have lost its mind. She made sure we got advance notice of each of his wild exploits before they hit the national news. Nora and B.T. had been together for 17 years. They were a team. Whenever and wherever B.T. worked, Nora was part of the package. She had seen him in every degree of disarray and triumph. In truth, she'd ceased long before to have a life of her own. She covered for him. She picked up the pieces. She lectured him, too often to no avail.

Her most outstanding and life-saving trait may well have been her sense of humor. She invited B.T.'s former girlfriends to his annual birthday parties. Such additions increased the guest list substantially, and to his chagrin and her delight, they all came. B.T. had amassed a 9,000-name long file of friends, relatives, and contacts. He had made a habit of remembering birthdays, anniversaries, and other special moments. Nora explained that she, too, got birthday cards and phone calls, but she was left to pick out her own flowers and sign her own card appropriately.

And I remembered:

"Happy Birthday," he had fairly chirped on his annual call. "So, how does it feel to be half a century?"

"It feels old."

"But, Maureen, you *are* old."

"Hmm. Well, just make sure you live this long and that you look this good if you do!"

"Maureen, I always look good and I'm going to live forever."

He lied.

My son, Patrick, stepped forward with an enormous Rolodex in each hand. He was in tears, but made no apologies for his show of emotion. He said he had learned "from my grandfather and my uncle Brien that real men do cry."

My husband, Victor, stood to tell the crowd that, "B.T. Collins should have been named 'McCoy' because he was uncompromisingly true to what he believed was right." He didn't mention that B.T., ever the protective brother, had had him investigated before we were married. Apparently, the results of the investigation were satisfactory, because when Victor had a heart attack shortly thereafter, B.T. sent him the following impeccably worded note of encouragement: "Asshole. It took my sister all these years to find someone who would love her for what she is. Don't f_ it up by dying, or you'll never get laid again." Victor, born in the Bronx, and a once Navy underwater demolitions expert, had responded in kind, "It's Mister Asshole to you!"

Ruben Garcia, a former Green Beret, had gone AWOL to find B.T. in a field hospital in Vietnam. He told us of B.T.'s demanding that a nurse come over and powder his butt! Ruben suggested that we had all powdered his butt at one time or another. And true to the Collins' charm, he had convinced us that we were lucky to have even been asked.

A crusty octogenarian, Lillian Allen, in a striped tam-o'-shanter rose to lead us in a cheer, "B.T., he's our man!" It was a repeat performance of her role during his campaign visit to a senior citizens' center. He had apparently approached her and said, "When I give the signal, you call out." She gave the signal and we all called out, "B.T., he's our man! B.T., he's our man! B.T., he's our man!" I smiled as I remembered his effect on women of all ages. In his presence, they blushed; they flirted; they forgave.

Ed Rollins changed the mood with a few all-night drinking stories. On one California visit, in the wee, very wee hours of the morning, he had foolishly left B.T. at a bar with strict instructions to wake him for his return flight to Washington. Amazingly, B.T. came through. He appeared at Rollins' door with a liquid breakfast, several shot glasses full, on a hotel tray. He had, on his own, re-scheduled Rollins' flight. He also, we were told, regularly called Ed's father on the elder Rollins birthday. Due to the time difference, he reached the father before the son. Then he'd whine in his New York accent, "It's your father's birthday and you can't even manage a phone call."

John Philp, whose white hair supposedly dated from Vietnam, explained that B.T. had seen a lot of action—most of it in the parking lot of the Valley Forge General Hospital. "B.T. was," he continued, "a shining example of the skills of the prosthetic arts. He had the most advanced false leg known to medical science, whose air value he used to make rude noises, an expensive arm that we taxpayers were still paying for and other false parts too sensitive to mention." According to John, "B.T. had languished in the hospital until, faced with expulsion into the real world, he had found succor in the academic community. There, he told hawks he was a war hero, and doves that he had been injured falling on the tracks of an underground-railroad while fleeing to Canada."

Each speaker began by telling when, where, and for how long they had known my brother, and I realized that only I was there when he was born, his chubby face framed with tufts of orange hair, deep in his ruffled organdy bassinet. But I was also there when he was re-born, when sliced off and smelling of rot, he lay on a slab of sheets in agony. So I closed with a story that no one save my sister would know.

Brien had been fastidious as a toddler and not terribly bold. Those who roomed with him in law school would have found this hard to believe; that booming voice, those half eaten sandwiches in the desk drawers! Mother dressed him to complement his red hair. On one occasion, she had sent him outside to wait for her in a pale yellow linen suit, with the severe admonition that he was not to get dirty!

Secure in his fussiness, she felt confident he could stay clean for the few minutes required. However, he came in minutes later, covered with mud, crying his eyes out.

"What happened?" my mother asked.

"A little girl pushed me!" he managed between sobs.

"A little girl pushed you?" "What did you do?"

"I said," Brien replied indignantly, "you are a very rude little girl! He did have impeccable manners when the occasion demanded.

II

THE FUNERAL

I'm going to have the last laugh.
By the time they get through talking, you won't know
the difference between Mahatma Gandhi,
Mother Teresa and me, Baby!

B.T. Collins regarding his own funeral

The next day, his friends' last hurrah was a hero's send off. The freckle-faced kid from White Plains, New York, had made it to the big time.

The funeral was a gut-wrenching, sad, and sometimes hilarious grand affair. Except for the laughter, you would have thought we were burying a Kennedy. Thank God, my mother didn't live to hear my description. Irish Catholic though she was, she was Republican to the core. She never forgave old Joe Kennedy for his affair with Gloria Swanson, or my father, also a Republican, for voting for Jack. But that day, whatever the comparison, Mother would have been touched beyond politics. I doubt my ever-tender father would have survived. Much later, I came apart as I re-lived the funeral on videotape, but that day I tried to simply stand tall, to bear witness, to make my brother proud. There were no tears. It was all too terrible for tears.

It was not the "fun funeral" described on the front page of the *Wall Street Journal*, but we did laugh as speakers imitated his sarcasm and body language, recalling his merciless wit and outlandish behavior. Rain had been forecast but the day dawned California perfect—warm, but not hot—no doubt on orders from headquarters.

"Nobody," B.T. must have boomed from above, "is raining on my parade!"

Bagpipes played us into Sacramento's Sacred Heart Cathedral to the tunes of the great wars, while a contingent of Green Berets gathered in the courtyard. Inside, a cantor sang *Danny Boy* so sweetly it's a wonder we weren't knee-deep in shards of broken hearts. A class of eight-year-old children, wearing royal blue tee shirts emblazoned with hand drawn American flags, filed to the front of the altar to sing about a hero. The children were the third grade students of Bambi Tidwell at the Pershing Elementary School in Orangevale. Six months prior to his death, the class had invited him to a play they had written about the Pledge of Allegiance to the flag. Although it was near Election Day, he had refused the offer of photographers, saying that this was the children's night and that nothing should detract from their efforts. He was impressed with their performance and touched by their patriotism.

September, 1992
Mrs. Tidwell's Third Grade:
You have no idea what your play meant to me. Twenty-five years ago, Americans burned and desecrated our flag . . . and it broke my heart. Your devotion to our flag moved me to tears. Thank you all so much. You are so professional. How in the world did you learn all those lines?
B.T.

After his death, they wrote in return as only children do—awkwardly, openly, from the heart:

I felt sad when he passed away. I didn't know if I should cry or scream. I'm sure he felt important when we sang to him. Probably when he heard us sing. He was cheering like crazy!
Stacey Slotnick

I don't doubt that my brother "was cheering like crazy!" He loved children. In their eyes he was magic, a sort of miracle man who had wonderful parts with which he could do marvelous things.

He willingly showed off his prostheses, explaining in some detail how they worked. One child even wrote to ask how he too, could get a hook and a wooden leg.

There were three sets of pallbearers that day; one to carry him, this time without protest, into church, another to bring him to the Capitol Rotunda, and still another to follow the caisson and rider-less horse that were to take him to the Capitol Park. A thousand people attended mass. Someone suggested that the first 20 pews could have been filled with the walking wounded, referring to the many women in his life who had loved and lost.

The Bishop of Sacramento, Francis A. Quinn, a priest from Ireland named McSweeny, and Reverend Locatelli of Santa Clara University celebrated the mass. The Bishop had often attended fund-raisers for my brother or for his various charities, but B.T., in his assumed role of non-believer, was sensitive to the appearance of such support. So, he sent the Bishop a note that read, "If you don't stop hanging around, you're going to ruin my bad reputation!" Quinn continued to do precisely that.

"He was no stranger to God," declared Locatelli, "nor was God a stranger to him." We learned from Father Locatelli that B.T. had given 10% of his salary to Santa Clara University every year since his graduation. That year, due to his meager California Assembly-man's salary, he had written a letter of apology to the University for giving so little. "Thank you, Governor Wilson," Locatelli said to the first pew, and tears aside, we laughed in blessed relief.

The mass over, the pipers accompanied him to the Capitol Rotunda. Breaking with historical precedent, the California Legislature allowed B.T. to lie in state before the memorial service.

Bob Forsyth, an aide to former San Francisco Mayor Jordan remarked that in his 20 years in Sacramento, he had never remembered a public funeral like the one for Collins. "It was really the kind of outpouring," he admitted, "that you would find for a deceased president."

A reporter added that B.T. had been so honored because he treated everyone the same. "It didn't matter if you were a United States

Senator, or the Governor, the guy who parked your car, or homeless—I *mean* he treated everybody the same. You can't do that for the period of time that he was in this town without people noticing." As Mark Shields reminded us in *The Washington Post*, "B.T. was an old time pol who knew all the cops and elevator operators by their first names." True.

The Capitol Rotunda faces a beautiful park, lush with roses in appropriate seasons, and shaded by massive palms and Irish yews all year round. There is a walkway, large enough for vehicles, if necessary, which leads from the Rotunda to the Vietnam Memorial that B.T. played so large a part in building. The morning of the funeral, that road was lined with California Correctional Officers, members of the California Conservation Corps that B.T. had brought to life under Brown, and California Highway Patrolmen. All stood at attention. My sister and I, my husband and children, walked the quarter mile in the sun and near silence, broken only by the sound of horses, jingling harnesses, and the creaking wheels of the caisson that bore his body.

The park was filled and still. The honor guard arrived, their soft-shoe mini-steps guiding the coffin into place.

Rabbi Lester Frazin stepped forward to offer the invocation. Frazin had never contributed to or spoken out for any political candidate until B.T. ran for the State Assembly. He then agreed, on one occasion, to give the opening prayer.

B.T. had introduced the Rabbi by saying that the Governor had asked him to get the Pope, but as His Holiness was unavailable, Frazin was the only logical substitute.

Now, deftly unraveling B.T.'s claim of non-believer, he began:

> *B.T. Collins declared, 'I am an atheist.'*
> *But he believed in small things.*
> *In the gentle smile that warmed the moment,*
> *The holding of hearts sharing the truth,*
> *The proud anthem of human union,*
> *Fat laughter vibrating among friends.*
> *He believed in small things*

A word, solid, unbent
A thought undisguised,
A hope resolute, intense.
And dreams too often buried in muddy,
Bloodied soil hallowed by silent laments.
He believed in buddies that went to hell with him;
He believed in them.

The uniforms of every rank and service stirred. The camera caught the rows of ribbons on the navy blue and olive chests, the insignia on the rolled up kaki sleeves, the wheelchairs, and the tears that slid down shaved and whiskered cheeks.

The Rabbi continued.

He believed in small things:
The indulgence of service,
The deed, not the promise,
The gift of the act, the exaltation of self in deed,
Selfless deed.
The bodies beading blood,
The pulsing heart, the quickened pulse,
The stolid labor of the human spirit, unsullied by sycophants
*   and sybarites*
Selfless service without end. Amen.

Members of the California Conservation Corps present turned toward the speaker, their eyes shadowed by workman's caps, their stained hands clenched.

"I will never thank you," he had shouted at them. "I will work you to death. If you don't like it, the bus leaves tomorrow."

They thought, *We'll show this son-of-a-bitch*. And they had.

Frazin looked out at us, face after face, silent row upon silent row fading toward the distant Capitol. His voice grew deeper.

He believed in small things
A simple stripe of white, a smooth slash of red,
A star-lit field blazoned with blue,
And you, and you, and you, and me.

The mourners were absolutely still. I could hear the fabric of the flags slapping against their tall poles, pushed by the light wind. Rabbi Frazin paused, then proceeded. His voice rose and fell. He spoke with such intensity, he risked a passion overflowed and listeners drowned in a sea of poignancy.

> *He declared I am an atheist,*
> *But he believed in small things,*
> *The freedom to be,*
> *The freedom to be free,*
> *The freedom to be 'We, the people.'*
> *To be us, to be the US,*
> *To be the U. S. of A., the United States of America,*
> *The dream that is yet to be,*
> *That depends on us*
> *That trusts us to be us,*
> *In the fullness of goodness that we can be.*

He concluded in little more than a whisper, and we leaned forward listening with our hearts.

> *He believed in small things,*
> *The holy soul,*
> *The human spirit,*
> *The divine mind.*
> *He believed in people, colorless, raceless,*
> *The faithful and the faithless—*
> *He believed in you.*
> *He believed in me.*
> *He believed in us.*

The Governor, Pete Wilson, was the first of many speakers. Wilson had put B.T. in charge of the California Youth Authority. The appointment bought B.T. national limelight and a brief suit from the ACLU.

"The easy bargain," the Governor began, "is for us to carry the precious memory of this man, this gruff, irreverent, gutsy soldier who did, in fact, give his life for his friends, his country, for what he believed in." Wilson was known to be brief, and direct, and to appeal to the facts rather than to the emotions. That day, he was in serious trouble. Tight-lipped and close to tears, he halted to regain his composure. "I'm sorry," he managed, "If B.T. were here today, he'd say, 'Candy-ass Marine!'"

"B.T.'s definition of living well," he continued, "consisted of bringing to any debate on any question a kind of unsparing honesty, decency, compassion, generosity of spirit, and uniquely irreverent sense of humor that you knew was pure B.T. If you spent 10 minutes with him and you were not hooked by the hook, something was lacking in you." Wilson had indeed been hooked, but it was mutual.

My brother believed in Marines. When his *company commander* had asked him personally to run for the California State Assembly, B.T., exhausted and in ill health, had, nevertheless, signed on.

"Much has been said of his being an agnostic. By God, I never met a man who was more Godly in all the important ways. We cannot repay you," the Marine faced the coffin and saluted. "But we can, at least, try to be a little more like you." Once again, he stopped. Those listening sensed his search for the courage to say what came next. "Good-bye, dear friend. I will always remember you with love and with laughter."

Former Governor Edmund G. (Jerry) Brown for whom B.T. had been a legislative aide, and later chief of staff, followed. "I didn't hire B.T. Collins. He just showed up. I don't know what he did most of the time. He was supposed to keep the legislature happy. That's the way we ran the government in those days. He was always trying to get me to appoint Republicans. 'It's all about relationships, Governor,' he said. 'Something you'd never understand.'"

The remark rang true. B.T. had underscored his feelings in an interview for *USA Today* during the 1992 campaign when Brown was a potential presidential candidate. He decried Brown's seeming insensitivity, claiming the governor wouldn't know his cousin Guido if he met him on the street.

"One of the strange and paradoxical qualities of this man," Brown continued, "was that he could so devote himself to governors of two different political parties and do it with the same gusto, loyalty, and uniqueness. He was there in the eye of the storm, absorbing the negative thrust intended for the government and for me." There was something else the Governor had to make clear. "B.T. Collins didn't invent the CCC (the California Conservation Corps); he saved it." In truth, B.T. had not only saved it, but re-invented it, and it was one of his proudest accomplishments. "He never thanked me," Brown joked, "He just criticized me. He blamed me for appointing him."

Those present who had witnessed the B.T.-Brown era first-hand knew all too well about the kidding and unbelievable behavior on B.T.'s part that went on during those years. Yet according to Brown, B.T. "Took the spirit of the CCC and made it a badge of honor, something of pride. He made it sort of a mixture of a Marine boot camp, a Jesuit seminary, and an Israeli kibbutz." Brown then suggested that a new group be established within the Corps and that it should be given the toughest jobs. It would be called "The Collins Brigade."

"There's a piece of life that's gone. B.T. Collins was an anachronism in his own time . . . all that stuff about honor and keeping his word, calling a spade a spade, saying it like it was, not being worried about what was politically correct or incorrect. Yet, underneath all that was a very tender, sensitive man—a marshmallow," the Governor concluded.

Brown might not know "his cousin Guido," but he knew B.T. Collins.

Tom Griffin, a former high school classmate and FBI agent, stepped to the microphone. "The FBI," he said, "mourned the loss of its biggest source of inside information."

B.T. was connected. He knew what was going to be on the front page of the *New York Times* and the *Los Angeles Times* before it was printed. Tom explained that he and Brien had met as freshmen at Archbishop Stepinac High School in White Plains, New York. "I was loath to miss school," Griffin continued, "because I never knew what Brien might do. There were regular arguments with one Father Murray about the virgin birth," he remembered, "and everyone present fully expected the oft-threatened bolt of lightening, voice from above, or Brien turned to stone where he sat."

Dave Porreca had met B.T. in a foxhole 27 years before, during B.T.'s first tour of duty in Vietnam with the First Air Cavalry. "I knew a lot of guys that talked a good game, but when they got hit, it took the starch all out of them. Not this guy. B.T.'s saving grace," he continued, "had been his total lack of self pity and a wickedly honed wit."

Young and reckless, B.T. and Porreca had made a bet about which one of them, if injured, would wind up selling pencils on a street corner to make a living. My brother had called first. "Hey, Porecca," he demanded in his New York accent, "Ya wanna buy some pencils?" The conversation, Porreca explained, hadn't ended there:

"B.T., my God! Where are you?"

"I'm AWOL in a wheelchair, drinking with my buddies, having a much better time than a dull, intellectual twit like you."

"How are you doing? Have they given you prostheses?"

"Yeah. Now you, I imagine would be satisfied with one of those plastic hands. Me, I'm going to have a shiny silver hook that gleams in the light of every bar from here to San Francisco, and when I stick it in the bar, man, I'll be drinking free forever!"

The Porreca-Collins relationship lasted a lifetime. Dave explained that he had a company in which B.T. invested, with the admonition that he was expected to make B.T. rich. Six weeks before he died, they'd discussed B.T.'s expectations. "How much time do I have?" Porreca asked.

"Less than you think," was the reply. Prophetically, B.T. continued, "You'll be forced to be there, you know, when they say all these great things about me. And I'll have the last laugh because by the time they get through, you won't know the difference between Mahatma Gandhi and Mother Teresa, and me, baby!"

Mother Teresa? I don't think so. Mahatma Gandhi? Hardly. But that day we believed him—at least those of us who knew and loved him. We forgave B.T. his faults; the loud mouth and worse language, the drinking, the broken hearts, the pigheaded refusal to change his opinions, and his life-threatening habits. We only remembered the tears and the laughter, the hopes, and the dream that the world could be a better place and that, together, we could make it happen.

Former Army nurse Ann Cunningham had served two tours of duty in Vietnam. B.T. revered the Anns of the world, and credited them with saving his life. At twenty-three, she found herself awash in blood and body parts and dying boys. If the war had made these soldiers men, they were chronologically boys, 18, 19, 20-year-olds who, in another time, would have been in college or laboring at a first job. "I never knew what eventually happened to my patients," she explained softly. "Knowing B.T. validated what I had done. He had a way of putting things into perspective. He would say, 'There are two ways of looking at this. Either I'm missing an arm and a leg or I've got an arm and a leg.'" To underscore B.T.'s perspective, she recounted the story of an October 1978 television interview with Sacramento television journalist, Doug Kreigel on just this topic.

Kreigel began by asking B.T. how he felt about his handicap. The question was followed by silence, a deadly, on-air silence.

Finally, B.T. responded, "What handicap?"

Long pause.

The reporter, recovering, stuttered, "You . . . you've lost your arm and your leg."

Another awful silence.

"Ah," B.T. replied, as if he hadn't quite understood. "Now if *you* were missing an arm and a leg, you'd be handicapped. But, hey I'm good looking, I'm Irish and I'm from New York!"

Taking care of B.T. Collins was not the job of nurses alone. Everyone he knew bore some responsibility for his wellbeing.

John Banuelos had been both nursemaid and dance instructor. He stepped out from behind the podium to demonstrate B.T.'s legwork. It was a hilariously accurate imitation of B.T.'s lack of grace.

But Banuelos was more than my brother's Arthur Murray. Once, when B.T. was ill, John was left in charge, equipped with a rubber glove and a suppository. "If he starts to faint," were the instructions, "give him the suppository."

He had leaned close to B.T.'s ear, he told us, suppository in view, and said quietly, "If I have to do this, you're going to die!"

Then, he closed with the lines that B.T. used so often to describe what really mattered in life, "It's not the sharpest car; it's not the foxiest lady; it's not the finest house. Is the world a better place because you were there?" We knew the line by heart . . . *Is the world a better place because you were there?*

Former California State Treasurer Tom Hayes, his Irish complexion the color of porridge gone cold, came next. He spoke quietly, hesitantly, as though each memory brought him further down. "When B.T. had come aboard as Deputy Treasurer," he began, "the first thing he did was to tell reporters that I was 'as dull as oatmeal.' He called me 'a dumb Marine who just might have been able to get into the Army if only my parents had been married.'" The crowd let go. "Yet," and Hayes paused too long, "he frequently sent clippings and letters to my parents and my kids singing my praises. He was a hero who had heroes: parents, policemen, teachers. When I lost my bid for re-election, he gave me a plaque: '*Semper Fi*, No Regrets.' That's how he lived his life—with no regrets.

"How many of us knew," Hayes continued, "that totally privately, without any press, B.T. traveled to Travis Air Force Base on a moment's notice to meet the remains of the MIA soldiers and Marines coming home from Southeast Asia?" I pictured my brother at attention, rusting inside from the tears held at bay, assuring the fallen by his presence that they were not alone. "How many knew," Hayes repeated, "that he canceled his schedule more than once to rush to the bedside of strangers who had lost limbs to reassure them that they could still have full lives?"

Tom reminded us that 11 days before, another very close friend, Jack Dugan, had died. Dugan and B.T. were inseparable and everyone knew it. B.T. had given Jack's eulogy, and Tom Hayes described it. "B.T. appeared visibly destroyed and spoke from a written text, which was a first. He had asked the priest, he said, 'to open the coffin so that he could see the face of his good friend, Jack Dugan one last time.' B.T.'s words, Tom said, "caused a superhuman struggle for self-control among those listening. It was a dual hurt; mourning Jack and worrying about their friend. B.T. paused to let the full weight of his statement sink in, then continued, "Jack" he said "looked terrible!"'"

Tom described the listeners' audible gasp followed by a burst of laughter. "B.T. went on, 'Where was Jack's fine Irish smile? Gone! Where were those rosy Irish cheeks? Gone! And those smiling eyes? Gone too! Ah,' and he paused again, 'but those eyebrows!' (Jack had a set of unforgettable bushy brown brows.) The mourners laughed harder! B.T. concluded by admonishing the listeners, 'never put yourselves in the position of wishing you hadda. When you really care about someone,' he said, 'tell him or you'll wish you hadda. I didn't and I wish I hadda.'" It didn't end there. According to Hayes, B.T. had worn a musical green tie to the funeral and, inadvertently, folded his arms across his chest causing an unscheduled, tinkling interlude of *When Irish Eyes Are Smiling*.

B.T.'s close friend, Stan Atkinson, anchorman at Sacramento's KCRA TV, concluded the eulogies. B.T. and Stan had met during the Brown administration, after hours in the city's infamous *Torch Club*—a kind of deliberately run down den of iniquity frequented by legislators. Tan, impeccably dressed, with just a touch of white at his temples, Stan is the quintessential television personality. "B.T. was forever the warrior," Stan reminded us, "but he was a warrior who had been spared. And he repeatedly asked, 'Why?' He never lost touch with the reality that he had been allowed to live. That reality had become the driving force in his life. He had been spared so that he could serve, and we had all become beneficiaries of his passion to do so with honor."

The memorial in Capitol Park ended with taps, the firing of guns, and a helicopter fly over in "missing man" formation, preceded by an old Gaelic tune, a sad one, about battle and guns and drums and loss of limbs. It was my song, one I had sung for Brien on so many other occasions. But this would be the last time and it had to be the best. I stepped trembling to the microphone, faced the crowd, trying not to look at my family in the front row, and sang my New York Irish heart out.

> *While on my way to sweet Athy,*
> *With a stick in me hand and a drop in me eye,*
> *A doleful damsel, I heard cry,*
> *Brien, I hardly knew ye!*
> *With their guns and their drums and their drums and their guns,*
> *The enemy nearly slew ye!*
> *Oh, Brien, me dear, ya looked so queer*
> *Brien, I hardly knew ye!*
> *Where are the legs with which ya run?*
> *When first ya went to carry a gun?*
> *Indeed, your dancing days are done.*
> *Brien, I hardly knew ye!*
> *With their guns and their drums and their drums and their guns,*
> *The enemy finally slew ye!*
> *Oh, oh, Brien, me dear, ya looked so queer.*
> *Brien, I hardly knew ye!*
>   *Brien, I hardly knew ye!*

> *A parody of an old Irish folk song*

I felt it was neither guns nor drums that finally slew him. His enemy was within. B.T. died from an overdose of intensity, of passion and patriotism, of a need to be needed, to succeed, and to be forgiven for having lived when so many others had died.

A reporter asked Marialis what B.T. would have thought of all this. "His only regret," she replied, "might have been that he was not present to give his own eulogy."

It occurred to me, listening, that the question of his reaction to the eulogies was moot because no one would have dared so praise him in his presence. I had watched him, by dint of biting sarcasm and displays of supposed ego, patiently refine the art of keeping even those closest to him at an emotional distance. To laud the deed was allowed; to praise the man was not. He seemed forever on the alert, dukes raised against the affection he both needed and actively sought. I believed he hid a lifetime behind a self-made emotional dam, and if ever he were to have weakened his resolve the feelings would have poured forth—and he would have drowned in a floodtide of his own vulnerability.

And if dead men shed tears, that day, I thought, *he would have cried a river.*

Afterwards, there was one hell of a party. Supposedly, he had so wanted a real bash that he left money for it in his will. In fact, he left no will—denial, perhaps, in the face of an ever-encroaching reality. My father used to say, when speaking of his inevitable departing of this earth, that he "wanted a band." It was his way of saying that he did not want to be the cause of any sadness. I'm afraid Daddy got a buffet; B.T. got the band, and the California Association of Correctional Peace Officers, plus several others, the bill.

It was a true Irish mourning with music and abundant tears and laughter. He was there parked to one side of the dance floor, and with him, his ashes not yet scattered nor laid to rest, his close friend, Jack Dugan. Jack's Tam O'Shanter and B.T.'s Green Beret rested side by side on B.T.'s flag-clad coffin.

Friends had made an exhibit of memorabilia: the bullwhip given to him by his classmates at Santa Clara, the Kennedyesque, massive rocking chair with its brass plaque from the California Conservation Corps, pictures of B.T. learning to ski on one leg and to skydive. There were the handshakes with various presidents, and my Dad in his Navy uniform, and the family and B.T., round-faced and freckled, as a little boy. People waited in long lines to see what B.T. would have laughingly referred to as "the shrine."

The Governor's wife, Gayle Wilson, had written her own version of *I Enjoy Being a Girl* from Rodgers and Hammerstein's *Flower Drum Song* when B.T. was campaigning for the Assembly, and she sang it again that night.

New York gave us Brien Thomas
With his tough talking repartee,
With his swagger, soft heart, and promise.
Give a cheer now for B.T.

I remembered when he told me in a soft voice, minus his usual New York-Bronx imitation, about her initial performance. I wish I could re-create in print the sound of his wonder. This man who had dined with the denizens of the Oval Office, met generals, major media personalities, and movie stars, commanded men under fire, and sat on a battlefield dying, could not believe that the wife of the Governor of the State of California would write lyrics to a song for him, let alone sing it herself.

A videotape tribute created by Jan Young, friend and member of the staff of Sacramento's NBC affiliate KCRA, ended the evening. To the background of an old Kenny Rogers' recording, we watched as B.T. went from sailor-suited toddler, to a bearded, 130 pound, bed-ridden, double amputee, to swaggering chief of staff. Dan McGrath, a reporter with the *Sacramento Bee* wrote "Yes, a one-legged man can swagger if he's a one-legged man with B.T.'s presence and *bonhomie*."

The tribute closed with some of B.T.'s largely unprintable remarks cushioned by Sinatra's famous *I Did It My Way*.

I saw that tape again in New York on June 20th, B.T.'s life day. That "nice Jewish kid" from New York, Steven Galef, my son Patrick, and others organized an East Coast gathering in Manhattan. We met at an Irish pub to drink and tell B.T. stories. The following day, a single piper played at Prudential's amphitheater. As I entered, there was B.T. on a ten-foot screen.

Among the on-site speakers was Michael Hernandez, a Cuban-American who had hired B.T. at Kidder-Peabody for the brief period when he was absent from public service. Hernandez broke down soon after he began speaking and never completely regained his composure. At one point, someone came from the wings to offer him a handkerchief, such was the quantity of his tears. He stopped to blow his nose. The harder he cried, the harder we laughed.

Hernandez confessed to being rather sensitive about his noticeable five o'clock shadow, which resisted regular shaving. It seems he had been photographed for a major magazine that emphasized this condition, and had taken a lot of kidding as a result. Thoughtfully, B.T. had clipped the picture and had it laminated on a plaque on which was engraved, "Whatsa matter, Hernandez? They don't sell razorblades in Cuba?"

In truth, it was amazing that B.T. had even been hired. Learning during his dinner interview that it was Hernandez' wedding anniversary, B.T. had lectured his potential boss on his responsibilities as a husband, then left. By the time Hernandez had returned home, B.T. had already called his wife to apologize, and the next day, of course, there were flowers from old you-know-who.

My brother was finally buried on the fourth of July. After a debate about Arlington National or another public spot, we had decided on a beautiful old cemetery in Sacramento where people could pay their respects more privately. There were no bands this time. No piper played. But the Bishop himself was there. "It was near the feast of Saint Thomas," he explained, "and Brien, though hardly a saint, had, like Thomas, a good many doubts about the goodness of God." Yet, Bishop Quinn understood what had caused Brien's lack of faith and blessed him in spite of it.

We had taken care to see that his grave was shaded by a mighty tree, and that Brien Thomas was in the company of other noteworthy Republicans. The headstone of India granite's polished surface matched that of "The Wall" in Washington. On the back were scrawled the initials, "B.T." as he always wrote them. Beneath those, "The World's a Better Place Because He Was Here."

And I, the New York sister stood, silent, watching in the California sun. "When I tell his story," I thought, "they'll think I made him up."

III

THE FAMILY: GROWING UP COLLINS

Yours are the ideals the world needs—the courage to do
and say the things that need to be said and done
and to leave the world just a little better for
your having been down its highways.

James J. Collins to B.T. Collins

All this brouhaha hadn't come out of the blue. It began simply in a
suburb of New York City, in a family whose priorities belonged to
another generation, whose roots, like those of most Americans, first
sat in the soil of another land.

The Family Collins

According to popular lore, we were nobly descended. The Collins
can be traced back to Milesius, King of Spain. The founder of the
family was Cormac, King of Munster, A.D. 483. The chief of this
tribe was McCarthy Moore, Prince of Muskerry, King and Prince
of Desmond, King of Cashel and Munster. The ancient name was
Cullen, and the Chief of the Clan Cuillean had large possessions in
the present county of Tipperary.

However, the official genealogy is minus any mention of my
brother, Brien Thomas, surely the most colorful Collins, better
known by some as just B.T. Son of Margaret and James and soldier
of political fortune; he charmed and bullied his fellow man and
woman to the top of the heap.

Californians believed they and Vietnam had created him. They
hadn't.

He'd been formed by a unique combination of love and patience, grounded in ethics and values, models given, and faults endured. If Vietnam became his crucible, the ingredients for survival placed therein had been provided by a loving family and an exceptional mother and father. California just gave him the opportunities to strut his stuff.

The Collins Family

For over half a century, we Collins children were privy to a remarkable personal relationship. Our parents were lovers. They were also friends and partners long before it was the fashion to so be. And they were "in love;" the Antony and Cleopatra, the Romeo and Juliet of the 1930's and for all the fifty-six years that remained of their extraordinary marriage. If my father didn't sing beneath my mother's windows, he did laughingly call her "Lotus Blossom" when trying to coax her from bed on a winter morning. And he brought her small gifts for no reason at all—a single rose, a silver bracelet made with his own hands, out of which he carved her name, "Peg." He took out the garbage without being asked and washed the dishes. My mother was the envy of the neighborhood.

Independent to be sure, they were nevertheless two hearts that beat in single time. You might get to one by speaking to the other, but decisions were rendered *a deux*. You knew as a child that you were dealing with a team. My father once explained this by describing Mother and himself as the "king and the queen," and Brien, Marialis, and me as the "subjects."

Though neither of my parents had grown up in a family of means, my father's family was the poorer. There had been seven children. My father was the only boy in the surviving five. There was an older sister, Helen, whose son would be posthumously awarded the Silver Star for bravery at Normandy, a younger sister, Amelda, and the twins, Margaret and Mary. The girls all sewed beautifully, and Margaret, commissioned to make hats for the wife of President Harding, had actually stayed overnight in the White House. My grandmother also sewed, painted picturesque farm scenes in the style of Grandma Moses, and once even sang in a chorus in Carnegie

Hall. The Collins women's finesse with a needle and thread was the family's main means of support.

They lived on a farm in Valhalla, New York. The *home of the gods* it was not.

Husband and father, John Collins, was an accountant in New York, but there were 19 saloons between the train station and the house. He rarely made it home sober. He was not a happy drunk, and the children too often hid under the dining room table only to be dragged out, cuffed and shouted at, at his return.

Because of his father, Daddy never, never drank. Not a drop. Not even at weddings. On his fiftieth wedding anniversary, he held a trembling glass of champagne to his lips to let a sliver of the bubbly escape. I doubt he even swallowed. In the toast that followed, he told us that he had never provided us with much of a bank account, but that he had nevertheless given us two wonderful gifts: a passionate love for our country and the best mother motherhood could provide.

The only member of his family to have a college education, he had earned his way through school by re-finishing antiques and teaching shop courses. He had gone off to college with everything he owned packed in a straw suitcase, his tennis racket strapped to its side. With these meager accouterments, he parlayed his way into the positions of President of his fraternity, President of his class, and Captain of the tennis team. Eventually, he would earn a doctorate from New York University and be named one of his undergraduate and graduate institutions' most distinguished alumni.

Daddy was physically a small man, 5ft. 10 at most. A study in efficiency, he rose early, working before work and after. If he sat, he read or wrote. His one recreation was playing golf. There too, his pace left you huffing and puffing. He had a swing like a whip and the ball took off like a white bullet heading with murderous intent towards the faraway green. He had a great reverence for "old things" things with a history, and for history itself, the latter his legacy to Brien. He talked often of the great wars and great men, of how life was and how it ought to be. He regaled us with tales of candles set on automobile dashboards during winter storms and brick-warmed bed sheets which led to a great story of one college vacation. Arriving home late one night, he stripped buck naked, jumped into bed, only to find that his 80-year-old Aunt Rose was already there.

He loved language and had a rich store from which to draw. He quoted the great poets and patriots at will, and sprinkled his ordinary conversation with a celebration of idioms. Even at the end of his life, when he could not remember his way from the kitchen to the dining room, he could still recite long passages from Milton's *Paradise Lost*. He had great respect for women, and liked them strong-willed, independent, intelligent, and feminine. A man well ahead of his time, he found none of these adjectives at odds.

Our father was very tough on the outside, stern and seemingly inflexible, yet, soft at the core. He loved to ground zero—his love so intense, it made you hurt. He was a romantic, and heartbreakingly sentimental. When he was only seven, I was informed via an ancient aunt, one of my father's twin sisters, Margaret, that his mother told him of Abraham Lincoln's great troubles, and he burst into tears. When I played the lead in a college musical, he traveled 400 miles to see the premier performance. He sat in the front row, his pride streaming down his cheeks.

Mother was born Margaret O'Brien, the daughter of Frank O'Brien and Kathleen McNulty, years before an appealing child star would borrow her name. Her father was known for his great sense of humor and his love of practical jokes. Her mother, unusual for a turn-of-the-century woman, had a college degree. Mother was the oldest of four children. There was a single brother, movie-star handsome, hair like coal and eyes bluer than the lakes of Erin. He had a voice you could hear for a block, and he hugged hard, like my father. He died at 52, like Brien. There were two sisters, Katherine and Alice. It was Alice who later managed to slip Brien through the gates of Santa Clara University under the noses of faculty Jesuits who should have known better. Katherine lived past ninety, her longevity due to clean living, an unshakeable faith in God, and a heaping dose of the famous O'Brien sense of humor, traits our mother possessed in abundance.

The family lived in northern New York, in the little town of Potsdam, home to two universities. There, the winters were and remain long. The snow fell deep, and they scooped it fresh into cereal bowls to flavor with real maple syrup for snacking. Mother snow shoed, skied, and skated. The house was large, and student boarders filled the extra bedrooms. It was rumored that if you were too late and the college dorm doors were locked, you could slip into a first floor bedroom at the O'Briens via a window left open for that purpose.

My mother's family, together with her cousins, the Murphy's and the McNulty's, were a riotous bunch who delighted in each other's company. Their parties continued all the years we were growing up and beyond. We'd sing and tell stories, and make fun of everything and each other. The O'Brien brand of humor was sarcastic and religiously irreverent.

Mother was beautiful as a young woman, and more so as the years passed. Her nearly aquamarine eyes were set in an elegant, high cheekboned face, and she walked with the runway swagger of someone half her age. She laughed often. I remember the sound of it. I could always distinguish Mother's undisciplined, almost raucous laughter in a crowd. Strong, independent, and intensely loyal, she was as alive as anyone I have ever known.

Even as the years passed and she became frail and ill, she seemed endowed with a constant *joie de vivre*. She had attitude long before attitude mattered. No mere imitation of the women of her day, Peg Collins was every inch her own person. She had opinions, and they mattered. Mother had mental energy. She read and learned and partied with passion. She greeted each day with optimism, her cup perpetually "half-full." With little money, she managed to do things with panache. Her dinner parties were a smash. Everything she touched had her own stamp of class and style. At 70, she had her ears pierced; at 72, she mounted a camel to ride across the Egyptian desert.

We kids were born against a backdrop of patriotism and national peril. I came first and held court without competition for five years before Brien arrived. I ate my morning cereal to the radioed sound of Hitler's screaming. While my baby brother slept, I watched my mother cover the evening windows with blankets, enveloping us in protective darkness. At school we were assigned colors by neighborhoods, and regularly drilled on how to return home safely in the event of a bombing. At home, we saved chips of soap to make suds, flattened our tin cans, and saved all our newspapers.

The poster in the barber shop window proclaimed, "Uncle Sam wanted *me*!" and the Nazis goose-stepped their way into Poland. An anxious world stood by, but the state of the world not withstanding, Brien Thomas remained at the center of our, if not yet the nation's, attention. Daddy and I sat by his bassinet and just watched him.

Marialis followed 13 months later. She was named for Mother's sister, Alice, and Daddy's sister, Mary. My parents didn't want her called simply "Mary," so they spelled her name phonetically, with the result that strangers can never pronounce it. Daddy nicknamed her, "The Duchess." She was, in fact, royally dainty, and her head was crowned with a mound of splendiferous, tightly coiled red curls. Although there were redheads on both sides of the family, Daddy was blond as a young man and mother a brunette. Brien's red hair and my sister's could be traced to the local high school football coach, or at least that was the explanation I gave, as a six-year-old, to anyone who asked. If my lack of sex education raised a few eyebrows, I did have a good sense of color. The coach, who lived near by, had locks the color of boiled carrots.

The nation's "Day of Infamy" arrived a month before Marialis was born. The planes came, and the ships burned, and the men died. The president spoke. My father responded.

Monday, December 8, 1941
Letter to the students of Alexander Hamilton High School.

Within the next few hours, the United States of America will be officially at war with a group of vandals whose trickery and dishonesty, as evidenced by their meetings with our Secretary of State, sinks them below the dignity of the name, government. Already men's lives have been lost, and this is only the beginning. Two of our graduates are stationed in the Pacific. Let those of us who are safe here at home conduct ourselves in a manner that will give credit to the danger they endure for us.

How fortunate we are to be able to say that we are citizens of the greatest nation on earth. Let us not fail her now in her hour of need. From this day forward we must conserve every article we use in school. We can do our part here at home. Any form of sloppy or lackadaisical work from today on will brand that student as a slacker who is holding back his country from its ultimate victory.

Instead of England's "Blood, Sweat and Tears," let us have as our motto: "Dignity, Honesty, Hard Work" (and plenty of it!)

The Skipper (J.J. Collins, Principal)

Our father's first official pronouncement would not be his last. For the next forty years, he would defend his country and plead with her citizens to do the same. As a high school and later elementary school principal, he sent letters home every Veterans, Memorial, and Presidents Day.

"Freedom's battles will always be fought by freedom's children," he told the parents. He asked that they "prepare their children to advance the common good of mankind wisely, and to do so in the home." Too many people, he believed, "were concerned with civil rights rather than human rights." If we believed in human rights, civil rights would automatically follow.

Daddy's thoughts were not only for public consumption. Growing up Collins meant growing up proud to be an American. We were of that generation born to duty, in the midst of a great war when loyalty to one's country reigned supreme. Although those feelings waned in some over time, ours would endure. Long, long after the last shots were fired, the last lives extinguished, the last fresh tears shed, our sense of obligation and the recognition of our privileged status prevailed. My father lectured us on the benefits of being Americans. He forever spoke reverently of the brave men fallen in battle. These human sacrifices had been made for us. We understood that we dared not *carelessly* enjoy freedoms that had been so dearly won.

Daddy joined the Navy. We all went to war. At thirty-five, married with three children, he was not required to enlist. Unable to bear being separated from him, my mother put the furniture in storage, packed us up, and followed my father wherever the Navy sent him. On D-Day, we were at The University of Notre Dame with a slew of other naval families. We had reached South Bend, Indiana, via the Pacemaker out of New York's Grand Central Station, standing room only. There were suitcases in the aisles and sometimes, being little, we sat on them or on the borrowed knee of someone in uniform. Those days, we rarely saw a civilian male.

The Navy had not provided adequate housing, so we bunked with various families. When the troops hit the beach in June, 1944, we were living in the home of an old professor, a widower, who had already lost one son to the war and was awaiting the news of another, a pilot, who was missing.

Then my cousin, Danny Mulligan, was killed. He had made it to St. Lo, where at 19, like so many others of that generation, he fell silent forever. All six feet two of him, auburn curls and laughing eyes went down in a heap in the French countryside. Daddy was given a leave and we went back East. My aunt and uncle were inconsolable. I can hear the sound of his mother's mourning still. "Daniel, Daniel," she wailed. It made an indelible mark on my nine-year-old memory and, I imagine, on my little brother's. Brien was four.

Within a week of our return to South Bend, another War Department telegram arrived. The professor's second son had been killed. Daddy took us into an upstairs bedroom, lined us up, and tried to explain that "something very sad had happened again."

I remember that the old man didn't cry. He just hung his head, and his sheath of "Robert Frost" hair fell forward, hiding his face. The wife of the young airman with the baby he'd never seen moved in with us. And there we were—total strangers huddled within the context of a common misery; Danny so newly dead, and with him this young father, son, and husband we knew not at all. His wife sat in a rocking chair, day after day, nursing the baby and crying. Her dead husband's picture was perched on the top of an old piano. He was wearing a leather aviator's cap, smiling, looking off, I suppose, into his own wild blue yonder.

After South Bend, we moved to Princeton, New Jersey, where we lived off campus in a giant Victorian whose rooms were divided among four Navy families, then on to the language school at Ford Ord, in Monterey, California. We lived, or rather, camped out, in motels taken over by the Navy along the famous Seventeen Mile Drive near Monterey. We slept all in a single room, Marialis on a trunk. Daddy rigged an old grenade box and a block of ice for a refrigerator. Mother cooked on a hotplate.

Then one day we were on our way back East, alone. This time, Daddy really had gone to war, on a ship. We would not see him for a year. Our mother must have been frightened. Dying for your country, she knew from personal experience, was not just something that happened to other people.

Back East, she fed and clothed us and rented a two-room apartment on Daddy's meager military salary, with the stipulation that she had neither pets nor children. We were told to take off our shoes upon entering and to stay out of sight. Two months passed before Brien and the landlord first met.

"Who are you?" he demanded.

"I'm Brien Collins," Brien replied. "But don't tell anybody. I'm not supposed to be here."

The meeting cost Mother an extra ten dollars a month rent.

Our father came home. Smiling, teeth white against a face tanned walnut from the Pacific sun, and trim in his dark blues, he looked, to my 5th grade eyes, like a movie star. In time, of course, we would fight another war, and another, and the son would go instead of the father. He too would come home, pale as a winter moon, but alive.

After the war, we settled in White Plains, a suburb of New York City. Because our father was handy, any house we owned was in the ultimate state of fresh paint and repair. Daddy, the original environmentalist, went regularly to the dump that he called the "Gift Shop," from which he rescued and remade various practical treasures. Our home was filled with refinished antiques, old silver, maps, mementos, and books on every subject. My grandmother's 1860 cameo-back love seats, on which we were not allowed to sit, as children, were in the living room. The house was pretty and in order. Both Mother and Daddy were scrupulously neat and organized, a trait, none of us, unfortunately, inherited. In front of any house in which we ever lived an American flag was flown.

We were a middle class family with more class than money. We wrote proper notes of appreciation, said "please" and "thank you," and asked to be excused from the table. We used the right fork, most often by candlelight.

Attendance at the evening meal was required, and dinner was lively. Our father worked at keeping us constantly intellectually on edge. He made us think about what we thought, and why. During the civil rights movement and the assault on communism, he deliberately provoked arguments with politically incorrect statements and we rose to the bait every time. "We didn't live in the South. How do we know what the real situation was? Maybe those white southerners have a few beefs coming."

We were outraged.

And on communism, "Why shouldn't everybody share things equally? Wasn't God philosophically a communist?"

We weren't a noisy family but we shouted at dinner. Daddy once had me sign a paper that I would believe in the economic principles of communism by the age of nineteen. I have it still.

Jim Collins *loved* his country, but he *adored* my mother. She was the center of his universe. We understood as soon as we were able to understand anything that Mother was the single most important person in our lives. Daddy told us so in dozens of ways.

When I left home for the first time, he gave me the following letter. I was 17, a French major, off to spend the summer with a family in Orleans, France.

June 1953
Dear Maureen,

This is just the first of many letters I will write you, but in this one I wanted to tell you the most important things to go away with. Mother has done so much for you. Of all the women I know, there is no one so fine and true, no one I would rather have you emulate, no one I would rather have you be like.

Mother loved him in return. "You should have seen your father in his tux. You should have heard him speak. Don't eat that last piece of pie; I'm saving it for Daddy. Dance with me, Jamie," she'd plead after supper. And, his cheek to hers, he'd lead her around the living room furniture to the rhythm of an old Guy Lombardo tune, while we watched from the dining room table.

My first year of teaching, when Brien and Marialis were still in high school, Daddy called us together in the fall and explained that there was something he really wanted Mother to have, something he felt she truly deserved but that he just couldn't afford . . . fur . . . mink! Not a coat, mind you, merely a stole.

It was a challenge. If we lived among inherited porcelain and polished antiques, mink was still a little out of our league. "Maybe," he proposed, "if we all found some way to contribute, we could swing it for Christmas." For his part, he would take extra job at night. Principal of a school in a nearby town, he already worked one other job in the window of a local hardware store on Saturday afternoons, demonstrating the uses of woodworking machinery. One by one, the rest of us found something, and the required sum was accumulated. Thanks to a local furrier who gave us a discount, an Autumn Haze mink stole was purchased. Marialis and I modeled it in front of the showroom mirrors until it was finally enfolded in clouds of tissue and boxed for Christmas. I didn't think we'd live until the "giving."

We gathered in the living room on Christmas morning—
Mother, in a quilted robe on one of my grandmother's loveseats.
Daddy carried in the large box and placed it across her knees. And
Mother, measuring it mentally, must have imagined a nightgown, a
blanket, or maybe *two* sweaters. We leaned forward in near-
excruciating anticipation. She removed the lid and peeled away the
paper layers to the softness below. At first she didn't even lift it from
the box, she simply touched it. The sight of her face! She was
simply so surprised, so totally surprised. She cried.

My God, we felt good!

And then there was the hat.

Mother loved to wear hats. My father believed in them. Real
women wore them. They were the ultimate romantic accessory.
According to Daddy, if a hat didn't cause others to stop in their tracks
and stare, it wasn't worth wearing. And so Mother's beautiful hats
over the years were legendary. One year, shopping in a well-known
New York store, Mother found the perfect Easter bonnet. It was
pale lavender Milan straw circled with moss-green velvet, trimmed
with silk sweet peas in magenta and violet, and all pale shades of
pink—a wearable Monet-Renoir combination, and much too
expensive. While Mother tried it on, my father took the salesgirl
aside. Slipping her what cash he had, he asked that she go to my
Mother, say that there had been a mistake, that the hat was on sale,
dropping the price by twenty dollars. She gamely did as he requested.

Totally in vain.

Mother burst out laughing.

"My husband spoke to you, didn't he?

"Ma'am?" The girl blushed.

"You realize," (turning to my father), "we won't eat for a month?"

The hat was purchased for Daddy, because Mother knew how
much it meant to him for her to have it. It was worn to a chorus of
"Ooo's" and "Ah's" for years. We had hot dogs a little more often,
but we did eat. I can still see Mother's face framed by that beautiful
brim, and our father's eyes as he watched her wear it.

Money was tight. "You would not be able to go to college if it weren't for your mother," Daddy reminded us. Mother was an elementary school teacher who took courses every summer, and at night during the school year, to increase her salary. When we returned from buying school clothes, he always asked, "What did your mother buy for herself?" The answer, "Nothing," never varied nor did the message sent.

"Mother," Daddy explained, "was not a domestic." True, although she shopped for groceries and cooked, kept the household accounts, decorated the house, threw parties, and bought our clothes. Per his instructions, we divided up the remaining household chores. There was no "electric" dishwasher until the last of us left home. Daddy washed the floors, waxed them, and we, in pairs of his old socks, polished them by "skating" from corner to corner. He also defrosted refrigerators and scrubbed ovens. Ours were the cleanest in the neighborhood.

Marialis and I folded laundry, dusted, and vacuumed. Brien's jobs were to make breakfast and clean the bathrooms. He did pretty well in the kitchen. Besides breakfast, his specialty *du jour* was a darkly chocolate batch of brownies. He also made evening snacks, like pudding, which he carried to his room and ate from the pot, leaving the remains under his bed to grow strange and malodorous gardens. These habits, along with throwing dirty socks, underwear, and various degradables to the far corners, called for messy search and destroy missions long before he wore a uniform or raised his hand in any salute.

He was routinely in trouble. The rules were many. He broke them all. He was alarmingly awkward. He backed into some things and fell over others. He did not become a character; he was born one. Even as a baby, he bit our dog for stealing his cookie. He cut my sister's scarlet curls to her scalp, unfortunately all on one side of her head, before he was even officially out of a crib. And she let him do it! Barely walking, he was already bending others to his will. By third grade, she was carrying his fourth grade trumpet to band practice.

My cigar-chomping, bar-thumping, heart-breaking younger brother was also a bit of a wuss as a child. For starters, he was forever fainting. His face would go white, every freckle on that pale surface standing free like a single copper coin. I'd say, "Mother!" and over he'd go. He fainted on trains and often in church. Perhaps his antagonism to religion had earlier roots than we imagined. Both places had crowds. Maybe he was simply claustrophobic. He was afraid of bugs, something he luckily had gotten over before traipsing his way through the jungles of Vietnam, and he would cry out, "Get those skins off me!" if so much as an ant crawled his way.

It follows that Brien was a difficult adolescent. He began drinking in his teens. It was what my father feared the most. Consequently, Daddy was especially strict. Brien then drank more. When he finally stopped cold in later life, we were all relieved. But before the final abstinence, there were multiple misadventures, one of which created a life long bond between younger brother and older sister.

Brien returned home in the early morning to find the doors locked. My father, furious, would not let him in. So he appeared at my second story bedroom window tottering on a ladder, trying to coax me into pulling him through its narrow frame. He was too big, too drunk, and the casement window much too small to execute the requested maneuver. I didn't dare go against our father's wishes, but I was afraid Brien would fall to the pavement below and be seriously hurt or worse. So I gathered up my bedding and ran downstairs. Holding the ladder, I talked him down. He slept in the garage. He never forgot the incident. He just never forgot.

Brien and Daddy crossed swords many times over his behavior. Mother, though upset, continued to dote on her only son. Fair or unfair, Brien would forever steal the show. Marialis grew up to study, earn good grades, play superb golf, and very smart bridge. I won school elections, sang, and received awards. Brien misbehaved and got a major share of the attention. Mother forgave his every fault. The two traded love in the form of insults long after he had left home.

"So, Ma. I hear you're in the home."

"I'm not in the home, you brat. I'm in the hospital."

"Well, the next stop's the home, Ma." And you know what?"

"What?"

"They'll give you an afghan," (Mother wasn't big on afghans), "and a walker, and a tin cup, and they'll give you gruel, Ma, but to get it, you'll have to bang on the walker with your tin cup."

Mother, (now laughing), "Oh, really. Thanks for letting me know. The flowers are beautiful."

"You like them? I got them off the used rack in the supermarket."

As always, Daddy thanked him in a letter:

June 1978

Dear Butch,

The flowers you sent Mother are still fresh—that was a beautiful bouquet! And she showed your card to everyone but the cop on the corner. Those days she was in the hospital were very sad for me—I got almost morbid about it—I would notice a piece of clothing lying around the house and I would become so lonesome for her, I would almost weep. I didn't give you kids much in the way of material things, but I sure did give you a good mother! Sometimes I get to thinking of how well you turned out—responsible, honest, upright, with a spit-in-your-eye attitude. I know she had a lot to do with that.

IV

The Family: Act II

———•◦•———

"What are you doing?" I asked.
"I've been thinking," Mother replied.
"I've been thinking . . . I had it pretty damn good!"

Margaret O'Brien Collins, age 82

So, as the years went on, and when we were able, we bought Mother many things, and realized that every time we bought her a gift, we bought Daddy a present too. And although Marialis and I were dutiful daughters, Brien's imagination and humor bested us on every occasion.

Our parents retired to Florida. One Mother's Day, he took out a full page ad in a Palm Beach newspaper in the form of a letter. It had supposedly been written from prison and was all about sending home his laundry and other nonsense. Naturally, many of her friends saw the paper and the phone didn't stop ringing for days.

She loved it.

But Brien's *piece de resistance de* Mother appreciation was when he spoke at a commencement which coincided with Mother's 60th college reunion. I was present because I had been on the faculty of my Mother's alma mater for 25 years. He stepped to the microphone *chewing gum*! I watched him from the front of the auditorium in my scarlet doctoral robes. I couldn't believe my eyes, and hoped Mother's were too bad to see what he was doing. Knowing about his diabetes, I thought maybe he had needed a little last minute sugar.

Wrong.

He was not chewing discreetly, more like some errant bovine that had wandered from the nearby fields into the hallowed halls of the "Academy." Ah, but the worst was yet to come! Purposefully, in full view of his listeners, he retrieved the gum, positioned it on the podium before him and began to speak.

"Now, that I have totally embarrassed my Mother and sister and have your full attention," he paused, "I can begin." His public show of affection was often embarrassing. In the past, Mother had been singled out as the lady in the front row with the dirty ankle, ("One foot in the grave and we all know who put it there!")

I was more than a little nervous. I never knew what he might say. The faculty was not at all amused. The students roared. He did have their full attention, and he spoke directly to them. He suggested that they might have heard stories about veterans shooting up supermarkets and damning their country, but that there were other kinds of survivors as well; that serving one's country was a duty, not a chore. He stated, forcefully, that he did not consider having been to war an excuse for committing anti-societal acts.

"You hear a lot about Vietnam veterans," he continued, "Well, you're looking at one of them and this is what he did with his life. The question is, 'What are you going to do with yours?' The only thing that really matters," he remonstrated, "will the world be a better place because you were there? Monuments were covered," he continued, "with the names of young Americans who would never be a minute older than those who are graduating today, and others who had never made it to a college classroom on any campus."

The arena grew very still. I looked out at his audience. Some leaned forward. Some heads tilted to the side, arms folded, eyes front. Everyone was listening.

"You have no right to waste your lives," he said quietly. "You owe. You owe this country the price of liberty, and your parents for giving you life. The next time you have a birthday, send your parents a present for giving you the greatest gift of all. And because this is Mother's Day, I would like you to meet my mother. Stand up, Ma," he commanded, "Stand up!"

There was a collective whoosh as 4,000 people turned to get a good look at Mother standing in the second row. Her tiny body was set off in royal blue. Her hand went to her forehead, tanned brown against her snowy hair. She smiled broadly in embarrassment.

"This is my mother," he continued. "All that I have been able to do and may yet do that is good, I owe to this woman and to my father, who cannot be with us today."

There must have been some closing remark. I cannot remember. The people rose as one. The applause was long and thundering. It was the first standing ovation in the college's 170-year history. The faculty did not understand. They thought he was there to impress them.

In fact, I would not have been sitting there in my gold tassel and velvet mortarboard if it hadn't been for Brien. He had lent me the money to finish my degree.

On my 50th birthday, I was alone at Indiana University in Bloomington, Indiana. My miniscule graduate student apartment was filled with flowers, among them the 50 long stemmed roses sent by my younger brother. The whole scene looked more like a funeral parlor or the Kentucky Derby than a place to sleep and eat. The phone rang. It was Brien.

"So, what are you doing to celebrate your birthday?"

"I'm going to the library."

"Sounds like fun. How about having dinner with me instead?

"Right. Aren't you just a tad too far away?"

He was downstairs in the lobby of my apartment building. He had flown from Sacramento, California to Bloomington, Indiana—the last leg of his journey in a plane designed only for midgets or those agile enough to fold themselves in half—to take me out to dinner. When we got to the restaurant, he banged on the bar and addressed a roomful of strangers:

"Hey guys! It's my sister's birthday. Whadda ya think? She look pretty good for 65?"

Later, he said, "Maureen, I'm going to buy you a computer. You need a computer, right?

"Well, sure, but Brien, these things are really expensive."

"Yeah, so find out how much. It's my Christmas present. But you have to remember this is it . . . for four or five years, this is it."

Next year.

"So, Maureen. What do you want for Christmas?"

"But Brien, I already have my present, remember? Really."

"Right, so what do you want for Christmas?"

His show of affection did not always involve spending money. Mother's sister, Katherine, had open heart surgery at the age of 75 in Syracuse, New York. Brien flew across the country to see her. Arriving after visiting hours, he stomped through the Cardiac Care Unit waving his cane, trailed by nurses clutching charts and frantically calling, "Sir! Sir!" in his wake.

Finding Aunt Kathy, he paused at the end of her bed. Without preamble, he bellowed, "Thank God you're still alive! I've come about the will!"

The nurses' jaws dropped to their pastel smocks—a Life Magazine cover complete with caption. Aunt Kathy laughed through and around her multiple tubes and electronic monitoring. When she returned home, she found a very old dollar bill. She threw it in the washing machine—several times. Then she pinned it to a note and sent it off to Brien:

"I'm afraid this is all there is but since you're so anxious, I thought you'd better have it now." He framed the dollar and hung it on his kitchen wall. She outlived him by six years.

Both our parents were caretakers. A cousin with an alcoholic father confided, "We wouldn't have grown up, if it hadn't been for your mother." She was indeed always watching over somebody—friends, neighbors, older relatives, the cranky ones whom no one else would have to dinner. Mother actually retired from teaching early because the teacher's union would no longer allow her to stay after school on her own time and tutor kids in reading for free.

Daddy wrote us every week from the time we left home until just a year before his death. We each had our collection of favorites. The letters were rife with lessons: write letters, get and stay in touch,

communicate. Be proud. Say so. Say, "I love you. Write it down."
He believed in the written record. Long after the phone calls had
faded from memory, the letters would be there to remind you of the
things that really mattered; kindness, duty to one's family and
country, taking a stand, making a difference, remembering important
dates, not only in history but in the lives of others, while creating a
portrait of the person who wrote, and of an era. He saved all of
Brien's letters from Vietnam. I saved all of our father's letters to us.

Daddy worried that fathers, particularly the corporate type who
populated his school district, did not spend enough time with their
children. So, he implemented a policy of "Class Fathers" in the
elementary school of which he was then principal. He spent night
after night in his workshop making birdhouse kits which were, he
hoped, to be put together by fathers and sons or daughters. He was
concerned about his students' writing skills—being able to write
well, he believed, was the key to their future success—so he
conducted a writing contest, always on a patriotic subject, each year.
He then personally read every one of the 600 entries.

He also wrote articles complaining about the loss of pride in
one's craft, as well as the protection of the indolent and incapable
worker. He believed these people had destroyed the competitive
standard which made America great. He pleaded for smaller classes
in which teachers could teach and students could learn—a classroom
in which the teacher reigned supreme. He asked that more time be
spent on reading. He denounced "purchased parenthood"—buying
child rearing from schools, camps, and recreation departments, and
called for parents to spend more time with their children.

But finally our father's voice stilled. Parkinson's disease made it
impossible for him either to write or type. The thoughts were
there, but he could not record them legibly. He lost his motor
control. He stopped talking. Used to fixing things, he continued to
do so. With a hammer, he smashed picture frames and window panes,
vases and various other treasures. Mother tried to keep him thinking
and active. She made him play bridge and sent him on errands. Then
one day he lost his way and a stranger brought him home in tears.

He began regularly to take off without warning. Firemen and policemen were called in to find him. He had to be followed, watched. He looked at pictures in the newspaper and imagined they were of Brien in battle, hanging upside down, dead or tortured, and he cried.

He turned night into day, making any rest for Mother impossible. "Sleep," he explained patiently and hilariously, "makes one mentally deficient." I took him for walks to give Mother some respite. He now held my hand as I had once held his, trotting along childlike beside me. He could go at an unbelievable clip. He was hurrying back to Mother. He never wanted her out of his sight.

"Where is she? Where is she?"

"Who, Daddy?"

"Tell me—is she gone forever? Is she gone forever?"

My God, he thought she'd died!

"Oh, no, Daddy. No!" I replied, my eyes filling with tears. "She's just home waiting for us." But I was not to be believed, and he pulled me ahead with amazing strength.

Daddy, always so swift, so sure, so alert, lived increasingly in a world of which we were not part, talking to people only he could see. He hadn't lost his mind, though we nearly lost ours; he had misplaced it. His circuitry had gone awry, wires crossed and plugged into the wrong places. It was exhausting for all of us who loved them both. Mother just grew increasingly tiny and breathless. Her doctor mandated what we all knew was coming. We were killing her, he told us bluntly. Daddy had to be placed where he could receive adequate care.

Marialis went to Florida and did all the legwork. Brien and I agreed to be there the day the awful deed was done. It's a terrible thing to give a father away; to see him unclothed, his used flesh draped on a clothes hanger frame, while nurses check for any bruises he might have brought with him, calling him "Honey." This elegant, slender man was my father.

"He has a Ph.D!" I snapped under my breath. "Call him *Dr.* Collins!" Mother and I got him settled and went to pick up Brien at the airport. Brien always took charge. I thought once he arrived that everything would fall into place. We would get through this nightmare with a modicum of grace.

Not so.

When we returned, Daddy called to us from the far end of the hall—his voice more wail than cry, a human sound I had never heard before nor since, reed thin, yet thick with every shade of despair—a hundred nails scraped along a corridor-long slate. MY S-O-N . . . MY D-A-U-G-H-T-E-R!

He believed he'd been abandoned.

Brien limped behind me. With the sound of each uneven step, I felt his hatches batten. I could hear his barricades rise. I knew my younger brother. I knew his heart was breaking. We wheeled Daddy to his room, weeping. His bony shoulders rose and fell to the rhythm of some wrenching inner misery. He cried harder. He sobbed. Never, ever, had we seen him in such a state. I could not imagine what Mother thought, seeing him so wretched.

It turned out to be Brien. Guilt over Brien. Brien's sacrifice for Daddy's patriotism. He thought he'd been too strict; that he'd been a terrible father.

Brien didn't move. I imagined that his guilt matched Daddy's own. He had disappointed this man, flunked out of college, managed to get half his body blown away, and more. Didn't he know that his father had forgiven him ever so long ago, that he was so proud? Neither man had forgiven himself. So big B.T. just listened, hand and hook to his sides, switch off, his face an ashen imitation of his childhood fainting days.

I felt sick. I knew Brien mustn't hear this; that this might be finally more than he could bear; that such hurt might crumble the carefully constructed façade upon which his bravado depended. Brien needed to fix things, to make things better. And now no act of kindness, no amount of money, no happy surprise, could bring Daddy back.

Frantic, I knelt in front of my father. Covering his hands with mine, I pleaded for calm. I told him that he was making everyone sad, that what he thought simply wasn't true. "You were a wonderful father to Brien, wonderful and he knows it! We all know it!"

Somewhere in that muddle that now passed for his mind, he heard me. He stopped cold. Will of iron still intact. Like son, like father.

The last time I saw him, I told my father how much I admired his kindness and the man and the father that he had been.

"When you love someone, tell him. Don't only wish you hadda."

Those days he spoke in code. I never knew whether my words registered, or if he would be able to respond intelligibly. I told him again and again that I loved him, trying to reach through that brain run-a-muck. We had always talked, and I needed to hear him one more time. Finally, I gave up. Then, turning away, I heard his voice behind me, clear and steady:

"I know you love me."

"You are a wonderful father!" I replied.

"Yes, well, you're pretty slick yourself!"

We would not speak again.

The most precious are the final messages. I never had a final conversation with Brien.

A month later, Daddy was gone. He couldn't live away from his Maggie.

I remember Mother's voice when she called to tell me, the sound not yet steeped in sorrow, the fact too bitter, the news too fresh . . . utter dismay laced with disbelief. "Daddy died!"

The message was clear. He can't. This isn't to happen! No! In an eerie after-echo, my voice would imitate hers exactly, just four years later. "Brien died!" I blurted into the phone, with all the fury of despair, denial, and yes, indignation. How could he do this!

It was Brien who led Mother to the coffin for the first time. Courage restored, he was back in charge. That night, he took Mother, Marialis, and me out to dinner. The restaurant didn't accept credit cards so Brien asked if he might write a check. Lest the manager refuse, Mother informed him point blank of Brien's position.

"Do you know who this is?" she demanded.

"No, ma'am."

"He's the man who runs the state of California."

Brien, eyes rolling upward, murmured, "I'll bet the Governor would be glad to know that."

Mother had uncharacteristically consumed two glasses of wine. The check was accepted.

Daddy's funeral mass, offered by a just-off-the-boat Irish priest, was on the fourth of July. It was a fitting day for a patriot of his intensity. Marialis, Brien, and I all spoke of his affection for Mother. The magnitude of his love laid bare was an awesome thing. We were privately afraid that our remarks would hurt rather than comfort her, that they would tell a story too poignant. How we struggled, painfully picking through our memories.

All to no avail.

Later, after everyone had left, Mother told me that I must tell her what had been said. She hadn't, she confided, worn her hearing aid!

In the months that followed, Mother became gossamer, someone to hold down as she crossed the street lest a gust of wind blow her away before we could bear to let go. She fell asleep beside me in mass and in mid-sentence. Once, she hung over her passenger seatbelt in traffic. My heart stopped but hers was beating still. She was merely napping. We hated to see her stand in the sunlight for fear we would see through her near-transparency to the angel waiting. She seemed more fairy than human. One half expected to see wings, should she turn around. And we dared not speak too loudly lest the mere expulsion of our breath blow her back to the dust from which the parish priest said she originally came. Yet, even parchment thin and short of breath, Mother was never *old*. She was simply too much fun.

However foolish it may sound, Brien, Marialis, and I thought she would live forever, or at least a couple of years . . . some time without the worry and care of Daddy, some days in the proverbial sun. We counted on it. We planned for it. Brien already had his tickets for Florida for Daddy's birthday, the first one she would spend alone. He thought about things like that. But she fooled us, and she and

Daddy spent it together. Something about a golf match on Heaven's green. The truth of the matter—life without him just wasn't worth it. In May of that year, she had nagged the doctor about getting back on the golf course. In October, she was, in our father's words, "gone forever."

Her funeral mass was celebrated on B.T.'s birthday. We covered the casket with a child's bouquet. At 82, she weighed a whopping 84 pounds. Brien went before the assembled mourners for the second time in less than four months. He stood tall, fixed his "baby blues" on the back row of octogenarians and shouted, "Turn up your hearing aids! I'm going to talk about my Mother!"

The last time I saw her, she was sitting on the edge of her bed fully clothed, facing the window. Her silhouette in the morning sun was so young! Her slender legs were crossed and her arms were to the side, each hand grasping a bit of bedspread. I asked her what she was doing.

"I've been thinking. I've been thinking," she repeated, and she thrust her chin forward as she spoke.

"I've been thinking I had it pretty damn good!"

Hadn't we all.

V

VIETNAM

Defending our nation on and off the battlefield
has never been easy. It never will be.
If service to the country is a casualty
in this symbolic war, greater horrors will follow.
Would I go again? In a heartbeat!

B.T.Collins

The Collins family had "had it good," with the exception of the Vietnam War. For each of us, the action in Southeast Asia represented a problem of a different dimension.

My younger sister struggled to achieve her own identity in a Republican, impassioned, and thoroughly opinionated family. She was a closet dove and Democrat. To express her feelings openly within the family would have been little short of high treason.

My mother, like every Mother, was simply afraid that B.T. would be called, and like my cousin Danny, killed. I, too, was afraid. My memories of the Second World War sat in my subconscious, along with my father's repeated lessons on duty to country.

Yet Daddy's turmoil may well have been the worst. He believed that being an American was a privilege, one that was to be earned. He had not been afraid to sacrifice himself for freedom's cause, but to risk the loss of his only son? That, indeed, might exact too high a price.

The nation's posture was even harder to bear. For a large proportion of the American public, the war in Vietnam was a war without purpose. We were not ourselves under attack, but supposedly mindlessly meddling in the affairs of another nation. The interconnectedness of world peace was not a popular view. Fear of the spread of communism had dimmed; the domino theory was no longer widely accepted.

Though the era's shoeless, unshaven activists believed otherwise, America had never gone easily to war. It took an overt act of aggression by a foreign power to get our attention. In 1941, we had to be slaughtered while sleeping; our sons, brothers and fathers buried in an American harbor's watery grave, before the American president won public support to enter a war in which the United States was already surreptitiously involved.

In the past, once the country was committed, most American men had gone willingly to war and, when possible, American women followed to support them. Not to do so was looked upon as an act of cowardice and civil disobedience. To "run away," to profit from the privilege of being an American, then defy the commander in chief were not acceptable options. During the Vietnam era, in some ironic twist of public perspective, those who turned their back upon the troops were seen as conscientious ideologues, while those who served were spat upon, called murderers, and otherwise taunted by their noncombatant counterparts. Those who dodged the draft hid in Canada or on the university campus; those who did not were forced to hide their uniforms in the closet and their veteran's status from an angry and often violent "peace-loving" public. This national mood struck a blow at the very heart of all that my brother had been taught as a child and all that he had learned from his copious reading of history.

Nevertheless, the popular claim that the war in Vietnam was different from all others was, at least partially, true. Beyond the lack of public support and purpose clearly understood, this was not a war of territory taken and defended, but a daily competition, a constant comparison of quantities killed. Territory taken was taken back, and the always elusive enemy was often unrecognizable. Their bare feet, youth, size, and gender were misleading, for they were fierce, wily, and unusually creative. They fought with beehives and bamboo sticks, with traps and trip wires, snakes and re-made explosives. They could drop from sight in the middle of a battlefield, only to re-appear at the edge of a clearing or under the belly of a fenced-in animal, thanks to an intricate network of underground tunnels.

Yet, the most dangerous enemy the troops faced was neither in the bush nor behind a child's innocent smile. It was an attitude expressed by an ever-increasing number of Americans via the media. Their message was loud and clear; "You shouldn't be there; we aren't behind you."

B.T. Collins marched to a different drummer. Former Governor Jerry Brown had him pegged when he referred to him as an anachronism. B.T. belonged to another time, another America; one in which issues were clear, and duty had but one definition. He should have landed on the beach at Omaha, or flown with Chennault's Flying Tigers, or been with Doolittle for those "Thirty seconds over Tokyo." B.T.'s allegiance had been to the generation of '41. Going to Vietnam was part of a payback to those who died in defense of a freedom he never took for granted. Had he lived, he would have been at Normandy for the 50th anniversary of D-Day, to see it all, to relive the glory of an America he understood. The worst tension he faced that day would have been controlling the free flow of tears. Heroes made him cry.

As a teenager, B.T. was fascinated by the lessons of history's greatest leaders. He read Churchill more readily than comic books. He devoured military campaigns from all the great wars. Yet he would not do his French, could not do his math, and had no particular interest in other required areas of a liberal education. How many verb endings I supplied, how many papers Marialis and I edited, I do not remember. Not enough, for he left the second university (at which my father had painstakingly managed to get him registered) after one semester and joined the Army.

B.T. was not *drafted*. He ran away to war. I have no memory of his saying goodbye. The news came through my mother. Although it was not yet fashionable to be "finding oneself," that is most likely what he was doing.

Initially, it was a lark, an adventure. Perhaps, at some subconscious level, he saw himself playing out the roles of the patriots about whom he had read. With luck, he too would make history. With luck, he would make my father, the ultimate American and fiercest patriot, proud. No question, his behavior to that point had upset my parents badly. His drinking, his leaving school, his seeming refusal to follow any rules, didn't fit our family character. Daddy knew Brien had brains and was at a loss to understand why he didn't use them. He had become impossible. My father was upset. My mother was worried sick.

I could not imagine my brother in the Army. He did not respond well to authority, did not adhere to schedules, and found discipline in any form abhorrent. He hated to get up. At home, when mother called him from downstairs, he would swing both feet to the floor, stomp a couple of times, and then swing them back onto the bed. One morning, while Marialis and I watched, she threatened that if he did not get up immediately, she would pour a glass of ice water on him. He didn't move. She poured. The water ran down the groove in the center of his back and dribbled onto the sheets. Still motionless, he murmured, "O.K., I'll get up." Five minutes later, he raised himself to a sitting position. I wonder if the sergeants at Fort Sill had my mother's sense of humor.

The Army did change Brien in ways we could not have imagined. The guy who wouldn't write a term paper wrote well crafted, revealing letters.

Fort Bragg, NC
1964
Dear Folks,

I have finished 6 books (over 1,700 pages) since last Monday. Consequently, I'm all fired up to go to war again. I want you to save my letters. Perhaps, someday they will be my Iliad or Odyssey. Patton once said, "One of the great privileges of citizenship is to bear arms freely in defense of one's flag and country." I suppose it is better for him that he did not live to be heartbroken by the vacillation of our foreign policy or the hapless naiveté of the "Ban the Bombers."

How soon we forget: Bataan, Corregidor, Dunkirk, Dieppe, Metz, Kasserine Pass, Casino, Tobruk, Tarawa, Iwo Jima, Okinawa—meaningless, more and more. I asked every guard during the guard mount yesterday where the town of Ste Mere Eglise was. (There's a drop zone here named after it.) None of them knew. Yet, how many people their age and younger, how many hopes, how many dreams, how many lives were extinguished in the spring of their years in this small town in France? Nobody knows anymore and, more ominously, nobody cares.

I am now 5 years older than Daniel* when he died . . . 5 years older and I still consider myself young. Perhaps more an *enfant terrible*? If it is true that "the best go first" and "the good die young," don't we owe them something for what they stood for or what they did? Yet we fritter away the heritage they died for at the conference table by acquiescence, by taking counsel from our fears, our good senses blinded by the myopia of fear. The horror of total war has cataracted our sense of what is right and wrong in our bungling of international affairs. We allow countries to spit in our eye, to break treaties, to refuse to honor written words, and still we seek to negotiate. How Caesar must be laughing at us. We cannot buy ourselves out of our responsibilities, our legacy, only into further disillusionment.

Let me not bother you with my maniac prophecies. My natural fear of social censure keeps these same utterances written, rather than fallen on deaf ears and barren minds. My thoughts find expression easily on paper, at least in the company of understanding or appreciative communicants. I'm just rattling on, content in my lunacy. Now, I really must shine my boots and put some order in this hovel. Looking forward to your arrival.

---

* Daniel Mulligan, first cousin, killed at St Lo, France, in June, 1944, at nineteen.

The family black sheep finally graduated from Officers Candidate School at Fort Sill and was now a Second Lieutenant. His first assignment was Santo Domingo, where US troops were maintaining order after a revolution. We were somewhat relieved. At least he wasn't in Vietnam.

27 May '65
Santo Domingo
Dear Folks,

Just went in to offer the Major my *US News and World Report*, which I had devoured. He gave me a cigar and we got into a discussion about Latin America. I'm really proud of myself. There is no topic of general interest on which I can't hold my own. It's unfortunate that there aren't more military minds as broad as MacArthur's and Marshall's, or who are equally as articulate when speaking. In *Life* magazine I just saw a painting of Andrew Wyeth's that I had seen in New York's Museum of Modern Art. No education is wasteful or absurd—even if it is the characterization of a whore in Mickey Spillane's journals, or a painstakingly erudite page of St. Augustine, or the wrath of fanaticism in the pages of *Mein Kampf*. Everything you hear or see is an education. Too bad I'm so lazy because I know I'm more articulate, more perceptive, more understanding and more tolerant than many of my contemporaries. Big deal. Well enough of this philosophizing and patting myself on the back. I must rest up. I'm sleeping only 12-14 hours a day. War is hell.

12 June '65
Santo Domingo
Dear Dad,

Sure wish you would reconsider and see what you can do about getting me to Vietnam. Had my first jump from a helicopter last week; really great, except that I closed my eyes as I jumped out— there's less prop blast. You sit in the door, which is really scary at 1,500 ft. Then when the jump-master says, "O.K.," you just shove away with your hands, point your toes downward and away you go. It was about 5:30 AM, no wind, long ride down-90 seconds. But I didn't slip right and I landed one foot from an asphalt road. That can be non-habit forming.

I really appreciate your letters, and the more time I spend in the Army, the more I appreciate what you've done for me. It's unfortunate that I didn't take advantage of it. I want you to know that though I have argued with you, I've never lost my respect for you. For years, I've bragged about you and the dedication you've exhibited. So, to make a long story short, you're okay as a man and as a father.

They say we'll be getting A-rations shortly. It pricks my conscience, because I'm a field soldier and all this softness is degrading. What really hurts, is that I'm missing Vietnam. I know I'll get there one of these days, but I want to go now. I know I haven't been much of a source of pride to you these last twenty-five years but I certainly couldn't cause you any embarrassment that far away. Please do what you can to get me out of here. I'd be forever grateful.

B.T. did get what he wanted, and all on his own. When he first joined the Army, he asked to go to Vietnam. The officers in command laughed. After graduating from Officers' Candidate School at Fort Sill, Oklahoma, he put in for Vietnam again and was sent instead to Fort Bragg, North Carolina for Jump School. In the midst of the aftermath of a revolution in the Dominican Republic in 1965, he applied once more and was told, "You're not needed over there; just cool it."

Finally, he found out that if he would extend his tour three months, he could go to Vietnam. Division headquarters, in exasperation, apparently reasoned if he were that anxious, let him go. So, while other young Americans sought to avoid combat, B.T. bargained his way into battle.

Only my father knew initially knew about his change of assignment. Brien concocted an elaborate scheme to have a friend in Santo Domingo send his mail on to An Khe, South Vietnam. He sent his letters to the family via Santo Domingo. It didn't work.

Two months into the scam, we discovered where he was. It was not good news.

When he arrived in Saigon, he was concerned that there was no mention in his orders that he was going to the 1st Air Cavalry Division. B.T. wanted the 1st Air Cav because it was a new concept, one about which he had read a great deal. The Air Cavalry was changing the face of modern warfare; the U.S. military was going "air" mobile. Helicopters, which had been used in Korea mainly to carry the wounded to field hospitals, now transported troops at 110 miles an hour to their Vietnam combat destinations to undertake search and destroy missions. The copters became fighting aircraft, some armed with rocket launchers. The use of helicopters also meant landing nearly 200 men out in the middle of nowhere, totally dependent on radio contact with the outside world.

Yet in some respects, the troops were actually far less isolated than they had been in other wars because there was now a faster means to bring them supplies, ammunition or replacements, or to transport them to the nearest hospital. It was a battlefield without "front lines." The enemy was essentially everywhere and nowhere; the trick was to find him. When the jungles were exfoliated to strip them of their hiding places, the helicopters were similarly denied cover, making them easy targets for enemy fire.

A 1992 article in *USA Today* described how B.T. finally made it to his preferred destination. Landing in Saigon, he had gone to the captain in charge and explained that he wanted to make sure he was going to the Cavalry. The captain countered, "How'd you like to work here? We process troops six days a week, ten hours a day—we have a villa, women and COLA!" The latter was apparently the ultimate perk. B.T. replied that he'd been trying to get to Vietnam for two years and that he wanted to "go north!" "North" meant to the combat area. The captain, in disgust, turned to the clerk and said, "That's it! Send him to the mud!"

His first tour of duty, from December 1965 to December 1966, was with the 1st Air Cavalry Division as an artillery forward observer attached to the infantry. This meant serving with relatively large groups of American troops whose primary duty was combat. The entire division was based at Camp Radcliffe at An Khe.

The town of An Khe is in the Central Highlands between Pleiku and Qui Nhon, split by Highway 19. The highway was actually only a dirt road that served as the main route for military traffic between the sea and the bases on the Kontum Plateau. The camp was secure, its perimeter enclosed with barbed wire and watch towers, and its inhabitants backed by air support and artillery fire. Approximately 16,000 men, (two divisions and support staff), were based there. The camp was usually maintained by a couple of battalions left behind to "hold the fort," (called manning the barrier), while the remaining troops were air assaulted out.

B.T. would soon discover that "the mud" was no careless army slang, but a very real consequence of the seemingly never-ending rain. Unrelenting, it fell in sheets, swelling the rivers, manufacturing slime. Clothes dripped, feet peeled away, rifles rusted, and the men shivered in the night air, uniforms clinging to their clammy skin. There would be times when trying to keep himself dry was second only to staying alive. Eventually, he learned how to light a cigarette and keep it lit, how to make and drink a cup of coffee while marching, and how to dry his socks by holding them under his armpits.

His first combat experience was well beyond the boundaries of anything he had ever known or imagined. He had never seen anyone dead, let alone blown apart. In battle, he acted on auto-pilot; the trembling, sheer terror, and throwing up began back at base camp. He constantly walked the line between dashing into combat, and cutting and running for his life. Yet, some days and nights were spent totally without contact, the sound of a sniper, or the sight of the enemy.

Young and undeniably cavalier about their own mortality, the troops thought of themselves as invincible until someone they knew dropped at their feet or became airborne before their eyes, victims of a single flying piece of shrapnel or a land mine. At other times, they faced an action so fierce, a chaos of bullets and bodies, heaped and mangled, dead and dying so unbelievable, they felt nothing. The worst tension came from not knowing when those times would occur. Some measure of escape was to be found in focusing upon seemingly trivial things. A discussion of twenty ways to cook a "real" egg could, for example, take up an entire morning.

Waiting for the worst to happen, B.T. read innumerable books on history, on the "great wars," and on the war in Vietnam from every angle. Marialis furnished a continuous supply of quips and quotes, articles, magazines, and books. He wrote letters—about 150 a month. His friends, friends of the family, everybody's relatives wrote to him, and he replied. It became a lifetime habit. He rarely described action to anyone but Daddy.

At home, we had all stopped watching the news. We never discussed the war. It was too frightening. B.T. specifically did not confide in me. He was the comforter and I, the comfortee. I would learn about combat after his death, from the books that described his war, and from the men who served with him.

27 December '65
An Khe
Dear Dad,

About an hour ago, we air assaulted into this valley. The way these people operate—it's really amazing. First artillery 8" and 175mm, then two air strikes, then us—come in on helicopters 4 abreast about 20,000 meters from base camp—all kinds of gear on our backs—start to go in and the chopper gunners open up and all I could think was, "What the hell am I doing here?" Choppers land and everybody gets out and starts running, shooting—we were the lead platoon. 3 Cong were killed, and they were North Vietnamese. I helped undress one before we buried him—awfully gory. The artillery is now here—they have rocket helicopters also—all in less than 2 hours. Just lifted "A" company 3,000 meters at tree-top level, in a matter of seconds.

Now 2 days later. Yesterday, we moved out so fast, I didn't have time to write to you. We had to go about 4,500 meters to get into position. I can hear all the elements on the radio—it's fascinating. VC evidence everywhere—red ants everywhere—

pack weighs a ton, feet always wet. The rice paddies are better walking than the jungle, but the water is hard on your feet and your helmet gets heavier as the sun goes down. Really got to hand it to these kids. They carry MG's, ammo, radios, all kinds of grenades.

Two days later—New Year's Eve—we're the last element to pull out, providing security for a battalion of artillery that's waiting to be lifted out. Haven't seen "Charlie" for 3 days; got sniped at, but walked and walked rice paddies, etc. 'Bout 11,000 meters yesterday—was really tired. It's an expensive war. I don't know how much it costs but probably hundreds of thousands of dollars— if you *think* you know where a sniper is, they'll shoot anything from 105 to a jet air strike on it. But you never see Charlie. It's his war—nothing but trenches and concealed foxholes.

Found an ambush site, "spider holes," we call them. They're so effective you can't see them until it's too late. These people are experts at camouflage, and the jungle is so dense. It's easy to get lost—very easy. Every village just women and children. They can see us coming for a mile. I think we really go about it the wrong way. Total score: 4 VC killed, 4 Americans killed-4 days. What can you do? This place is infested with North Vietnamese Regulars—find ID cards everywhere.

Helicopters are used quite effectively over here—re-supply, med-evacuation, pick up captured documents—just throw a smoke grenade out and down they come. I keep a liaison recon aircraft on my frequency all the time and as we search and sweep, he recons the area to our immediate front. It's hard to sleep with all the guns shooting all night. They don't have targets, they just shoot "H and I's," Harassment and Interdiction fires, at likely fronts of approach. Sometimes you get so tired and hot and there's red ants biting you and you don't know if Charlie is in that bush. The tension of the situation tires you more than anything else and then you look at these kids—mostly draftees, with radios on their backs and MG's and mortars, extra ammo, and they keep going—makes you feel ashamed. I'm glad I went to OCS. I live much better as an officer. It's worth it, though I'm a dead aim for that sniper. Although, I wear no rank, the Cong can see the map in my shirt pocket, plus I'm close to the radio.

I keep thinking of Ernie Pyle's words on the cover of *Here's Your War*, 'bout people back home never realizing how tired these kids are. I guess you just have to experience it yourself. I wonder what goes through their minds. Patriotism is the last thing, I'm sure. I don't think they realize the dangers of communism or what it is. Some of them, I suppose, get a joy from killing, especially those who were at Plei Me. They hate Charlie and I don't blame them. Been reading *Armageddon*, by Uris about the post-military government in Berlin—really fine. He has come a long way from the days of *Battle Cry*.

Don't take this as an offense, Dad, but I'm not lonesome. I'm where I belong. And though we've been at odds at times over the years, I've never been ashamed of you. I'm so proud of you. When people smile at me because I volunteered for Vietnam, I remember you—that you didn't have to go and you did. Tell Mom not to worry. I'm having my usual inexpressible "ball."

28 February '66
Dust Bowl
Hello Dolly!*

Got to read *Time* and *Newsweek* yesterday, which I devoured like a madman and spent the rest of the night raving like a lunatic about what stupid sons of bitches Fulbright and Wayne Morse were. Just once, I'd like to put those pompous, theorizing asses over in a village that is under Cong control and let them see the fear in people's eyes—see the starving, bloated bellies and all the while the camouflaged barrels of rice that stand there, untouched because that rice belongs to the Cong and the people don't dare touch it. My personal mission is to burn and destroy all the rice I find. And now these compromising bastards want to run out on these people. That would be just great. I

---

* Dolly refers to our mother whose first name was Margaret.

suppose civil rights and the "Great Society" are more important than our word and solemn pledge to these poor, starving, pitiful people. Sure we hate it over here—nobody wants to live like an animal and worry constantly about never returning. I've seen a wounded sergeant, blood flowing out of him so fast, it took four of us to keep him alive and all the time he's vowing that he'll return. You can't beat people like that. Don't worry about us, just the "Doves." I've had to think that all these young Americans over here have died for nothing.

Enough of that. It just gets me down sometimes when people act so ignorantly, throwing the lessons of history out the window. My thoughts are always of you and Dad and all the things you have done for us kids. What I wouldn't give for some iced tea and cold potato salad and steak and corn like we used to have in the back yard. Seems like centuries ago in a faraway place.

1 March '66
Dust Bowl
Dear Mom and Dad,

Very bad day today—hot, dusty—no shade—helicopters blowing all over the place. Must have been 120+. God, this place is a miserable existence. I'd rather be on an actual operation, regardless of the hazards. Everybody is so damn dirty. I had to throw my dinner away after a chopper just coated it with sand. Maybe I'm cynical and jumping to conclusions, but I get so goddamn bitter about the dissension in the US—especially when we're so miserable over here. These troops want to leave too. They've got kids they haven't even seen and young wives who need them. It's such a mess.

Next morning: Well, started to shave and the choppers coated the shaving cream on my face with dirt so I looked like I had a mud pack on. At 2 AM, had to go out on patrol to check out alleged artillery rounds landing near by. It turned out the VC had thrown a grenade into a household and killed 5 people-3 adults, 2 children—not very pretty, and just now I read that Wayne Morse is bitching about us using tear gas as inhuman on the Cong! I should have sent him the little girl's body. She couldn't have been more than 8 or 9. How senseless, but it keeps the people scared and reminds them that no matter how many Americans are around, the Cong are still here. Every time I look at these poor victims of terrorism and then I read about Fulbright, Morse, the pickets and draft dodgers, I'd like to break every one of their stupid, blind little necks. Can't wait 'til the sun goes down. I think one of these days it will dissolve my nose. Could always use an ice-cold beer.

30 March '66
Highway 19
Dear Mom,

Just a short note to make sure that you receive a Happy Easter greeting from me, <u>on time</u>, for a change. I'm sort of in a bind to get my "old lady" a gift or flowers, so this will have to do. My thoughts are of you and your Easter breakfast and early years of Easter egg hunts—especially of your crazy hats—but I do remember that my shirts and shoes were many and your hats and pocketbooks were few and far between. I've now seen too much that you've never seen *but remember this:* I remember. Too late perhaps, but I remember and I *appreciate* what you have done! Well, Happy Easter, Young Lady. Hope you knock 'em dead with your hat!

As an officer, he soon found that the practice of rotating the troops after a year in the field meant constantly working with inexperienced men. Troops were hardly efficient during the first few months, and less than enthusiastic the last two. Because he served relatively early in the war, he did not face what for him would have been the ultimate blow—mutinous dissension in the ranks, lack of respect for command, or disregard for the life of your fellow soldier or the Vietnamese whom you were supposedly there to protect. Instead, he formed lifetime bonds and learned lifetime lessons. With a bunch of kids (B.T., at 25, was one of the old men), he sloshed through interminable rivers and rice paddies, while his fair skin burned to a crisp. Leeches crawled up his pants and inside his shirt, attaching themselves so securely that only contact with a cigarette's red-hot ash would force them to drop. He cut through razor sharp elephant grass. He made his way through snarled walls of brush through which the Infantry literally had to hack passage.

There were hills; exhausting, almost vertical climbs that led to landing zones so rife with the unseen enemy's fire that no helicopter could land safely.

And there were monsoons, malaria, and heat, unmerciful heat and humidity, plus something common to all wars and to most soldiers . . . bad food and boredom. Booze and women for the moment, forgotten—anything dry, or a shower, steak, ice cream, sheets, and sleep assumed an enormous importance.

VI

SAM BIRD

———— · ⋄ · ————

To describe him gives me a lump in my throat.
His spirit is undying, his thirst for responsibility
unquenchable, and his compassion for others unlimited.

Letter to Sam Bird's parents, B.T. Collins

With the First Air Cavalry, as an artillery forward observer, B.T. was *attached to* but not *in* the infantry. Upon completion of Officers' Training School (OCS), he had chosen the artillery as his branch of service. The artillery handles the large weaponry. Nevertheless, he was a "Grunt" (infantryman) in every way but actual assignment. He ate, slept, fought, thought infantry. It was, he believed, the heart of any army. To be in the infantry was to be in the thick of it, at ground zero, where the real soldiering took place.

11 April '66
Base Camp
Dear Dad,

My infantry Battalion Commander paid me the highest compliment today. Said if I'd change my brass to Infantry, he'd make me a platoon leader . . . impossible, but a nice feather in my cap. I live and fight like a Grunt. It's in my blood. You'd probably never understand. It's like this. On my first operation— 4 day job in Binh Dinh Province—I went in on 1st lift. Scared I'd fall out of the chopper. I had jumped before, but only with a parachute. Now when I get close to LZ, I sit on the floor, rifle in hand, and before the chopper lands, I'm out. I love it! So, I'm crazy. By the way what ever happened to the idea of hanging a star in the window for someone who's at war? I'm doing my best, believe me. If one of the silent one's should get me, I want to know I died for a worthwhile cause.

Although B.T. longed to be an infantry commander, his best skills were not the physical skills of soldiering. His friend, Dave Porreca, kidded him, "I'll carry the grenades, you carry the food, but keep your ear on the radio. Don't ever throw a grenade!" (A sadly prophetic admonition.) "You throw like a girl."

However, his mind, his intellect, his imagination, his gift for spatial reasoning were, Porreca explained, perfect tools for the task of an artillery forward observer.

"The forward observer in the jungle has to have an imagination. Hell, he can't see the guy on his left or his right, yet he's supposed to know where their perimeter is. He must know where 180 guys are out there; how they're spread out in their foxholes, then create, in his mind, a fire support plan for them; call in the artillery rounds and surround this perimeter with on-call fires. Just based on the messages he's receiving on his radio, he has to be able to understand what's going on in some part of the perimeter that may be 200 yards away. He must know what the men need and what the terrain is like. He must have a 3-D model of it all in his head so that he can call in artillery fire within 30 yards of these people to keep the bad guys away. If we were attacked, B.T. did these calculations in his head. At the same time, he's sweating and dodging bullets like everyone else, but he can't let his emotions run away with him because he has a special set of problems that he has to deal with for all of us.

"The forward observer is dependent on information he gets from somebody else. Maps were made by a Defense Department mapping agency which mapped terrain all over the world, using aerial photography, some ground surveys, and old French maps. These maps were not always correct. When the FO first calls in a set of coordinates, the guns will fire spotting rounds, (like blanks) a round that will burst above the trees just so that he can make sure the guns are aligned and hitting the region he wants hit. The adjustments have to be made by what he hears not always by what he sees. B.T. had, then, to "hear" where the fire was hitting and adjust this now-identified location with his own spatial coordinate system. This calls for gifts that most guys in the service never have. B.T.'s ability to do this was just incredible."

B.T.'s friendship with Dave Porreca was to last a lifetime. In conversations and letters, Dave described their relationship to me in detail. Early on, when combat allowed, he and B.T. argued the nights away. The natural horrors of war and the tension of omnipresent death created ties between them well in excess of similar contacts in the outside world. They shared a love of philosophy and the stimulation of honest debate. B.T. was careful to keep any intellectual bent undercover. He preferred, in Porreca's words, "to paint himself a neer-do-well with personality." It was far more acceptable in that environment to appear macho.

Both men were educated; B.T. because of his voracious reading, Dave because of formal course work and a degree. Both disliked the rigidity of academe and the church. They appreciated the world of ideas, but not always the institutions that were their appointed guardians. While B.T. would have worked within the institution, changing it through people, Dave would have done away with the institution and started from scratch.

They saw what would later be called "political correctness" as another form of rigidity. The either-or, polarized views of the major political parties were also without merit. Problems, they believed, have multiple causes and therefore, demand multifaceted solutions. Through people, however tainted the institution to which they owed allegiance, anything was possible.

B.T. witnessed this time and time again in Vietnam. So, it was the ultimate paradox that while he recognized the potential for perfidy, hypocrisy, and dishonor in all of us, it was forever a surprise and a cruel disappointment when he uncovered it.

The fact that he and Porreca didn't see eye to eye on everything was part of Dave's appeal. All his life, B.T. would surround himself with people whose views were different from his own. It was the family dinner table all over again. Evenings were spent finger pointing and table pounding, with raised voices and raucous laughter. Everyone was thoroughly opinionated—B.T. most of all. No conclusions were drawn nor consensus reached, so the debate would soon start again. Dave's debating skills and their nightly discussions surely drew them closer, but then Dave Porreca had also saved my brother's life.

For every man in every war, there's a battle that is burned into the memory, a unique combination of horrors on a particular day or night that is by the sheer depth and breadth of its brutality beyond human imagination. For B.T. Collins and for his radioman, Andy Anderson, that battle was known as "Crazy Horse." Andy described it to me on tape as soon as he could bear to do so after B.T. died:

> It began on May 16, 1966. When Bravo Company jumped from the helicopter into the elephant grass that day, it was pierced with pungi sticks, an ingenious weapon designed to spear troops upon contact. A seemingly insurmountable mountain rose before them. It had been raining for days. They made the climb taking two steps forward, three back, sticking their rifles in the muck to keep from falling. Their soaked combat boots, oozing mud and water, seemed to weigh 20 pounds apiece. They crawled —at times, the space between the loosened roots and the tangled overhead mass was too small to stand. Though daytime, it was dark. The jungle laced against the sky shut out the light. They reached the ridge in near silence: the only sounds the boots drawing mud, the exhausted sighs and the occasional whispered expletive.
>
> Two minutes later, the unseen enemy let loose. The bullets came from everywhere, crossing and crisscrossing, trapping man after man in their deadly intersections. Hell and Armageddon combined. No time to think, only to react. B.T. took Andy's radio and ordered him to dig a foxhole and get in. He called out coordinates for artillery fire but to his horror the fire hit the trees and the shrapnel fell upon his men. He heard their screams.

He would hear them until the day he died. He tried delayed-fuse rounds, ones that fired, would explode upon hitting the ground, but the slime that passed for terrain just sucked them up and put them out. There was nothing they could do. The maps were old. The coordinates were off. They had climbed the wrong mountain.

May 17th: B.T. lay all night, cheek to the mud, ear to the radio. From Andy's foxhole he could see the bodies downed. A young soldier dragged them by, and every time he passed, their eyes locked in shared terror. They were running out of water and ammunition, stranded and under-strength due to malaria and previous casualties. Someone said, "It's fixed bayonets next." And still the soldier dragged the bodies by.

May 18th: At 4 AM, a bugle sounded eerily in early morning half-light. It was intended to spook the men and it did. They believed it was the enemy's call to battle. They expected immediate hoards of brown faces and with them, the fire and agony of hundreds of rounds of ammunition hitting their mark. They waited.

Silence.

Bravo Company was on the verge of being slaughtered without knowing when. The Company Commander called for support, and Porreca, although severely under-strength as well, volunteered. He burst into B.T.'s position at the very moment the enemy stormed the area. "That mad minute," and those that followed, are described in S.L.A. Marshall's book, *Battle and the Monsoons*.

When it was over, they slid down the slope, 20 or 30 men left out of 85. They passed the poncho-covered mounds splattered with mud and blood, rubber sheets under which their *family* lay. B.T. never said a word. He just reached out to Andy and, for a minute, laid his hand flat on Andy's chest. Solemn gesture. If I can feel your heart beat and you can feel my hand, then I know both of us are still alive.

22 May '66
After Crazy Horse*
Dear Folks,

I was in Qui Nhon yesterday to see the sick and wounded. It was really heart-rending to see the troops and their spirit, no matter what their wounds. One sergeant who saved our lives broke into tears when asking about his men. His squad was almost entirely wiped out. The Division surgeon has been to see the General to make sure we get a rest. It's the talk of the town. The 2/12th is burned out. 25 cases of malaria daily, not to mention gunshot wounds, snake bites, and one heart attack. We look like country boys staring at the food . . . torn and faded fatigues. We need so many more people over here. We have to win and the only way to do it is to use everything we've got. We're so under-strength. A lot of the old hands are thinking of upcoming rotation, so naturally they don't want to go on operations, especially since a lot of them have children they've never seen. I'm so very tired. You'll never know how much I appreciate your mail. Thanks.

9 June '66
Where, I don't know
Dear Folks,

After 3 miserable days of humping through the thickest stuff I've ever seen, tremendous heat and rotten muck, I finally got washed and got the slime out of my ears and fatigues. Just walk in the stream fully clothed and start scrubbing your clothes right on you. I have a cold and I feel like I'm 40. Maybe all this is finally getting to me. I still feel like I've got my harness on. My poor RTO. I know he's really beat, but I have to keep him going. We're quite a team. He's got 97 days to go and then he goes back to the farm. We're almost up to strength but all new men and they can't take this heat day after day. Malaria is still taking 2-3 people a week. Tomorrow we go way the hell north back to

* "Crazy Horse" is my addition. B.T. never referred to it.

Kontum for a real grinder. I'm very leery of the whole thing. The terrain is very, very hilly and a hill in VN is a hill! A Mount Everest! The main reason I write is that I want to remember how my emotions and spirit can change so much in just a few hours. If ever I have a family, I'll know I was there and I did my part, however minute it was. It is enough to say I wouldn't trade this experience for a million dollars. One of the Sergeants whom I wounded with artillery fire wrote the CO and told him that I was the finest FO he'd ever seen. Little things like that keep you going, although I know I can never erase from my mind some of those terrible incidents I've witnessed. Regards to *Lynn. No one appreciates the gift of life more than I, so I feel akin somehow to the tragedy of her dying at such a young age.

25 June '66
An Khe Perimeter
Dear Folks,

54 cases of malaria . . . all my people. Lost my radio operator from ND—105.2. He was like a son to me. We had been together for 7 months. I want to cry. We got 89 replacements during the operation, and came back with 94 people.** It's a losing battle. Lost my Company Commander too . . . 105. Funny, you remember that you were tired, scared, dirty, but when it's over, cleaned up, rested, you can't remember *how* tired. Guess a lot depends on your resiliency. Sometimes I get so tired, I could lie down and weep, but when I come in from a hot patrol or after a fire-fight and I notice the looks of silent appreciation, I know I've done some good. It's a battle of endurance, mental and physical and, you know, I don't really care whether anybody cares because *I'm* doing my share, so they can demonstrate all they want. I've had Montagnard or popular forces attached to us who I swear were no bigger than the boys next door, plucky

---

* Lynn Thomas, a young mother, living next door to my parents, who was dying of cancer.
** Full strength for a company would be between 180 and 200 men.

little soldiers—14-15 years old. Be lucky if they see 20 . . . very lucky. De Gaulle really ticks me off. I knew, sooner or later, we would have to bear the brunt of the fighting over here. But remember we only spend one year here. Gotta run.

One year, only a year . . . for us it seemed a lifetime. At home, we were counting the days.

13 July '66
Highway 19
Dear Mom,

Got your letter tonight. No need to be so proud—not a very high decoration, plus I've been in a lot worse situations where I thought I might get something—but the real reward is the knowledge that the fire I bring in perhaps saves some lives, and the compliments that I receive from the men in the company I'm attached to. I'm no hero. There's millions of people with Bronze Stars. But it is nice, and my Battalion Commander is kind of proud of me. The sad thing is I was only doing my job— nothing more, nothing less. Hardly worthy of a medal.

I'm reading a book by Costain about 18th century England— pretty good—also, Barbarossa (German-Russian Campaign '41-'45). Sure do miss your BLTs. Haven't seen fresh vegetables in sooo long. I wrote to Lynn. How's she doing?

And then there was Sam Bird. Whatever B.T. had witnessed to that point, no event nor any individual would impress him more than this spit-and-polish Captain from Kansas. B.T. met his new company commander one hot July day in 1966. As B.T. wrote in *Reader's Digest*, "I was filthy, sweaty, and jaded by war, and I thought, *Oh, brother, get a load of this.* Dressed in crisply starched fatigues, Captain Bird was what we called 'squared away'—ramrod straight, eyes on the horizon. Hell, you could still see the shine on his boot tips beneath the road dust." Looking at Sam, he thought, "Who in the hell is this guy anyway?"

They were the same age; Sam, a corn-fed, purebred from Kansas, and B.T., a street-smart, wisecracking Irish-American from the suburbs of New York. Sam had graduated from the Citadel and B.T. was a college drop-out. Sam and God were on good terms. B.T. and the Almighty had been on the outs for some time. And Vietnam had done nothing to improve the relationship. But both men laid claim to the traits and loyalties of a different generation. Each one grew still at the sight of Old Glory; each shed a tear when the anthem was sung.

In the months that followed, B.T. would come to revere Sam Bird. His lessons in leadership would have a profound impact on the way B.T. lived his life and led others, during and after the war. ". . . he packed a lot of lessons into the six months we served together. Put the troops first . . . Respect every person's dignity. Always be ready to fight for your people. Lead by example. Reward performance . . . Sam wouldn't ask his men to do anything he wasn't willing to do himself. He dug his own foxholes . . . [he] patiently worked on their pride and self-confidence. Yet there was never any doubt who was in charge." He had the qualities B.T. valued most: honor, selflessness, and meticulous devotion to duty. Sam was everything B.T. admired— a hero's hero, a soldier's soldier, the top of the line. He even cared about B.T.'s teeth!

> 2 August '66
> An Khe
> Dear Folks,
>   Made a beautiful air assault yesterday. Held up in one village, rounding up all males 14-65. Kids very friendly, unbelievably cute, trying to search us, always so hungry. God, I get tired of seeing these starving kids. The countryside very nice—palm trees, lots of rice paddies. Lots of rain. Last night we all spent about 3 hours talking about food. I bragged and bragged about your pies and the chicken tetrazini and the clam dip—your fantastic potato salad. We just drive ourselves crazy. My teeth are falling out. My CO* is my same age and only has 2 cavities.

---

* Sam Bird

He stands over me and makes me brush every day. He really is a 100% all-American guy—always squared away—has the men's welfare on his mind and goes out of his way to make himself known to the troops. Right now, our job is to stay around and protect these people rather than leave them to the mercy of the Cong. These poor people. I can go home to my Rheingold and clam dip, but these waifs of the human race really don't have much of a future.

Ironically, the time I spend meditating on "world-shaking problems" is usually when I'm on a Chinook or Huey C-31. Noise is so great, can't talk, so everybody is full of reflections. I know one thing. I've had enough bullets whiz by me and seen enough dead American kids. I value life. There's no glory dying in some rice paddy. I'm being careful.

By August, B.T. had remained in the field longer than any other forward observer during his tour. FO's were usually returned to the Battery for On-The-Job-Training (OJB) every four to six months, but B.T. convinced the Battery Commander that he had no intention of making a career of the Artillery and was going to ask for a branch transfer to the Infantry. Because much of the training was administrative in nature, (its intent was to train future artillery commanders), and because B.T. was so good in the field, he was allowed to stay in place. He became, according to his Radio Operator, PFC John Turnbull, "one jam-up" forward observer.

18 August '66
LZ "Tom"
Dear Mom,

Short note to let you know your favorite son is always thinking of you. Been here 2 days securing engineers while they blew a monster hole in the jungle that they now decide they don't want. No coordination whatsoever. It scares me. I'd like to get back to my own battalion. You look well in your pictures, all tanned and ready to raise hell. Save your strength for me. I want nothing but cheese soufflé and lemon meringue pie and cold beer. I'll even go upstairs and get your reading glasses. Deal? Keep having a good time. Don't worry about me. I'm fine though I smell like a goat. My two RTO's are back from malaria. They asked to come back with me. Both had a choice, plus they had been with me in some pretty nasty happenings, so I felt kind of honored. A lot of the enlisted men who are going home have come up to tell me I was the finest FO etc., which is pretty nice considering I've hurt some of them with my fire. Things like that make it worthwhile. Please don't worry. I'm the biggest coward going—want to save myself for all those women who are waiting to be ravished.

I got a nice letter from Lynn. It helps me to keep from feeling sorry for myself. Everything is always relative. If I should die now, I know it would be quick, but to have to go her way, with so much to look forward to, just doesn't seem right. What a great thing—the simple gift of being alive and in good health. It gives me the spirit to keep climbing these hills.

6 November '66
Plei Mei S.F. Camp
Dear Dad,

We walked back yesterday to the LZ where we landed. Sort of a forced march. My RTO passed out again, so I carried the radio. The Captain told me that 10 kids from the infantry came up to him to ask if they could carry my radio. Put a lump in my throat. Have to go clean my rust stick (rifle). We fell in the river yesterday, so I'm sure it's a mess. Almost lost one kid. Have a really bad burn on my hands and face. Have to take a drug tonight so I can get some sleep. My nerves are holding up fairly well, though everybody says that an FO who's been in the field as long as I have is fighting the odds, but I'm doing OK. More cautious than I used to be—always checking. A favor. Could you have some flowers sent from me to Mom for Thanksgiving? Sign the card, "To My Favorite Bird Baster." Promise to pay you back.

B.T. hated cleaning his rifle. According to his RTO, Gary Ethan, he cleaned it so seldom that it was always jamming after the first shot so the troops began calling him "One Shot Collins." Not to worry. B.T. eventually got Gary to clean it for him regularly.

> 7 November '66
> North of LZ "Hammond"
> 15 November '66
> In the rain
> Dear Folks,
>
> As I understand it now, I should be transferred to Special Forces sometime soon. So, I just went from 22 days to 387 days. I'm sure my second year will pass as rapidly as my first. Leeches are 5-6" long—impossible to avoid them. The slop sometimes pins you up to your waist—have to get pulled out. Impossible to stay dry. Immersion foot has really done a job on some of the company. I don't know whether I told you or not, my old RTO sent me a lighter with the names of all the operations we'd been in together. Don't worry. I'm doing fine. Just a little tired but I'll be squared away in next couple of days. Just kind of tired.

His first tour was up. He decided to extend his time. He asked to be assigned to the Green Berets, the Army's Special Forces. More than a combat unit, the Special Forces' mission was to work directly with the people. This appealed to him. Also, he had to move on. As always, I was left out of the loop. Perhaps my parents couldn't bear to share this unthinkable news.

Green Berets and Artillery aside, what B.T. wanted most as the year ended was a Combat Infantryman's Badge. The "CIB" was originally intended as a decoration for the foot soldier, for the enlisted man who spent his life fighting it out in the field. Yet, it became a coveted decoration, a badge of honor because it represented those who had seen the worst of it—humping mega-kilometers through the mud, sleeping standing up on a rocky ledge in the rain, surviving the heat, the decaying feet, the snake bites, the daily pictures of men in pieces. B.T. was denied a "CIB" because he wasn't infantry. However, during his last days, Sam and the men of Bravo Company presented him with a handmade wooden plaque, bearing a replica of the Combat Infantryman's Badge and the following inscription:

> 1st Lt. B.T. Collins, "Concrete 3-7." From the officers and men of Company B, 2nd Battalion, 12th Cavalry. In recognition and appreciation of your outstanding performance and uncompromising expertise in providing 'solid walls of steel' as a forward observer from December 1965 to December 1966, we will always remember you as an "infantryman" and as a legend in your own time.

In a journal written after the war, B.T. recalls his last moments with the 2/12th: "The news was out that I was leaving. I made a mental note not to break down in front of my men."

It was not a promise kept. As he accepted the plaque, tears slid down his cheeks. The would-be infantryman was, for once, without words.

PFC Joe Forgione, remembers the ceremony and B.T. "He changed my life forever. I would have followed him anywhere. He never led us into anything for glory. Foremost in his mind was to keep men alive. He told it like it was; he never talked down to anyone."

PFC Gary Ethan, radioman and B.T.'s personal rifle cleaner, agreed. "He told me the very first day. 'I'm new at this. I've got a lot to learn. So, if you see me screwing up, just straighten me out.' He meant it. B.T. always told us we were making history, that what we were accomplishing would someday be in the school books. In battle, he became an infantryman, a soldier. He deserved a CIB. We gave him a standing O."

Later, because of the unusual number of days he had spent in the field with the infantry, B.T. did receive his Combat Infantryman's badge. It is worn on his uniform that has been donated to the Citizen Soldiers' Museum in Old Sacramento. The handmade painted plaque, now blistered with age, is there as well.

Leaving Bravo Company was very hard; leaving Sam Bird behind hurt even more. The night before his departure, he wrote to Sam's parents.

November 30, 1966
Dear Mr. & Mrs. Bird,

I am the FO for this company, and your fine son is the fourth company commander I've worked for, so when I talk about his qualities as an individual, I feel that I am qualified. To describe him gives me a lump in my throat. He worries about his men like a father, yet always accomplishes the most difficult mission. His spirit is undying, his thirst for responsibility unquenchable, and his compassion for others, unlimited.

If you could see the way he operates, the way he handles his men, the way he stays calm under the most adverse conditions; you'd bust your buttons with pride. It's really awe-inspiring. Working with people like Captain Bird makes you feel like there are some good, decent people in This Man's Army! A couple of days ago, he was up to his knees in the mud in the pouring rain, digging a drainage ditch. Yesterday, he was helping a private hold down his shelter to stop it from being blown away by a helicopter. He runs a good ship, flexible but not limp. His spirit is an example to these kids who have a miserable existence. They seem to know he won't let them down. I know myself. I would follow him to the gates of hell and back.

Well, must close now. Thought you would like to hear something about your fine son, because knowing him, I knew you'd never hear it from his lips.

PS Please don't tell him I wrote about him.

So the first year was done, and its mark was indelible. If the history of the great wars had fired his imagination, in no way could it be compared to the rush of the real thing. For war, even at its bloodiest and most dangerous is still a seducer of men. The wind whipping his face as he came in low over the trees, the sound of bullets spitting fire around him, the *son et lumiere* spectacle of artillery played against a night sky excited him at first. But that kind of feeling grows old in the field. The physical sensations, soon only sporadically pleasing, were replaced by sheer exhaustion, anger, and disgust.

B.T. told the family and others that he believed he had found his niche. He was saving some lives; he was improving the quality of others; he was helping; he was continuing the American tradition of duty to country. He was *good* at soldiering. The qualities that caused him be the center of attention as a teenager, he found, could be harnessed for the common good. He had the ability to make others listen, to make them follow. The traits of character that had been applied only to amuse now had a more serious purpose.

Underneath his tough-guy, nothing-gets-to-me exterior was a man to whom others really mattered, a man who would die for you, and the men around him knew it. They told me so.

The careless, he conned into believing that he was just a simple Joe; blunt, honest, nothing much beneath the surface. In fact, he was a complex man, this complexity only to be exacerbated in Vietnam. At its very core were a heartbreaking sentimentality, a lot of guilt, and a frightening capacity to care; frightening because it could so easily get out of control. My brother changed slowly from fiery idealist to impatient realist without ever totally losing his belief that life could be as it should be.

And at the end, he admitted, he was truly afraid. "It was getting really hairy . . . the pungi sticks . . . it even crossed my mind that something might happen to me."

VII

Special Forces

Vietnam? The best damn thing that ever happen to me . . .
The greatest weight reduction program I was ever on!

B.T. Collins

B.T. did come home between tours, stopping in Wichita, Kansas to visit Sam's parents and assure them that Sam was fine. He also drove to visit me in the wilds of Northern New York. I had never seen him so trim, so hard, so tall. What a relief it was to have him home safe and sound and in such great shape. He wore his uniform. My children were literally jumping up and down at the sight of him. And then he told me. He was not home for good. I couldn't believe it.

"My God, Brien, why?"

"You don't know, Maureen. The children . . . if you could see the children. You just can't understand how bad it is. I'm good at what I do. Maybe, I can save some lives."

When he left this time, Daddy took him to the airport. It was more than Mother could bear, although she was, in many ways, the tougher of the two. Our father watched Brien walk away from him in the airport. Looking at his back, he thought, *Maybe this is it. What if I never see him again?*

He shared his fears with Brien in a letter, and my brother, in a weak moment, later shared them with me.

The Special Forces would call upon all of B.T.'s people skills. He would be politician, arbitrator, comptroller, teacher, paymaster, field-soldier, drill sergeant, nurse, social worker—a sort of one-man government and more. Working with the indigenous people, his job was to teach them how to stay healthy, how to defend themselves, and their own villages, using modern weapons.

Prepared speeches were useless. B.T. had to draw from his previous experience with these people and recognize that they came from a different culture, one whose roots and ideas were still planted in the practices of a different century. The task would require extraordinary imagination and ingenuity if he were to turn them into a fighting unit. Unlike his assignment in the First Cavalry, he would be part of a team of only twelve Americans who would be in charge of nearly 250 indigenous troops.

B.T. was first assigned to a Special Forces team in the Delta. As his tour began, he was the Executive Officer (XO) of Company A-425. Later, he would volunteer to join a Mobile Guerrilla Company, A-432, the 4th Mobile Guerrilla Force stationed in To-Chau, in Hatien Province, Republic of South Vietnam.

The second camp was situated on the southwestern coast of Vietnam near the town called Hatien. This was strictly a volunteer job. The Mobile Guerrilla Company carried out missions in extended operations—each lasting at least 30 days. Because the men would be so far out into enemy territory, there would be no medical evacuation. They were dependent, therefore, on their own Special Forces medics and each other's training and skills to care for their needs if wounded.

Their mission was generally to be a thorn in the enemy's side, to go into areas which the Vietcong or the North Vietnamese Army dominated, and to conduct guerrilla operations against their forces. In other words, their intent was to hunt down their units, pick away at them by ambush and direct action against their supply lines; to search for their supply bases, call in air strikes against any concentration of their forces, and deny them free use of their area of operation.

In Special Forces, B.T. found lifelong friends in fellow Green Berets Henry Cook and Ruben Garcia. When Henry joined the unit,

B.T. tried to counsel him about the horrors of combat; what to expect from his first experience under fire, and how to deal with the emotional upheaval that followed.

It was, nevertheless, quite a bit worse than Henry had imagined and recovering from the ordeal required in-depth imbibing and no small amount of serious revelry. Henry had received a cut on his forehead that required 13 stitches. The "morning after," each man of the twelve-man unit contributed one stitch. Obviously, some showoff sneaked in "two." He still carries the scars of a night of Special Forces collective surgery.

Brien's letters continued, describing a different battlefield, almost a different war.

> 24 January '67
> Thung Thoi
> Dear Folks,
>
> I'm the XO of an "A" company detachment (2 officers, 12 fighting men) on the Mekong River, 5 K's from the Cambodia. This area was under water for 2 solid months! It's a mess. I'm in charge of all the funds (pay the VN troops—militia)—civic action, and pay operations.
>
> The area we live in is OK. We have a shower, toilet, a cook, and a houseboy. We conduct operations on boats right on the Mekong River. 75% of our area is VC controlled. We can only *advise* the VN under us—countless power struggles. Unbelievable amount of paper work. And I'm such an ignorant neophyte it makes it worse. Civic action programs bogged down—troops won't fight. It's really hopeless!
>
> What a mess—filth. We (12 of us) have an unbelievably large area to administrate (advise). Sure wish I were back up in the highlands working with the Montagnards. The Vietnamese I'm with now just use us to get anything, and the US government literally gives away tons of stuff and thousands of dollars. Maybe I can do something in spite of it all. I shall persevere. Keep this to yourself. It just helps me to get it off my chest.

29 January '67
A-425
Dear Folks,

Last night we came the closest I've ever been to Cambodia. We walked along the river border (Cambodia on the other side) and we could hear dogs barking over there. I was naturally disappointed that the VC had left. It's funny the way the other Americans keep telling me in a very paternalistic way how tough it is. Yet, I don't have to wear a "steel pot" or carry a backpack. I don't have to lie in the mud or the rain. I always have hot chow and can have a shower when I return. When I think of my days in the CAV and the misery, I am embarrassed at some of the comforts we have here. I feel like a slacker. Last night the cook made me a cheese omelet and later, we had chocolate cake. This A.M. spent some time with outgoing XO to learn more about my most important function. I'm going to be responsible for some $250,000-$300,000 American each month. Quite involved. As you can see, I really have a comfortable and safe life. I'm *not* lying to you. No point in it. Last year there was a reason as it *was quite dangerous up there*. But this, by comparison is a breeze.

30 January '67
6:30 p.m. Watching the Mekong float by.
Dear Folks,

I went down to Hon Ngu this A.M. to watch sick call. Two really dedicated S. F. medics down there. The problems they face are enormous. The filth, tradition, superstition, and medical practices stagger the imagination. The Special Forces people are training village health workers so they can do their jobs—treat burns—watched them suture a girl whose head was split open in a fight in the market place. I will learn how to do that, and to give shots eventually. The lads who do the work are only about 16-17 but real fine. The Americans coach them through an interpreter. If the cases are serious, they make bi-monthly trips to Long Xuyen, where a civilian hospital is run by an Australian medical team. Cleft palates, TB, hernias treated there. We pay the transportation. Yesterday, one of the VN troops killed himself with a grenade. Life seems pretty cheap to them. How about a box of Dutch Masters Panatelas for a Valentine's present? C'mon let loose some of that gold!

31 January '67
A-425
Dear Folks,

Really too tired to write but I had some thoughts I wanted to put down. We walked all night long—not bad terrain—but the lack of sleep got to me and I kept falling asleep on the march. It wasn't being bone tired or terrible fatigue; it was just lack of sleep. I felt kind of sheepish when I remember what I used to do. In the light of the activity and endurance requirements down here, I guess I, frankly, did go through a bit of hell last year. But it didn't seem that way at the time because you're alive. I think a lot—daydream while I'm walking or riding in a boat, a million thoughts go through my head, especially because there are no Americans to talk to. The CIDG, (indigenous), troops are just great until they get to the objective and then they just fall apart—talk, yell, shout at birds—really something else. We finished up in this village. God! That stink and the poverty! Every time I see it and smell it, I thank my lucky stars I was born in the good old USA. The eternal search for food, the stink of the fish, the river taxis, the market place; it's another world. I must have crossed 13 waist-deep rivers last night, but it's nothing compared to those hills.

We must have traveled 13-14 Ks last night, 70% of it in VC controlled territory, (That doesn't mean they're actually there) but they collect the taxes and make the people dig the trenches. The mosquitoes like to carry me away for ransom. I was so tired, I fell asleep on the boat going back. Another one tonight, but the old man flat refused to let me go, for which I'm glad. Instead of sleeping, I consumed this book, *In the Morning*, by the author of *A Tree Grows in Brooklyn*. It was great. The kind of story that Dad would like. God, if I didn't love to read, I'd be in a fix. I can read so fast. I never realized it, but I must put away a book or 2 a day in my spare time. I took a couple pictures of the kids today who were hanging around in adulation of Willy, who is a monstrous 6' 2", 240 lb. weapons sergeant. Some of them are very cute and others a real pain but what does a kid have to look forward to over here?

Funny, this time last year (exact date) I was in a graveyard in Bong Song, absolutely terrified, and now here I sit placidly. Well, hope you are well and raising hell.

1 February '67
A-425
Dear Folks,

We went up to one of our outposts to pay the CIDG. Quite an experience! We took Polaroids up there and these people go wild over them. The CO Commander of the fort invited us for tea-beer-chow-tea with chopsticks. I got the chow down . . . barely . . . and we chatted through an interpreter. Kids always amazed at my height. Living conditions very bad—brave people, even if they are mercenaries. At every pay formation, there are a few amputees—so young—life tough enough around here when you've got *both* feet! Today, I ran into another sad case. A 66 year old man who teaches the dependents of the CIDG. We hired him because his son is VC who planted a mine and blew his own father's leg off. Poor old guy who doesn't think the world owes him anything. Not a glimmer of hope. I told him my father's a teacher.

Next day: I just heard of Grissom and White's deaths on the radio. What a goddamn shame! Got another favor to ask you. If I'm going to just sit on my duff, I'd like you to send my Spanish and French books. Send the grammar books and then the novels. I never sold any of my books so they're there somewhere. Dad, thanks for your letter. There will be more homecomings and good-byes in the years to come. I just wanted you to know I was touched by your remarks. I hope you'll never have to be ashamed or embarrassed because of me. And about this being a hero bit, I swear to you that I'm doing nothing—absolutely nothing, dangerous.

Hero or no, we were proud, our father especially so. He went to a bar . . . he who so despised drinking. It was one of Brien's hangouts, just a joint . . . polished bar with a greasy floor, and that dank air that smells of stale beer and stubbed cigarettes. Daddy was wearing a hat, vintage Elliot Ness, and his raglan-sleeved brown tweed coat, long out of style. His white shirt was starched and with a tie. He slid onto a stool and called quietly to the bartender, drawing a tissue-wrapped package from his pocket. Then he folded back the paper to show the hidden pride inside. The ribbons revealed grew brilliant in the neon light, and the bronze circles shone like new coins in his trembling hands. "My name is Collins," he began. "I believe you know my son. I wanted you to see what he has done."

The bartender later told B.T.

And then the unthinkable happened. B.T. received a letter from Sam Bird's sister. Sam had been horribly wounded on his 27th birthday, his last day in Vietnam. In a cruel twist of fate, he should not have been there at all. His time was up, but he had conned his commanding officer into extending his tour a month. His men had planned a surprise party and a cake had somehow been flown in. But orders came down for Bravo to lead an assault on a North Vietnamese regimental headquarters.

When they flew in, the landing zone was "hot;" the enemy many and waiting. Sam went down two minutes after his feet hit the ground. Shots first shattered his legs, then siphoned off a quarter of his skull. His terrified, near weeping executive officer, Lt. Dean Parker, tried stuffing the leaking brain matter back into the cavity from which it oozed. Furious, his radioman, PFC Joe Forgione, tracked down Sam's would-be assassin and killed him. The clean-cut Kansan, who had carried JFK's casket on the Capitol steps, would never walk again, never see clearly, never have the use of both arms. He would suffer from unbearable headaches and pains in his legs all the rest of his days. He lost his short-term memory. The scholar and future general's IQ would drop to that of a child. The family knew about Sam and we grieved as for a son or brother though we had never met him.

B.T. was heartbroken.

13 February '67
Monday
Dear Dad,

I received some very bad news today—very, very bad. Captain Bird was critically wounded while air assaulting. His condition was determined by the attending physician to be a matter of grave concern. It happened on his birthday. Dad, he was like a brother to me. We were complete opposites. He was *the finest* commander, the greatest SOB I've ever met and I don't even know now if he is alive. I always thought of him as indestructible. I don't know why—I imagine some people think of me as thus blessed. Why have others died while I live? I just don't know. I just don't know. I want to believe that he is still alive, because if the will to live has anything to do with it, he will be. But not knowing—you know yourself, head wounds and belly wounds are not pretty and a slug can really do a job on your skull and its contents.

I know there's nothing you can do. I just needed a sympathetic ear. When you and Mom think you've made some sort of sacrifice by having me over here, remember the Birds. I'm no hero, nor am I invincible, but I can function under fire. These things I know, but I guess it doesn't make any difference. Generator going off.

Combat drew my father and brother closer. B.T. confided in Daddy because he had been to war. He would understand. And Daddy told me. He knew I understood as well, and while my heart went out to Sam's family, my fear for B.T.'s safety grew.

19 February '67
A-425
Dear Folks,

Doing my paperwork today. My heart's not really in this, because basically, I'm a field soldier. My friend Sam has taken a turn for the worse. His parents are with him in Tokyo, and naturally are taking it pretty hard. Five operations so far. One lasted 7-1/2 hours with his head packed in ice the whole time and still, no word whether he'll live from one day to the next. I finally got the word what happened, and almost every single one of the officers was wounded. My old radio operator is dead and one of my best friends who had seen more than his share was blown apart by a hand grenade. I feel quite hopeless and frustrated, as I am unable to do anything. I would feel better if I were in some kind of action. We really were a tight knit group in B CO and have remained so or perhaps the Captain's injury has strengthened old bonds. Maybe I made a mistake staying with one company so long. Who knows?

9 March '67
Thursday
Dear Folks,

We now treat 125 people a day at the dispensary and 50 TB patients. 1 sergeant plus the 4 VN nurses he has trained—it's a going operation. I'm working on a letter to the Lions Club because we need streptomycin, penicillin, and vitamins so badly. We need drugs for the TB patients daily. Yesterday, a woman died right outside the dispensary, about 40 yrs old. She'd probably had TB for years—her lungs just fell apart. You should see some of the cases that come in—but at least, they're coming in instead of going to Chinese medicine men (12th century witchcraft). These people are so apathetic and so filthy. It seems just hopeless at times, and I wonder what we're keeping them alive for. Maybe I'll transfer to the 173rd and get back in the war.

17 March '67
Dear Dad,

This will be the last letter for quite a while, as I've been reassigned to a different operation and for security reasons I can't tell you where, nor will I be able to write. You have to explain somehow to Mother. Just tell her something because there won't be any mail from me for at least 2 weeks maybe longer. But don't worry, I'll be OK—believe me.

2 April '67

Dear Folks,

Realize that you're probably upset at the lack of mail from me, but I am on an operation and probably will be on one until the 15th of April. I am with a special type of company. Haven't been doing much because 4 of our interpreters quit, and it's literally impossible to operate without them, and quite dangerous too. My new camp is on the coast on the Gulf of Siam. I will probably spend more time in the field from now on—troops are like children, constantly AWOL. They sell equipment—unbelievable! If the American public only knew, but there's nothing you can do. They're basically civilian mercenaries.

I had a letter from Sam's father. He's still alive. Really sad. He had such a tremendous future. At a *minimum*, he would have been a 2-star general. His parents are with him in Tokyo. Two more acquaintances KIA last month. Getting so I don't even want to look at the *Stars and Stripes* for fear I'll see the name of someone I know. I feel so ineffective sitting on my arse down here.

9 April '67

Dear Dad,

Went on a long 30K operation the other day—little trouble—but I'm okay. Just an administrative item for your information. You (at my request) will be the only one notified if I am critically wounded. If I were not expected to live, also, all correspondence of this nature will go to your school address. I think you will agree that this way is best. In the event that Mother should get a telegram and you weren't there . . . you are better equipped to handle the situation. Be advised: I am not pre-occupied with death, but I think these things should be in order (my military mind working again). Don't reply in kind with a lot of maudlin nonsense. I am fine and will continue to be fine, subject of course, to the normal rigors of VN: VD, cirrhosis, a generally bad outlook on everything. Take care, old man.

17 April '67

Dear Folks,

Just a quickie. Got to get a new company trained; no equipment, no ammo, no interpreters, all hoodlums, all came to this company because we pay outrageously high salaries. It's hard when you don't have the training facilities, plus the language. They are mercenaries—they can quit any time they want.

Somehow, I've got to get them ready for combat in about a month. It's enough to make a grown man cry. My indigenous Company Commander is from the experienced company. Although we don't speak the same language (he's Cambodian), we understand each other—set up 3 parachutes for classes tomorrow, try some basic English and hand and arm signals—close-order drills. Then we have a whole mess of paper work, but only 1 typewriter for 2 companies. It's my first chance at command, and it's tough. I have my own method of controlling my NCOs, but you have to get them to have confidence in you. There's only 6 of us with the company so far. I'll do my best, but the higher-ups just say, "Get it done." Just armchair generals. I'd like to see those bastards in a fire-fight when these troops run—and they will, I know it, I've seen them—leaving their own wounded.

Re: your letter. No need to worry if anything happens to me. You will know in detail the same day. When I say Gulf of Siam, our camp is on the ocean about 3,000 meters south of Cambodia. Very safe area. No Charlies here. Not trying to win the war by myself. Just doing a thankless, frustrating job to the best of my ability.

30 April '67

Dear Folks,

My new boss very good. We had whole shrimp last week, heads and all. I don't think you'd like them. They usually dry them on the street—flies included. We're getting the troops more and more under control. I understand they burned some flags in New York. That's nice, really nice. Nice crop of people you folks are raising or cultivating or tolerating back there.

6 May '67
To Chau
Dear Folks,

About the flag burning. I just don't know. Been thinking of writing the *Reporter Dispatch** my views but probably will not get around to it. Don't forget, the Bronze Star is the *lowest* thing you can get for valor. The Old Man is really trying to make an officer out of me. I seek his respect, but to earn it, I've a lot of work to do. Hopefully, some day, this band of miscreants will be mine. Not much time, but I've got 'til December, so maybe we can make a go of this thing yet. I'm just too easy to be good, I'm afraid. As an individual, I can stay alive, but as a leader, I fall far short of what this job will take. I guess I need a lot more self-confidence, or I'll never be good at anything.

You know what the hardest part about this job is? That I know I'll stay to the bitter end, even if it means dying for these bastards, knowing full well that they would never do the same for me. "*C'est la guerre*," right? Well, at least I won't have any trouble looking in a mirror after this tour. I'll have given it my best shot. Don't mind me. I gotta cry on someone's shoulder.

They were burning flags in my town too. I thought about Sam dying, with half his brains left behind to rot on the floor of some jungle. I thought of B.T. filthy and exhausted, always in danger. I thought about the pungi sticks and the landing zones where the enemy waited in the tall grass. And I was angry and bitter. As an academic, I had never quite fit the mold, and now I was significantly out of step. My colleagues were almost universally "anti-war," a term I detested because of the implied opposite. The students' behavior was an affront to everything I believed. My world was falling apart. The bad guys were winning. Even my cousins were in Washington

---

* Our hometown newspaper.

demonstrating. One day, as I returned from campus, a group of protesters set a flag on fire in front of me.

My first thought was to call my father nearly 500 miles away. He alone would understand. "Daddy," I wept. "My God, they're burning the flag!" It was a line never to be crossed; something, I, like B.T., could not forgive.

"I know, Puss," he replied sadly. "I know. I'm sorry."

16 June '67

Dear Folks,

I am on an operation. I rendezvoused with the Old Man today—waiting to infiltrate fresh troops—very tired—eating indigenous rations, rice and fish—water crucial—all water here is brackish. I'm doing OK—how long it's going to last—I don't know. Happy Father's Day. Don't sweat it.

June 20, 1967. The heat and humidity were unbearable in the marsh-laced, swamp-infected terrain of B.T.'s first and last mission with the Mobile Guerrilla Company. And he was tired—bone deep, to the soul, flat-out whipped. Later, he blamed himself for having stayed too long in one spot. When tracked by and tracking the Vietnamese, the rule was never to stay in one place more than 24 hours. And although he had not overstayed the regulation time limit, something had told him to move on. But fatigue and heat had won out.

The VC found him.

In the ensuing fire-fight, a South Vietnamese mercenary tossed him a live grenade. He saw the tremendous flash. Someone's screams hung dulled in the dust around him. A blinded sergeant hollered, "Give the Old Man my morphine!" And there was blood . . . so much blood. And it ran warm from him, but he was ominously chilled. He saw the medic running toward him, and he called out to him, "T-burg, T-burg, am I going to die?"

The school year was coming to an end in the Hartsdale, New York district in which my mother taught second grade. A message on her classroom intercom asked that she come to the office; a secretary was being sent up to cover her class. The war news had been so bad that week that I wonder what went through her mind at that moment.

My father didn't wait in the office but started upstairs to her classroom on the second floor. Mother saw him from the landing. It hurts me to think of the look that must have passed between them . . . these lifetime lovers, and Brien their only son. She knew surely, whatever the news, it would not be good.

And it wasn't . . . or was it?

Who could have imagined the life that was to follow?

VIII

VALLEY FORGE

I'm not putting up a front for other patients;
I'm doing it for myself and I'm tired of it.
I'm tired of not having an arm and a leg and
I'm especially tired of you and your
goddamn dressing changes!

B.T. Collins to Dr. Jim Sargent

They lifted him as gently as speed would allow, sliding him, now silent, across the blood-greased surface of an olive drab poncho. Nearly crying, they carried his body to the waiting helicopter.

Against regulations, his men had radioed a ship off the coast. The Special Forces Mobile Guerrilla rules were clear: if the man were too severely injured to be carried out, he was left. Anything else would alert other Vietnamese to the troops' location and put those remaining at even greater risk. The men understood privately that this was a rule never to be obeyed. The ship they contacted had a helicopter deck. Marines flew in and picked him up.

Above the noise of the engine, the chopper pilot pleaded with him, "Stay awake, Collins. Stay awake!"

In northern New York, the phone was ringing as I entered the house. I had begun to dread the sound. I was afraid to go out for fear of missing a call, and afraid to stay in for what I might hear when I picked up the receiver.

It was my Aunt Fran, my mother's only brother's wife. She was the one who always called when someone died. Her message was clear and direct. "Call home. It's Brien." I didn't ask for further information. I wasn't sure I wanted to know.

I dialed my parents' number and managed, "Daddy?" I heard my father's sorrow in the initial silence. He cleared his throat, and sighed from his very soul. He read the telegram. I caught the words, "double amputation," and I froze. No words of comfort or questions came to mind. I said that I would come to White Plains immediately but my father replied in a near whisper, "Not now. *When he dies*, you'll have to come home for the funeral."

Brien was going to die? When he dies! Nooo, Daddy. Nooo! A voiceless protest screamed within me, but before it gathered sound and force, my mother took the phone and cheerfully stated, "They always put them in a hospital near their families." (I don't know how she knew this, but she sounded quite positive.) "*When he comes home*, we'll all go to the hospital to see him. In the meanwhile, we'll just have to wait."

When he comes home . . . I could live with that.

I hung up the phone. The house was very still. I entered the next room and fell to my knees on the braided rug covering an old wood floor. Then I cried out—animal sounds—a creature caught in the iron-toothed trap of a truth too terrible to bear. I would never have believed such pain was possible. Instinctively, I ran to church. I lit every candle there. Again I knelt, alone in the center aisle, touching my forehead to the cool stone floor. Stretching out my arms, I beseeched the Almighty, proposing a veritable litany of "If You'll just, then I'll . . ." promises upon promises, impossible to keep. I wept until, fat-lipped, and slit-eyed, I was no longer recognizable. I was mortally afraid.

In the months ahead, our stern yet gentle father wore his anguish; evidence of his pride, his fear for Brien's life, his guilt. He, after all, was the patriot, who had so encouraged service to one's country. Mother, gracious lady of the candlelight dinners and impeccable manners, would teach us what courage . . . no, what having guts really meant. No crying, no carrying on. No "Poor Brien," or "Why has this happened to us," or "What will we do?" What mattered most was that he was still alive. And he would get well.

In Vietnam, B.T.'s fellow Special Forces officers, Ruben Garcia and Henry Cook, got the news while still out on their own Mobile Guerilla operation in the Seven Mountains area. When Ruben came out of the field, he flew directly to Can-Tho to render his operational report to the commanding officer. He then tried to find out where B.T. was and, in what condition. No one knew the answer to either question. Exhausted and hungry after thirty days of eating local rations and being under fire, he was furious. He sounded off to the officer in command. "When," he asked, "had Special Forces become so large and so uncaring that they would send men into combat, and then forget about them when they were wounded?"

Needless to say, he told me, "I got my butt chewed, but there was so much scar tissue there it really didn't matter."

Ruben left the officer standing, mouth open, stormed out of Special Forces Headquarters and walked to a nearby airfield where he inquired if there were any aircraft headed for Saigon. Saigon was simply a hunch because it had a field hospital. In reality, B.T. could have been anywhere, even already evacuated to the Philippines or to the States. The operations chief of an Otter about to make the four-hour flight to Saigon told Ruben that if he wanted to get on "that slow-flying son-of-a-bitch" and if the crew chief would let him on the plane, to be his guest.

The crew chief was not overjoyed. Ruben, caked with grime of a month in the field, smelled like dung. But owing to the fact that he was carrying an M-16 and looked in no mood to argue, the chief told him to climb aboard.

Arriving in Saigon, he found a jeep to take him to the field hospital that was about 10-12 miles away. He reached the hospital, only to find it dark and totally quiet. Nevertheless, Ruben managed to locate someone who knew B.T., and told him that he had already been evacuated in very serious but stable condition. A nurse, overhearing this conversation, offered that B.T. might still be at the evacuation holding bays at the airport; she thought he was not scheduled to be "evac" until 07:00 the following morning.

Ruben hitched a ride back to Saigon.

After having been stabilized aboard the *Sea Wolf*, B.T. was flown to the Third Surgical Hospital at Dong Tam. The initial report was not promising:

> Patient admitted ashen gray in profound hemorrhagic shock with severe fragment wound to the right leg and thigh and traumatic amputation of the right hand and lower forearm. Approximately 8 units of low liter type O blood were rapidly infused. Airway maintained and 100% oxygen administered. ph of 7.1 was treated with 6 ampoules of NaHco3 IV near the completion of the initial blood replacement. Patient regained consciousness. Prognosis grave.

"Profound hemorrhagic shock" in layman's terms, meant that B.T. was "bled out;" his blood supply was gone . . . thus "the initial blood replacement." His blood pressure registered 45 over nothing; his pulse 20. The supply of oxygen to his vital organs was about to disappear, and brain damage would begin. Sodium Bicarbonate was given to reduce the acidity of his blood shown by the low ph reading. Nevertheless, B.T. was alert and talking.

Mother once told Marialis and me that Brien had very little to say until he was three or four. Then he interrupted her afternoon bridge game with a long, complex and grammatically perfect sentence. He had, to use her words, "Never shut up a moment since." True to form, according to the nurses and doctors, he continued to talk whenever conscious throughout those first perilous days.

Twenty-four hours after his admission, his shattered right leg was declared unsalvageable, and a surgical amputation was scheduled. What remained of his right arm was to be repaired at the same time. When the nurses cleaned him up before surgery, it meant shaving his beard. Unbelievably, he put up a fight. There was no way he was going to lose his beard. "But you're going to lose your leg," the frustrated nurse explained. "I don't care about my leg," he replied. "The beard stays!"

The war in Vietnam was a particularly dirty war. While technology had increased the quality and delivery speed of medical treatment, it had also created more dangerous weaponry. The potential for lethal injuries was staggering. Rapid-fire arms increased the chance of multiple wounds.

Frequently, soldiers were hit in paddy fields or along waterways where human and animal waste collected. Whatever lay between the point of entry and the exploding mine, rocket-propelled grenade, booby-traps and or bullets (twigs, leaves, mud, bits of uniform, insects, and the like) was carried with tremendous force into the wound. Because of the subsequent danger of life threatening infection, the wound had to be "debrided," which means to remove painstakingly and painfully every bit of foreign matter. The "foreign matter" rose to the surface in infectious stages and, at each appearance, had to cut away. In WWII, the procedure had been to clean what was visible then suture the site. Many men died from infections after returning home because only the surface had been treated and the wound had not, in fact, healed. B.T.'s wounds would be debrided.

Injuries like B.T.'s in which a limb had been "traumatically amputated," (blown away by the force of an explosion), still needed to undergo the process of surgical amputation. The planned surgical removal of a limb is far different from the loss of one that has been literally ripped from its natural location. The remaining flesh and bone are neither evenly distributed nor naturally positioned to allow for complete healing and the eventual use of prosthesis. The amputation site must be "prepared" through skin grafts and bone reduction, extremely painful processes that B.T. would endure for months.

In the hours that followed his initial surgery, he suffered two cardiac arrests. A priest was called to give him last rites. He asked my brother if he were sorry for *all his sins.* Apparently, B.T. raised his head just enough to look the priest in the eye. "No," he replied, "not *all* of them!"

Surely after all he had seen and suffered, sin must have seemed the least of things . . . a sense of proportion that would remain with him and endear him not at all to his ultra right Christian opponents during his run for the California Assembly twenty years later. No question, his "meet-the-grim reaper-and-spit-in-his-eye" attitude made a difference, for dying was a very real possibility for B.T. Collins in those initial hours. The nurse in charge had listened to too many stories of girlfriends, hometowns, and families, only to have the man not make it. One look at B.T. and she assigned him to another nurse with the admonition, "Let this one die with you instead of me."

Fortunately, by the time of the Vietnam War, the combat mortality rate had been cut in half. B.T. was one of the thousands to be saved in this modern conflict; scraped from the muck in bits and pieces to be reassembled painfully, even cruelly, by the gentle, the caring, and the inordinately skilled. The use of helicopters brought rapid air evacuation. Most of the patients were young, and, other then their injuries, were in relatively good physical condition. Whole blood was readily available. Advanced surgical techniques and intensive care nursing were the rule in field hospitals that were as well equipped as their stateside counterparts. The Third Surgical Unit to which B.T. was taken was a self-contained, transportable hospital that had electrical power, heat, hot and cold water, air conditioning, and waste disposal facilities.

Regardless, the carnage was tremendous and the missing parts too many. After the war, surgeons began to question whether in putting these bodies back together they had done the right thing. Would these reassembled human beings ever again live whole lives in the outside world?

For those who knew B.T. Collins, the answer, of course, was "yes."

Back in Saigon, at the airport, Ruben finally found the Quonset huts that housed those about to be medically evacuated. He spotted one leaking light and heard the sound of voices. He knocked on the door and when it failed to open, kicked it flat. Streaked with dirt and still armed, he stepped into a long bay with beds on both sides. Every patient who was able was looking at him. Running toward him was an angry nurse giving him one of those looks that, according to Ruben, "only nurses know how to give." The door he had knocked to the floor was the one on which a movie was being projected. No matter, for back in the shadows, sixth bed to the right, his search ended.

Seeing Ruben, B.T. propped himself up on an elbow. Too tired to smile, he wept softly in disbelief and gratitude. His tears dried in place . . . no back of the hand left to brush them aside. Moving toward him, Ruben cried as well, white rivulets washing down his blackened cheeks. He sat gingerly on B.T.'s bed, and heads lowered in the darkness, one listened and the other told the story.

B.T.'s suffering was obvious. Even allowing for the color-draining darkness, he was unusually pale. His young face was pulled back against its own bones, his forehead creased and clammy, his ordinarily raucous voice hoarse from vain protests against an almost constant agony. He spoke about his terrible loneliness, the phantom physical sensations in limbs no longer there, the many transfusions, and, the fact that the acidity in his body kept rejecting the transfused blood. He felt lucky just to be alive, lucky that a Sea Wolf had been nearby and was willing to send one of its helicopters. He worried about an 18-year-old in the next bed with a serious head wound, who was in a coma and not expected to live. He spoke of the future. He would go back to school; he would do something with his life. His injuries, he said, were only momentary setbacks.

But his somber mood was short-lived. As Ruben got ready to leave, B.T. called out to a pretty redheaded nurse, to please powder his back and his rear. "Someday," he told her, "you can tell your grandchildren that you powdered Ole B.T.'s butt."

She laughed and said she was sure this would be the highlight of her military career.

B.T. never forgot that a friend had remembered. And though he knew that many, given the opportunity, might have done the same, Ruben was marked special from that moment. Vietnam taught him that pain becomes tolerable in the presence of compassion; that compassion plus irreverence, humor, and just plain orneriness were an unbeatable combination.

The next morning Ruben arrived at 0600. This stinking, sweat-stained, faithful friend clung to the ghost of the man he once knew, holding B.T.'s hand as he walked beside his stretcher. He helped carry B.T. aboard the plane that would take him to Clark Air Force Base in the Philippines. He waited while the nurse and medic locked the litter in place. They wished each other luck. Ruben had brought B.T. the cigarettes he had asked for and loaned him his lighter. Unspoken prayer and promise: If I give you my lighter, you must live to return it. Who knew if they would speak again, or where or when?

Ruben stood watching the plane lift off and began to wonder for the first time just how much trouble he was in for leaving without permission to go find B.T. What was the worst thing they could do to him? Send him to Vietnam?

He had known B.T. Collins for exactly two months.

I answered the phone in my kitchen. Its ringing still made my heart stop. Had B.T. died? I heard him over the static of the transferred call. He was at Andrews Air Force Base. The sound of his voice, however weak, was reassuring. He was alive.

"I'm fine," he insisted, his words cracking with pain and exhaustion. "I'll be in Fort Dix, the day after tomorrow. Don't worry. I'm okay. Don't worry."

"No, B.T. No, I'm not worried. I'm just glad you're all right.

This time, we both lied.

The first time the family saw B.T. was in a transit hospital in Fort Dix, New Jersey on the 4th of July. He had been examined at Clark Air Force Base then flown to Andrews, then to New Jersey. He would be at Fort Dix only 24 hours before going to Valley Forge, Pennsylvania, where he would spend the next 18 months. The family was minus my father, who had gone to Europe on school business. The airline had promised him priority status if he should need to fly back to the states with little notice. We were initially told that B.T. would probably not be home for two months so Daddy had planned accordingly. My mother decided to see what condition B.T. was in before letting my father know that he had come home.

In the hospital parking lot, we passed buses whose insides were stacked with racks of wounded. Although the orderlies seemed to lift them carefully, the narrow litters swung wide, rubbing against the doorframes, the injured bodies bobbing as they were carried down the stairs. Some cried out because they were so badly wounded that even such gentle jarring hurt them terribly.

I was nervous about going to the hospital. The family weeper, I was afraid I would lose control and make everyone feel worse. So, I had tried preparing myself for the visit by imagining Brien without an arm and a leg. But the man lying in the hospital bed was not my brother at all. I have cried many times since, reliving that scene, but at that moment the shock was so great, not a single tear fell. We tried lamely to be cheerful, but mostly we were absorbing the horror of it all; the sight of him, the sounds of his suffering. My mother said very little. Marialis was even more quiet than usual. She and her brother had argued bitterly about the war.

And now this.

The room was flooded with sunlight—bright backdrop for the living remains stretched out before us. I remember seeing something paper-like in human form, a nearly see-through silhouette beneath some sheets. The bandaged stump of his right arm and his remaining left leg were exposed. He smelled . . . not of sweat, but of decay. His hair was wild . . . uncut. Fat tufts at his forehead and around his ears contrasted with his cavernous face. His eyes were sunk so deep you had first to find them.

There were no hugs of welcome. We dared not touch him for fear of hurting him more. Wide drops of waxen perspiration rolled down his forehead to his chin where they collected and tremulously hung. Periodically, his eyes rolled white to the back of his head. I would come to recognize this as a sign that the painkiller was wearing off. There must have been some initial greeting, some tender words that said what we were thinking, "We love you. Thanks for holding on, for living, because if you had died, we would have too."

Did he know, we wondered? Did he understand?

Brien seemed to be talking on a non-existent radio. He explained to no one in particular that he had warned one young member of his company to "Watch out!" but the soldier had not and was killed. A nurse came in to administer a quick injection. He gave us an imitation of a smile and we smiled back.

I felt sick.

Frantic because of the smell of his wounds, I went searching for a doctor, but the ward floor was crazy; people in white half-running in every direction, living bodies being loaded and unloaded. Finally, I stopped a nurse and borrowed some scissors. Then I went to work on Brien's hair, thinking by cutting away that tangled mat, I could somehow unearth my younger brother.

Marialis had contacted his closest childhood friends when she learned of his arrival. About four o'clock that first afternoon, they came marching into the room with a box of cigars and a six-pack of beer. They filled the room with laughter and wisecracks and he rose to the occasion, making an effort to react to their make-believe cheer.

"He was," one of them later told me, "so diminished."

Still another confessed he was relieved because Brien was obviously "too badly hurt to go back."

We left him with his buddies. Walking to the car and during the two-hour drive home, no one spoke. Later, Aunt Amelda, my father's youngest sister, called to ask about Brien. Mother said to me, "Tell her the truth; tell her how bad it really is."

The next morning, bags packed for a longer stay, we headed for Valley Forge, Pennsylvania. The hospital, closed in the late forties, had been re-activated for casualties of the Vietnam War. Of all the military hospitals, it received the largest volume of Vietnam wounded, especially those who required extensive stays and multiple re-constructive operations. Brien fit both these categories. He was in a private room, which in an Army hospital meant a space only slightly larger than a nun's cell. These accommodations would later allow for too many one-way conversations, a place in which he could talk himself into a sewer, Brien to Brien, with all the lack of perspective, pain, and loneliness that limited space made possible.

He would be under the primary care of three doctors: Dr. James Sargent, Dr. William Stewart and Dr. Richard Sullivan. Sargent was an orthopedic surgeon who had been drafted over the phone. He had just finished his orthopedic training at the University of Michigan in Ann Arbor and had been in private practice only 19 days when he was ordered to report to Valley Forge. He arrived four days later, without a uniform, unable, in his own words, "to perform a proper salute." With Sargent on board, there would still be only three fully qualified orthopedic surgeons to take care of 1,500 orthopedic patients.

Dr. Stewart, also an orthopedic surgeon, was sent to Valley Forge with the understanding that he would be there only six months. However, when the Tet Offensive came in 1968, the number of casualties increased nearly ten-fold. He stayed, and eventually became the acting Chief of Staff.

Dr. Rick Sullivan, in contrast, had been with the First Cavalry in the field for a year. He had received a Bronze Star, and identified closely with the patients under his care. He had lived their lives before coming, battle-fatigued himself, to Valley Forge. He occupied the bachelor's quarters in the hospital and, therefore, was available at night to talk with patients when the pain and fear were at their peak. Sullivan's specialty was skin grafting.

It was lunchtime when we arrived. Mother took Brien's food and, seated next to him, attempted to feed him.

"Eat your carrots. It will make your hair curl," she coaxed.

I imagined that my brother had seen enough to make his hair forever stand on end, let alone curl, but they were only practicing a childhood ritual. He said that now he would never marry, and my mother shot back, "Those girls who have been after you all these years must have been interested in more than your body!"

He had always seemed quite cavalier about "girls," as they were then called. Back in high school, they would call the house regularly. Sometimes he would go to the phone; sometimes he would not. I wondered, privately, if his disfigurement would make a difference.

I pictured my three year old son, who had fallen several months before and severed the muscle that held his lip in place. He was such a handsome child and until it healed, he was a mess. How I had worried about this minor misshaping. And now my mother was feeding her son because his hand was no longer there. The stump of his leg lay next to her. She smelled the festering wounds as she smoothed his hair and spooned mashed carrots between his cracked lips. What could she be thinking? It made my chest hurt to watch her.

Dr. Sargent entered. He was young and handsome, tired and rumpled. His white coat was starched. His brown shoes were studded with lumps of plaster, a small yet deliberate act of defiance. This lack of spit and polish was a matter of principle. He was a doctor. He wasn't really "Army."

"Am I going to die?" Brien asked flippantly.

"Hell, no! You're too ugly to die.

"So . . . ?"

"So, you don't smell too good. I'm going to have to take a look at those wounds." He paused. "This isn't Nam, you know. I have to schedule the OR here in advance, and I can't wait that long to examine you thoroughly. I'll give you everything I can," he hesitated, "but this is going to hurt you pretty badly."

"Hey, you do what you can do."

Translation: there would be no general anesthesia. Brien's eyes had widened in a flash of fear. Dr. Sargent looked down at his ruined shoes. As he raised his face, I saw there were tears in his eyes. I wondered how, after all he must have seen, he could still care enough about one terrified, redheaded loudmouth to cry at the thought of putting him through any more.

We were directed to the hospital snack bar to wait. On the way, we walked by a line of blank-faced men in blue pajamas. The only sound as they passed was the shuffling of their hospital slippers.

I realized that despite all that had happened, the Collins family was luckier than many others.

Seated at a table, I worked to keep my mind off what was happening to Brien at that moment. Out of the corner of my eye, I saw what I presumed was a mother and her son. The young man's face was half blown away, his healing so hideous that I had to make an effort not to gasp out loud. Yet, worse was the expression on the mother's face as she tried to look at him without reacting.

Watching this mother and son, I realized how little attention is paid to the consequences to the non-combatants at home, who are as much a part of the reality of war as any military action. The fallen men were fathers, brothers, husbands, and more, before and after their lives were taken or their bodies mutilated. For every arm or leg missing, for every pair of eyes that no longer saw, for every disfigured face, for every man who would never return in any condition, there were broken hearts and changed lives among those who loved them.

The Collins family was no exception.

Brien looked exhausted when we returned, his face, the color of putty. Mother explained to Dr. Sargent that my father was in Europe and that she had taken it upon herself to size up the situation before calling him home. Sargent was adamant that Daddy not be called.

"He doesn't want his father to see him in this condition," he told us. "Facing his father at this point," he warned, "might actually slow down his recovery."

Did Brien think he would disappoint Daddy once more, or did he understand, as I did, that the sight of him so horribly injured might have been more than my father could bear?

Dr. Sargent explained to us, in layman's language, the preliminary plans for Brien He had an open wound on the stump of his right arm and a large, gaping hole on what remained of his right leg. The bone was exposed at mid-thigh. The surgeons were going to cross graft his legs to get enough skin to cover the bone in his right leg. All infection, contamination, or dead tissue needed to be removed to prevent an insidious infection. Although Brien would be given medication to dull the pain, these horrific procedures would sometimes be required twice a day. Brien's ragged wounds would be sutured with wire that was less likely to cause an inflammatory reaction.

In the horror of the healing process, former patients have explained, pain is a grim and determined enemy. It takes over. It radiates from the site of the hurt, leaking out over the entire body, even reaching limbs no longer there. In a military hospital, pain, disability, and disfigurement become great levelers; sergeant, captain, private, colonel become equal victims of the ravages of war. Officers who had once been in charge now relinquished their command to drugs.

The Percodan, Demerol, and Morphine came at four-hour intervals, and as the third hour came to an end, Brien would be seized not only by pain of greater intensity, but by the fear of what he knew was coming before the next shot. Facing an operation or a debriding, he anticipated the hell that would follow. Nighttime and the periods immediately preceding a procedure were the worst. In the darkness, his mind focused on pain. He needed to scream, but held back for fear of frightening other patients.

It was a battle he did not always win.

As the men fought for each other in the field, so, too they fought in this sterile environment. They emptied bedpans; they ran interference with families and friends; they set daily examples of endurance, perseverance, and heroism. They survived by indulging in a MASH-type humor.

In the other private room on Brien's ward lay a man whose legs were strung up on pulleys, exposing open, oozing wounds. Everyone who strolled, limped, or wheeled by made comments: "You've got the ugliest legs I've ever seen!"

"Put your legs down. You're making everyone sick!"

Seated in wheelchairs on the lawn, the patients would deliberately throw a ball in the path of a passing nurse. "Hey, Lieutenant," they'd shout, "Pick up the ball!"

To which she'd retort, "Pick it up yourself!"

And they'd answer back, "What kind of person are you? You mean you wouldn't come to the aid of a bunch of helpless cripples?"

A blue-eyed, fiercely handsome Irishman, who'd lost both his legs below the knee asked me, "How'd you like to be six foot three one minute and five foot two the next?"

Indeed this black-haired Patrick with the long lashes was a bit of a rogue. He was known to "pat" the nurses as he passed in his wheel chair. I listened outside his door when the nurse came to change the dressings on the stumps of his legs. He asked in mock Irish brogue,

"Would you be after doin me a favor, Lieutenant Cullen?

"I don't know, Lieutenant Brosnan," the nurse replied warily. "What is it this time?"

"When I get my new legs," he joked, "Can I have hair on 'em?"

Patrick Brosnan was gorgeous. Legs or no legs, he was one of the handsomest men I've ever seen. In the hospital, these square-jawed, clean-cut kids were everywhere. Yet, when they turned around, each was missing something—here an arm, there a leg, two legs, the side of a head. It was as if the enemy had chosen to mutilate our best, our brightest, our most beautiful.

After each hospital visit, I would return to my university hometown to face bands of perfectly healthy, whole, and filthy college students. They shouted. They marched. They came to class barefoot. They verbally assaulted the war and everyone connected with it. They had little respect for the truths on which I was raised, those for which the men in Valley Forge had given so much. It was disheartening. I was disgusted.

The bonds between survivors at Valley Forge lasted forever. There, B.T. began his relationship with John Philp, "the Silver Fox," so named for the color of his hair and wily wit. Brien and John had first met in transit at Fort Dix, and were, at twenty-six and twenty-eight among the ward's "old men." The two shared a seething disrespect for the inconsequential. John referred to Brien as, "A legend in his own mind, and a bionic, walking (limping) advertisement for the oxymoron combat safety."

John had nerve damage and injuries to his upper right arm and knee that, though repaired, left him officially disabled. When he finally left the hospital, so the story goes, B.T. claimed to be appalled because John still had both his legs and arms and his disability was nearly as high as his own. "Fair is Fair," he hollered, "and if John is 60%, I ought to be at least 400%."

Philp replied acidly, "When Lincoln said, 'We should strive to care for him who shall have borne the battle,' he had no idea that B.T. would be wounded in action and attach himself like a limpet to the public teat for the rest of his life. In fact," he said, "Brien wasn't disabled at all because he still had his mouth." This may, the two agreed, have been the beginning of Brien's thinking about going to law school.

I witnessed other scenes when wounded veterans cut up each other so badly, the humor so ribald, so scathing; laughter at each other's expense so raucous, they made me gasp. I sensed that this take-the-finish-off-the-furniture language masked a love so deep that it could not be expressed any other way.

"Laughing comes to crying," my father used to say when we kids were horsing around. These men were crying, only no tears were allowed. At the slightest sign of warmth or caring, the tiniest show of affection—a hug, a handshake held too long, it would have been all over.

On rare occasions, however, some took that risk. John was scheduled to go home to Ohio for the first time on October 12, 1967. It was his birthday. After months in the hospital, this visit was understandably a major occasion. Coincidentally, B.T. was due to have a major revision of the stump of his right leg on the same day. As the anesthesia began to wear off after surgery, he cried out in distress. Then he felt somebody grab his hand and heard the whispered command, "Hang on, just hang on!" As he looked up, there was John, encased in plaster, leaning on crutches—still at the hospital.

IX

MENDING

———•—•———

*I see a chubby little boy desperately trying to tie
his own shoelaces. Now grown to manhood,
tall and handsome, he is learning to tie his laces all
over again, using one hand and a metal hook—evidence of
his contribution to freedom among men.*

*A letter to the parents and students at
the Midland School, Rye, New York
James Collins*

After the first, few terrifying weeks, B.T.'s mood was amazingly good. He was happy to be home and damn glad just to be alive. He was one of a handful of officers who was in the acute stages of his injuries, and therefore needed to be on the ward. He immediately established himself as a ward commander. As he had tried to protect those who depended on him in Vietnam, he now sought to save his fellow patients from an equally powerful enemy . . . despair.

The class clown became the ward comic. If the men were laughing, they couldn't be crying. No officer, whatever his or her rank, escaped his sarcasm. Everyone was kept busy reacting to his behavior, listening to B.T.'s stories, following his lead; less time to think about how you looked or what was going to happen when you re-joined the real world. He saw them through their mutual horrors. And, in so doing, he saved himself as well.

And then one day he'd had enough. In the whirlpool, which really isn't as soothing as it sounds—swirling waters tugging at unhealed wounds—he broke down and cried. Dr. Sargent found out about it, sent him back to his room and closed the door. For the first time, B.T. seemed genuinely depressed. He had had his fill of pain and suffering. Running emotional interference for the other patients had become a load too heavy to bear. B.T. crawled into bed. Sargent leaned against the closed door, folded his arms, and let him have it.

"What?" B.T. demanded.

"I wondered how long it was going to take you to get tired of putting up this "tough guy front for all the other patients."

"I'm not putting up a tough guy front for all the other patients." B.T. snapped. "I'm putting up a tough-guy front for myself, and I'm tired of it. I'm tired of not having an arm and a leg and I'm especially tired of you and your goddamn dressing changes!"

"Getting killed is one thing," Dr. Sargent replied softly. "Coming home like you is something else."

"Oh, really?"

"Yeah, really. Well, you have come home. You're alive and you will get well, but first we have some work to do. I'd like to schedule the surgery as early as tomorrow. Something else," Dr. Sargent turned before leaving, "you'll have to change your attitude, stop being a field commander, and start being a patient!"

"See you around, Doc!" B.T. replied, turning his face to the wall.

Getting well meant that he was going to require a major debridement on his leg; that, further, if they were going to close the wound, they would have to shorten his femur (thigh bone). The good news: he would still have enough leg to be able to walk with a prosthetic device. The bad: what lay ahead, however necessary, was going to be awful.

The next day, Dr. Sargent went in during morning rounds to see how the "ward commander" was doing. B.T. was sitting up in bed in a bright red shirt. There were pictures of Jean Harlow and Paul Newman and several *Playboy* centerfolds taped to the wall. A tennis racket was visible under his bed. And B.T. was smiling. He had not yet had breakfast. He admitted sheepishly that he thought he'd have some surgery instead.

Dr. Rick Sullivan had had a midnight chat with B.T. about "being whole;" that "being whole" was as much a mental as a physical state. He convinced him that whatever shape he was in, there was lot to be done, a lot he could do, a lot he should do, "should" being the operative word. The doctor knew which buttons to push. He had rearranged that day's OR schedule. B.T. was now Sullivan and Sargent's first case.

B.T. also came to feel that if he didn't get well, he would disappoint Jim Sargent. In a letter to Sargent's wife, he wrote:

Not dated

Dear Mrs. Sargent:

I have spent a good deal of my military life destroying things and people.

That was my job, and I never before had any real regrets. But I have looked at Jim's hands wistfully sometimes, thinking how wonderful it was . . . the constructive things that he could do with his as opposed to what I had done with mine. Should I ever have any children, I would hope that at least one of them would enter medicine. Perhaps then, I could, in some minuscule way, repay Jim for what he has done for us all.

The surgery turned out to be a more complicated than anticipated. The femoral artery, which supplies blood to the leg, had to be opened, and the bone cut two inches. The surgeons were able to move one skin flap, thereby decreasing the amount of skin grafting needed by one third. B.T. was doing fine the following morning. That evening, however, he began hemorrhaging. He went into shock, and lost ten units of blood before they could get him into the OR, The count was up to 19 units by the time they had the situation under control.

Jim Sargent had left for his first furlough in a year. This time, Dr. Bill Stewart saved his life. Nearly thirty years later, Stewart recalls that even in the midst of this crisis, B.T. was making wisecracks. "I'm living proof," he told the attending nurses and doctors, "that only the good die young."

On a nearly weekly basis, throughout the end of August, September, and October, 1967, B.T. continued to undergo the process of "thickness skin grafting." This meant taking skin primarily from his left thigh and abdomen, and moving it to cover the open muscle in his right arm and leg. Eventually, they were able to clean up his right arm well enough to close it and B.T. began moving about on wheels, generally misbehaving, making the doctors and nurses crazy and everyone else helpless with laughter. He charmed and flirted with the nurses. He did see a lot of action in the parking lot, as John Philp had told us at the wake, teasing even the senior women officers unmercifully.

At a party at Rick Sullivan's quarters, B.T. and John became frustrated because they were unable to leave for the ward. They managed to get out of their wheelchairs and throw them down a flight of stairs. Hearing the racket, those who had refused them rides looked with guilt and horror at the two empty "crashed" wheelchairs, wheels spinning on the landing below. John and B.T., of course, were safely seated on the floor propped up against a wall.

B.T. continued to make progress. He had plenty of help. Parents of the children attending my father's Rye, New York, school drove to visit him. One family brought B.T. a television. The letters and articles that my father had written, and still wrote every Veteran's and Memorial Day had born fruit.

To the Parents of the Children at the Midland School,
Rye, New York.
November, 1967

I would ask you to talk to your children about Veteran's Day. I would ask you to emphasize how dearly the rights we use so poorly were purchased. I would ask you to talk about the casualties of war—for they are not simply numbers.

For my own part, I see a chubby little boy desperately trying to tie his own shoelaces—and then I see him grown to manhood, tall and handsome, but now he is learning to tie his shoelaces all over again, only this time he is using one hand and a metal hook: evidence of his contribution to freedom among men.

Understandably, Daddy found the sixties unusually difficult. "These were the times," he wrote to the parents, quoting Thomas Paine, "that tried men's souls." He spoke of the "summer soldier and the sunshine patriot" who shrank from the service of their country. "How could we teach respect for the great American heritage, for the ideals of Washington and Lincoln, the courage of all those who stained with their blood the snow at Valley Forge, the sand at Omaha Beach, the jungles of the Mekong in a society which denigrated family pride and respect for the law, a people increasingly influenced by a 'the-government-will-take-care-of-me attitude.'"

This had to be heartbreaking, he believed, to the true patriot who risks his life or leaves part of his body so far away from home in a cruel and bitter war.

B.T.'s friends came bearing gifts as well. Not satisfied with the traditional flowers, books, or in B.T.'s case, beer, his childhood classmates decided they would blow him away with a surprise birthday show in his honor, for the whole hospital. The account of his birthday party that first fall filled four columns in the *New York Daily News*. Over 350 guests attended, with or without legs, arms, hands, feet.

Lynn Bennish, his grade-school sweetheart, and Joyce Payson, a longtime friend, found a young TV producer, Shaun O'Driscoll, as well as a pianist, a singer, a model, and a marketing field supervisor, plus a 17-year old drummer whose parents drove him into New York City for the late night rehearsals. And the O'Driscoll's Follies were born.

Musicians, dancers, singers, sets, and costumes were crammed into a charter bus, and headed for Valley Forge, Pennsylvania. The show was to begin at 8:00 PM, but by 7:30, a Red Cross worker asked if the audience could come in to watch the cast get ready. The men had been waiting outside on stretchers and in wheelchairs for an hour.

Many of the performers did not know B.T. Some had mixed feelings about the war. But they had begun to care about the guys, and "the guy" who had inspired all this hoopla. As the December, 1967 *Daily News* reported, "Rockettes they weren't, and the Supremes they would never be," but they danced their feet off and sang good and loud. And the men whistled and cheered in return.

The show was so successful, they planned another for Christmas. On the day of the Christmas performance, they met at 4:00 AM to pack the bus. Nearly twenty-four hours later, at 3:30 AM, they would head back to New York, many to be at work at their regular jobs by 9:00. The show began in the surgical wards, a sort of on-the-road preview for those too severely wounded to make it to the recreation hall that evening. The young performers who had been afraid of what they might find there soon forgot about everything but entertaining.

Long before 8:00 PM, the other patients were waiting for the main event. The hall was packed with men lying flat on their backs, sitting in wheelchairs, or propped up on crutches. B.T.'s entourage threw themselves into it, and the boys and men watching went wild. No *bona fide* celebrity, no running back, no long-legged dancer could have been appreciated more. B.T. presented a TV, a gift from the residents of a nursing home in South Amboy, New Jersey explaining that the newspaper publicity had brought about a number of new fans. He shared other gifts, as well as letters that told of brothers killed in Vietnam and wounded in World Wars I and II.

The show closed with everyone singing "White Christmas." The familiar music filled the room. And if "tree tops glistened," so too, I am told, did several hundred pairs of watching eyes.

Brien came home that first Christmas, in uniform, on crutches, with his pant leg pinned. My father changed his dressings that morning. The wounds looked hideous to the uninitiated, and Daddy was certainly in that category. I don't know who hurt worse. Brien was not ready for anyone other than medical personnel to "see" him.

Did he understand that I could have done it?

Never.

Later, we went to church. We were all so proud. I thought my father was going to cry. Returning, we sat down for dinner. The table gleamed with Waterford and polished silver. Though mid-day, there was candlelight. Steam rose from the oversized turkey and browned stuffing. If no one counted the legs under the table or the hands in the laps, it might have been like old times. Then the phone rang.

I rose to answer, and a *little voice* asked for B.T. It was Sam Bird, former leader of men under fire who now spoke with the tentative tone of an elementary school child. Brien got up with difficulty and we all sat silently at the table, listening to one side of their gentle conversation. No one had the courage to look at him or at each other when he returned. The meal ended abruptly. We could barely swallow. The joy of the day and Brien's return had run dry.

True to Dr. Sargent's promise, B.T. was getting better. Now fitted with his own prosthesis on his right arm, he practiced writing with his left hand, learned to tie his shoes, to feed himself, and unfortunately, to light a cigarette. Hour after hour, sweating with the effort, he piled blocks upon little blocks to improve his dexterity. He learned to use his shoulder muscles to control the movements of his hook. He learned to hold a glass firmly enough not to drop it, yet not so firmly that it would smash between his steel fingers. He learned to pick up a penny or turn the flat pages of a book. The hook became his hand.

There was psychotherapy too—or rather, there was supposed to be. The amputees attended regular counseling sessions at which self-analysis, introspection or even conversation was at an absolute minimum.

The first time B.T. attended, he steered himself awkwardly into the room in his electric wheelchair, bumping into tables, chairs, and other patients. After several moments of silence, he said, "Look, you guys are a lot farther along than me. Maybe you can help. I miss my arm. I miss my leg. Tell me it's going to be all right." His candor broke the ice; everyone opened up after that.

Using his new leg took practice. Legs can be more of a problem, because they are weight-bearing. It's a question of balance. B.T. was over six feet tall and the right side of his body was missing. The long and heavy prosthesis was attached to the stump of his leg by means of a vacuum. The suction was adjusted through a valve at the knee.

"Stump." How I hated that word, for the image it brought to mind and the pain it implied. He had two. And they were ugly—twin loaves of pale dough never to rise, crisscrossed with cranberry-colored scars. He looked at them every day, every day for the rest of his life.

Finally, he was walking. Somehow, in the back of his mind was the notion that getting better equaled being whole. And being whole, to him, meant being as he had been. Once he had been tall and lean. He had jumped into the elephant grass from a hovering helicopter; he had run ahead of his men up the mud-slide of a hill. He had played touch football on autumn afternoons and tooted a trumpet, marching in a school band. He had had slender hands and arms that circled for powerful hugs. And now, beneath his elbow there was but a bit of arm, just enough to slip into the cuff of a prosthetic device, and below his right hip, almost nothing.

He sat on the edge of his bed one day and he looked down at the six inch-wad of discolored flesh that once was his thigh. *Hey,* he realized, *this is the end of the line. This is as good as it gets. This is the best I'm going to be.*

Was he aware, at that moment, that he still had those "baby blues?" And that "mouth," that sometimes I could have done without? And that smile. And *the look*; he would tilt his head back and to the side and catch you from beneath his eyelashes. You were trapped. Then, he still had his mind, though he sometimes drove us out of ours. And he had his heart . . . too much heart.

Other milestones followed: The passage from screams to clenched teeth; from crutch to cane; the first time out of bed, carousing in a wheel chair, ordering the troops; the last operation for a while; standing rather than sitting; looking down rather than up; literally seeing others eye to eye; walking on the ever uneven pavement . . . even falling was moving ahead.

And always, *always*, there was an attitude. "Here I come! Out of my way! Don't mess with me!" Denying the pain, he hid his fear within the cocoon of those marked by a similar fate; wheelchair wagons circled round the fire of protective familiarity.

The world outside the hospital, however, was a whole different ball game.

As Labor Day 1967 approached, his closest friends planned for him to spend a weekend with them. Privately, he was terrified. He began making excuses, none of which was accepted. The trip went ahead as planned. Things went well. B.T. even had enough courage to ask his friend, Dick Ehrlich, to change the dressing on his leg, and Dick managed it without flinching. On the way back to the hospital, they pulled over to a roadside restaurant.

"What's going on?" B.T. asked, nervously.

"Nothing. I'm hungry. Don't you want something to eat?"

"No, really. We just ate for God's sake. Are you going to eat again?"

"Yeah. Anyway, that was hours ago. You're going to miss dinner at the hospital. Just have something."

"No, thanks, really. I'll just wait here in the car. Hey, no problem."

"Look, Collins. Look at me!" Dick turned toward him "I'm proud of you. Get it? Proud! What's say you get into that wheelchair and we'll try it. If it gets too bad, I swear to you, we're out of there."

As B.T. would recount in a 1988 article published in the *Wall Street Journal*, "It was my baptism of fire all over again. The first parachute jump; the first fire fight. And I survived."

The article, *In Praise of a Comrade Back Home*, was one of B.T.'s ways of publicly saying thank you. He just wanted everyone in the United States (including Dick) to know what a difference that kind of friendship could make. A year later, the same weekend, they went to the beach. This time the leg and arm came off and, leaning on his friend's shoulder, B.T. hopped to the waves and fell in. After that, he never looked back.

On the streets of New York, he made his way amid the cries of "Baby killer!" and "Make Love, Not War!" Head high, always in uniform, he was dismayed and embittered. The hatred seemed directed as much at him as at Vietnam. And he was as angry with those who stayed silent as with those who spewed their vicious epithets. He shared his feelings with an old friend.

April 24, 1968

Dear Judy,

I found people directly hostile to me. I was astounded. How can you ever talk to anyone about a war? It's like talking to a bunch of nuns about sex. When I am at parties, people ask me what the women are like, and what is it like to kill people? These guys just don't have a clue. The fact that I went first to a hospital upon returning home saved me. If I had come home alone and found out how people felt about me . . . Jesus!

He came to see me in northern New York—no easy task. He had to change planes. The second lap of the trip was in a tiny aircraft, one of those in which he had to bend to board and sit with his knees to his chin. I had arranged for a wheelchair. No need. He walked off the aircraft, limping slightly, shoulders back, eyes straight ahead.

How proud of him I was; how proud he was of himself. Had I not been afraid that he would mistake my pride for pity, I would have wept.

Like many combat veterans, he had become watchful, his hearing so sensitive he could have heard an ant breathe. It seemed much too quiet. He was acutely aware of where people were. Sometimes he thought he saw people hiding behind a simple grove of trees. In a room full of people, he placed himself where he could see what was going on. Conversations bored him. The topics aired by those his own age who had not been in Vietnam seemed foolish. He had become addicted to constant danger, so the sense of security at home left him uneasy rather than at rest. At times, he wondered how people protected themselves. They were, unarmed after all.

Eighteen months after he had been carried into Valley Forge, he walked out on his own, if not on his "own" two feet.

He planned to finish his education. First, he had to find a college that would take him. In this era before affirmative action, handicapped persons enjoyed no special status. And B.T. had been thrown out of one of the best eastern universities. His academic record was hardly his saving grace. Maneuvering the ice-covered sidewalks of New York was like walking a minefield, and the winter winds made his missing limbs ache.

After spending some time with friends and family, he headed for California. A new life and the warm weather beckoned. He made the trip across country alone, driving a specially equipped car. On the way, he stopped to see Sam Bird. This was not a first visit. Yet, the sight of the handsome young captain grown old, paralyzed, and partially blind nearly shut B.T. down completely. "Shutting down," however, was never an option. He would persevere for Sam, for himself, and for all those like him.

So, he rode off to the Golden State, to the greatest concentration of anti-war activists in the country. Eventually, he would fall in love with California. It was just the place for some politically incorrect idealist to carve his niche. But in that spring of '69, he was a terrified twenty-eight-year-old who had been to hell and back, facing his last chance to make something of himself. For better or worse, California's living legend-to-be, not yet a twinkle in any governor's eye, was on his way, his uniforms, war maps, and probably an American flag in plain view on the back seat.

X

SANTA CLARA

*You must know of my love and affection for everything
that embodies the selflessness and generosity
that is Santa Clara University*

B.T. Collins

B.T. managed to get accepted at Santa Clara University. The family, pleased that he was finally going to finish his education, was relieved that he was well enough to attend classes. In reality, he was going back to war. Only now he was a private, a beginner without rank, approaching a mental rather than topographical minefield, whose terrain he had yet to successfully reconnoiter. He faced a field of fire through which he would run neither unencumbered nor unafraid. He would need to establish a new chain of command, a corps to mobilize for the common good, all the while adjusting to life without dying—life without the fear of failing to protect those who depended on him.

According to *Webster*, a student is: *1. One who attends a college or university. 2. a. One who makes a study of something. b. an attentive observer.*

My brother was, loosely, all of these: a voracious reader who collected ideas, philosophies, and theories; an astute observer of history and of people and their interaction, yet one who never, however, gave in to the rigors of academic preparation. Thinking was an area in which he excelled; formal study was definitely not his forte.

He had indeed *attended* universities: The University of Pennsylvania, which he was asked to leave, and New York University, our father's alma mater, which he left to go to war. Again, he worked hard to conceal any sign of intellectual activity, in deference to some old fashioned and, unfortunately, out-of-date notion about what constituted being a "regular guy."

War changes those who participate. It had changed my brother B.T. profoundly. It cut a groove in his spirit like the imprint of a thick stick drawn through wet sand, but a mark no kind of tide could wash flat.

"Never explain, never complain, never look back," he said.

But he did look back. The stump of a leg and a curve of steel were cruel reminders, not only of his sacrifice but of the sacrifices of comrades left behind. Vietnam had indeed changed him, but when he arrived at Santa Clara, he was a change happening—a work in progress. Wherever he was finally going, he hadn't yet arrived.

If B.T. had gone to war believing he owed his country, he now felt he owed everybody. The debt was enormous. He owed all those dead kids whose opportunities to succeed had been stolen. He owed Mother and Daddy, and Marialis, and me for the nightmare we'd endured. Most of all, he owed himself. Life had a renewed value, one he must cease wasting. Finishing college was the first step toward turning that life around.

In time, he would take control. In time, Santa Clara's hallowed halls would ring with his balls of brass, and both students and faculty would knuckle under the weight of his searing wit. Soon, those hearing his music would dance to his tune.

But in the beginning, he only knew he had to succeed, and he wasn't at all sure he could.

To the outside world, the university, or the "Academe" as we insiders call it, is believed to be a deep, if not always profound, breeding ground of critical thought; an intellectual symphony hall wherein a cacophony of opening minds manages somehow to play a piquant tune. Sadly, it can be, and too often is, the stuffiest of arenas, in which neither fresh air nor truly new ideas flourish. Honest dissent, rather than that paraded for one's own aggrandizement, is fed with some relish to the lions of self-accorded superiority. Academics, even at their best, still see and understand the world within the context of books rather than life's experiences.

Enter my brother, the terrified rascal who dispensed bravado like a medicine man from the back end of a horse drawn wagon, the soldier to whom all huff and puff of professorial pomposity mattered no more than a wing-flapping gnat. Those who participated in his collegiate experience were afterwards really never quite the same. If B.T. were little prepared for college, Santa Clara was certainly not ready for the likes of B.T. Collins.

When asked why he had chosen Santa Clara, B.T. answered that the campus had the shortest distances between buildings. He wasn't joking. When someone is dragging 13 pounds of wood around, and it rubs what little is left of his leg raw, *distance matters.*

In reality, he chose Santa Clara because it was a small school; one in which he believed he could successfully maneuver physically and mentally. He had chosen well. Santa Clara did not fit the academic stereotype. That it was sensitive and intuitive in the extreme was evidenced by the fact that it laid traditional standards aside when it accepted B.T.'s meager credentials for admission. B.T. had found a school that passed his test. The University would learn it had chosen wisely as well.

Santa Clara University began life as a Franciscan Mission in 1777. In 1851, opening its doors to a dozen students, it became the first institution of higher learning in the state of California. During the California gold rush, it attracted Protestant and Catholic students alike, among whom were the sons of foreign consuls living in San Francisco, native Californians, international students, and members of prominent state pioneer families. "A prospective student's admission was almost guaranteed if he appeared at the door with sufficient bedding, an iron bedstead, and $350 to cover the year's board and tuition."

First known as Santa Clara College, it attained university status in 1912 with the addition of a School of Law and a School of Engineering. A School of Business was added in 1926. It achieved national prominence as a football power in the 1930's, winning back-to-back victories in the Sugar Bowl in 1937-1938. In the 1960's, the University accepted its first female undergraduates, making it the first co-educational Catholic university in California. By the 1980's, it would emerge as the leading Catholic university in the West, attracting the attention of William Bennett, then US Secretary of Education, for the breadth and depth of its curriculum.

In the late sixties and early seventies, Santa Clara University would not have qualified as a wildly activist campus compared to other California strongholds. Nevertheless, the turbulence which tainted other colleges and their surrounding communities touched Santa Clara as well. There were riots in town, sit-ins in the University President's office and lay-ins on the R.O.T.C. parade grounds. Whole neighborhoods in nearby San Jose were rife with drugs. A group of Chicano students took over the University's administration building. There was a general lowering of academic standards, a resistance to any kind of judgmental guidelines. Easily 40-50 percent of the law school graduates graduated *cum laude*. At one Santa Clara Law School graduation, a student jumped off the stage in exuberance to assure there was no possibility of a dignified ceremony.

Initially, when questioned about the activities of the anti-war activists, B.T. responded quietly that having the freedom to say what you wanted was what going to war was all about. You gave of yourself, when asked, to the country that made such conduct an inalienable right. His words represented only an acceptable public persona. The right to dissent may well have been guaranteed by the Constitution, but in this instance, to B.T., such behavior was unpardonable. It was an issue toward which he would never mellow. I could not then imagine him on a college campus, in California, no less, given what he had been through.

"How do you stand it? I asked.

"Hey, babe," he answered, sadly. "That's what it's all about. That's the American way."

Santa Clara's undergraduates were the traditional 18-22 year olds, not heavily into deep thinking, and without a wealth of real-world living. To his professors, B.T. represented a cooler mind in passionate times. He was older and more experienced than his peers. He was wise in the ways of life at its most serious and most dangerous. By then, he had substantial background in the subjects he was studying. Despite all his carousing, he had always managed to read volumes.

To his first classmates, he was somewhat intimidating: his height, his bearing, his captain's voice, those blue eyes that, at 29, had already seen too much. There was an aura about him—worn, wise beyond his years. Few of them had come face to face with the "real thing." Easy to look at a vet and see just another man who'd been to war. Yet, here was a human leftover from an actual battle. If he'd been wheeling around in a chair, slinging anti- or pro-Vietnam slurs, he could have been dismissed. But he stepped off the screen, out of the photographs, into their paths, loud, bossy, wearing his wounds like a badge of honor. He wasn't bitter; he was proud. He didn't hide. Everything about him said, "Look at me! I *am* the real world."

Was he angry? More than even he realized, but at a level so deep he could not yet bear to set it free.

No one who is physically whole has any idea what it's like to walk down the street with half a body. If we have become handicap-sensitized, thirty years ago we were far less so. However empathetic we have become, we are incapable of walking in the disabled's shoes. It's one thing to be with others like you—missing this, missing that—here a wheelchair, there a wheelchair, cushioned from reality in a cocoon of cripples. It's another to be with friends who've known and loved you all your life and are simply glad you're alive. But to walk into a classroom slightly late because you've had trouble getting there, all eyes watching as you try to urge your inflexible Pinocchio parts into a people chair, B.T. discovered, was a whole different story.

He had only been on public display for a short time when he arrived on campus. No matter what he led others to believe, he felt both stares and surreptitious glances. He was not only alone physically but, to a large degree, ideologically. He was in a new war, fighting while wounded, still learning to walk, writing with the wrong hand, running under the crossfire of foreign and, I'm sure he believed, misguided understandings of duty and country. Yet, without realizing it, he was observed and admired. He struck a chord in his peers and professors; he gave them pause. Gradually, he became big brother, thorn-in-your-side, and commander-in-chief in a single package.

He finished the remaining credits for his undergraduate degree in a year and a half, majored in History, managed a 3.0 and stood 82 out of 295 students.

Law school seemed a logical follow up, particularly if he planned a life of public service. Miraculously, he was accepted into the University's School of Law—not immediately and not without difficulty. His LSAT scores were marginal; his academic record, based on grades earned before entering the Army, was very weak. There was no logical reason for the University to give him this opportunity— except they believed in him. "They" being, among others, Mary Emery, then a Professor and Librarian of the Law School, and George Giocomini, Professor of History. First rejecting his law school application, Santa Clara reconsidered, based on Emery's intuition and the following empathetic letter from Giocomini:

April 2, 1970

Pursuant to our telephone conversation, I am writing this in hopes that it will give the Admissions Committee some bases for reconsidering its decision in the case of Brien [B.T.] Collins. He is a thirty-year-old disabled, retired Army captain who doesn't quite have the credentials for admission to law school. He does, however, in my judgment, have both the desire and the ability to complete successfully the requirements of the School of Law. Quite frankly, I believe he could use and deserves a break.

I have now had Mr. Collins for two courses in which he received an A and a B. I am not an easy grader and these are fair reflections of my judgment of his academic ability. I am impressed by his personal drive to overcome the loss of an arm and a leg in Vietnam. While learning to write left-handed, he nevertheless wants to be given written examinations rather than receive the special treatment accorded by an oral exam. A word about his LSAT scores. Mr. Collins generally appears in complete control of a situation—to the point of seeming cocky. I have never seen him so shaken as he was prior to the LSAT. He knew that a good score was important to offset his pre-military academic record—that, in some ways, his entire future rested on the test. He did not do well. I ascribe this to simple nervousness.

For me, one of the attractive aspects of Santa Clara is its size that permits faculty members to know both their students and their colleagues. Without embarrassment, one can ask or be granted a favor. Equally without embarrassment, the favor can be granted or denied. I am asking for a favor: that the Admissions Committee reconsider and act favorably on Mr. Collins' application. In my seven years at Santa Clara, I have only once before asked for such a favor. It concerned a student with a GPA of 2.2 whom I thought could make it. He was admitted and graduated 10th in his class. Mr. Collins could do the same.

I appreciate your willingness to bring this matter to the Committee's attention and I hope they will accept my strong recommendation to accept Mr. Collins.

They did.

By the time B.T. was accepted into Law School, he had become a known campus character. He was both deadly serious and frivolous; things mattered terribly or not at all. His behavior was unthinkable, yet totally without pretense. Somehow, people knew immediately they had to take him exactly as he was. Among the many lessons learned in Vietnam was the necessity of being pure. In combat, all men are laid bare. In the terror of the moment they are stripped to the soul and beyond. He would remain faithful to that essential truth and, in so doing, became, according to one of his professors, "One giant breath of fresh air in a bullshit world."

The class entering Law School in the fall of 1970 was the largest and the most diverse in the University's history. The heretofore incestuous mix of Irish and Italian Catholic Californians had expanded to include students from universities and colleges across the nation. Beaded or buttoned-down Brooks Brothers, they were almost universally against Vietnam. The undergraduate institutions from which they came were hotbeds of political dissent and festering anti-war sentiment.

B.T. knew the mindset. He'd seen it in action.

Many, if not most, of those protesting had never seen a bad accident let alone stood helpless in the moist rain of human remains. Some few might have known a near miss; a bad fall on the winter slopes, perhaps, a near-drowning in a summer lake. But combat is on-the-hour "near misses," and multiple "on targets." If the blast or bullet misses you, it may hit the guy next to you and his blood, if not on your hands, is on your face and your uniform and you step in it and over it, and the ground beneath you is red, not brown.

Nevertheless, B.T. knew instinctively that combat veterans and law students had similar problems.

Vietnam, especially, was a war of isolation. The combatants were physically separated from the larger ensemble of those who fought with them. The troops were therefore, of necessity, inalterably interdependent. They had a common enemy; they fought within a common context. In law school, there is also a common enemy— the intellectual and physical demands of the system: can I study this hard, learn this much, and stay married, stay awake, have a life, stay alive?

The class of 1973 was not interdependent. But under Captain Collins' command they would so emerge. B.T., who didn't know beans about law school, knew a hellava lot about "getting through," facing the enemy and coming out alive. He understood fear; he knew about fatigue. Beating the odds was a battle familiar.

The public perception of law school was then, and probably still is, personified by the film, *The Paper Chase*. Law students supposedly cowered in the presence of acerbic professors whose main purpose, in addition to imparting knowledge, was to humble those before them. Humility was not a strength from which B.T. Collins drew. Students, fiercely competitive and not universally kind, traditionally ate each other alive. B.T. was used to men who died for each other, who stood between him and the line of fire out of love.

Posture if you will, he thought. *I've held the blood red gray matter of a mother's son in my hands and stumbled over the scraps of a once-a-child in the tall grass. Talk on of trials and torts, I've lived the world's real wrongs and survived. Let's get our priorities straight!*

So, thanks to B.T., the fabric of life on campus came apart at its dignified seams. While other law students toiled in terror during the first weeks of law school lest they be called upon and found wanting, B.T was the first member of the class of 1973 to say, "Not prepared"—an unbelievable and, therefore, unforgettable event.

A fellow student recalled. "Many of us may not have believed we were prepared. B.T. said it. You could have heard a pin drop."

Other students remembered that he could be counted on to provide on-going comic relief. In the waning weeks of one semester, B.T.'s classmate, Barry Weissman, slipped into Corporations class to catch the professor's pre-final exam summary. His lack of regular class attendance was a recognized indiscretion. Noting his appearance, B.T. stood to explain to all assembled that the rumors of Barry's untimely death were greatly exaggerated. He then proceeded to introduce him to the professor and to each of the other students, insuring that Barry would have to attend all remaining classes.

Redheaded law professor Lillian Altry, now Bevier, had according to B.T. "legs to her shoulders, a great deal of patience, and her feet on the ground."

Unable, on one occasion, to answer her questions in class, he admitted he was unprepared then added, "That's a mighty fine purple sweater you're wearing."

It was—and Professor Altry *wore it* to perfection. Every student in the room, male, or female, exploded with laughter. Of course, he only said what everyone else was thinking. His behavior, outrageous by any standards in any surroundings, was even more so within the lecture halls of law school. To her undying credit, Professor Altry broke down and laughed hard with the rest of them. Not only did she not bring him up on charges she came to regard him with great fondness:

"There was this quality about him, as though it were important to let him be. There was never any malice to his remarks; he never went after people for the purpose of inflicting gratuitous pain. He just poked fun at himself and at an enterprise that too many took too seriously. You realized how far he had to have come to recover his spirit as he had. It made you think about the war. If a man this good had suffered this devastation, and still was not bitter, then it could not all have been for nothing. Actually, he was shy about women and not as comfortable about his physical appearance as he would have had people believe. "

Others agreed. "He made you think," said classmate Pat O'Laughlin. Pat was a longhaired, well-educated, semi-beatnik from Berkley, secure in his liberal ideologies, who had been in the thick of the anti-war movement. At 21, he had the baby face of an innocent 14-year-old, which made all-the-more amusing the fact that B.T. regularly referred to him as a bleeding-heart pinko, card-carrying communist.

"B.T. had specific old-fashioned American ideals, as opposed to our hip, anti-authority generalities. We had that ironic, detached notion that all this valor stuff was irrelevant, sentimental garbage. I have since read a lot of Vietnam literature, and I cringe when I think of what I was like. I had no idea of the realities of war. How generous he was! He could have shut us off with a "You're just naïve, snot-nosed brats," but instead, he listened. He didn't argue politics but, rather, by example, demonstrated that certain basic values never go out of style. He possessed an abundance of what we used to call character."

All of which may or may not explain why B.T. later held up pictures of O'Laughlin's children at a party and claimed to be their biological father.

Professor Marc Poche, who would later launch B.T.'s political career, was one of his first-year law professors. B.T.'s handicap first came to his attention through a superior court judge who sought oral exam status for his hemophiliac son with a wound on his writing hand. The judge told Poche that he also had a student with only one arm. Surprised, Poche called B.T. into his office and informed him that he would be allowed to take his exams orally. B.T., standing at attention, refused until Poche literally ordered him military style to "dictate his answers." Still standing at attention, B.T. responded briskly, "Yes Sir!"

He did agree to have a key to the elevator. Steps were especially tough because both of his missing limbs were on the same side. The shifting balancing act required was painful and exhausting. Watching him waiting for the elevator one especially hot Santa Clara day, a student remarked wistfully, "Wish I had one of those keys."

"Hey," B.T. replied, "No problem. All it'll cost you is an arm and a leg."

He lived comfortably on the edge. He took no precautions. Physically, he was without fear. He skydived until his hook caught in the chute's lines and dragged him half a mile on landing. He learned to ski. He broke his arm in the attempt. When the ski patrol came to his rescue, they nearly fainted. He had removed his prostheses before starting out on the slopes but they were unaware he wore any. They came upon this gravely injured half-man hidden in the snow. They were beside themselves. Good God! The discomfort of a broken arm not withstanding, he reveled in their obvious consternation.

When he fell, he insisted on getting back on his feet alone. His fellow students knew the drill. No help allowed. One rainy day, they watched from the Law Library's windows as he made his way up the walk. Slipping on the collected water, he went down . . . hard. He twisted his leg so that it turned backwards and he was able neither to get up from that position nor to re-attach his leg properly. In the movies, a similar scene evokes immediate tension and pity. The crippled man falls, he cries, and the audience cries with him. In contrast, this audience, and it was an audience, knew it would soon be laughing, that the first floor of the Santa Clara Law Library was about to be engulfed in unrestrained hilarity. The show was on: Red Skelton and Lucille Ball in a double amputee's body—slapstick on a university sidewalk.

Cursing in frustration and anger, he dropped his pants, yanked off his leg, jammed it furiously under what remained of his right arm, and crawled upright. Hopping on his remaining leg, he headed toward the library, mad as hell. Every time his one foot rose and fell, it whacked the waiting cement. The sound resounded throughout the court yard, the library floor shook in anticipation of the human storm that would inevitably follow this physical thunder—*thump, thump, thump, thump* up the steps, *thump, thump, thump, thump* across the floor to the librarian's desk. Then balancing himself on one leg, he withdrew his other from underneath the stump of his right arm— sword from sheath—and holding it aloft, he swung it down on the surface of the front desk with a mighty crash, and in utter exasperation, roared, "Goddamn it, goddamn it! I broke my f . . . ing leg!"

Did it hurt when he fell? When a three-foot, thirteen pound piece of wood and plastic is torn from the tender flesh to which it is attached, does it smart? When a six-foot-two man falls like felled timber to cement ground without a waiting arm to break his fall, does it make him wince?

Nobody thought about it.

He had succeeded in convincing them it was no big deal. But maybe, in comparison to the scraping of open wounds; maybe next to the withdrawal from Percodan or the agony in the first hours after surgery.

Maybe not.

In any case, pain was something he understood. During law school, he traveled to Bay Area and San Francisco hospitals to comfort accident victims and veterans. He'd hold their hands while dressings were being changed. He'd tell them that the pain would pass, and they knew he knew, and it helped.

"Be thankful you came back," he admonished those who were former soldiers. "No one said it was going to be easy. No one can take away from us the friendship we've shared."

At the same time, he was undergoing frequent surgery himself. He had re-occurring abscesses in his right ear due to the loss of his eardrum at the time of his injury. Finally, he was given an implant.

The stump of his leg was still being adjusted. Each new repair job sliced off a little more flesh, until he was left with considerably less to which his prosthesis could be attached.

While he took care of some, he managed to get others to take care of him. The great con honed in the hospital was born anew. The new troops were trained to do his bidding. "Remember me? I'm disabled."

During B.T.'s undergraduate years, Marialis had cleaned his apartment, washed his clothes, and typed his papers, often into the wee hours of the morning, while she worked full time. Now our Aunt Alice (Schmidt) ironed his shirts and hired two teens to clean his apartment. A young woman in his apartment building admitted to doing his personal laundry. (He literally threw his clothes down onto her balcony and she hauled them off to the Laundromat.) A team of fellow students kept a 24-hour vigil to insure that he would not fall asleep while studying. In fact, he needed the help, but would never have asked for it in the ordinary way.

Keeping watch was a necessary inconvenience. The energy needed to drag his parts around campus was debilitating, but so was his nightlife. B.T. drank more than his share. And when old "John Barleycorn" took hold, he remembered. He saw *their* faces. He heard *their* cries. He told *their* stories and he wept.

But it would be a lie to say he drank because of the pain, though surely it helped, or because of Vietnam, because he drank before and during the war. It was a dangerous habit, one that would help destroy his health and, later, almost cost him his career.

Unfortunately or fortunately, his well-documented consumption of alcohol was more often the cause of "fat laughter among friends," (Rabbi Frazin's phrase), than the result of remembering men under fire. He became, if possible, more loquacious than ever, and routinely, by word or deed, excruciatingly funny.

One night, after a particularly heavy bout of drinking, his friends close behind, he careened up the stairs to his apartment. There was the sound of a mighty crash. Worried that this time he might have hurt himself, his friends burst into the room. It was empty. The window was open, its curtains flapping ominously in the night breeze. No B.T. Too horrified to verify their fears, they neither moved nor spoke. Then the silence was broken by his frustrated mutterings; safe, but mad as hell, he had fallen into the closet.

In the bars or the classrooms, wherever, B.T. was making his mark, shaking up, and sometimes, for good causes, shaking down those who would become his lifelong companions. Relationships, as Governor Brown had reminded us, were to B.T.'s mind absolutely necessary to human progress, yes, and to human survival. Never a fair-weather friend, once he connected, he held on. He was there when he needed you and when you needed him, and sometimes before you were aware of either.

A classmate recalls the letter B.T. wrote him on the occasion of a family tragedy. "Within days of the unforgettable event, B.T. wrote me a lengthy letter, which to this day I keep in my dresser drawer. Since that time, I have made it a practice to step in and offer my support to friends who are in crisis. Often I wonder, 'What would B.T. think or do,' and I try to act in kind. Thus, even in death, for me he is forever alive.'" He wrote:

> After debating for a week whether I should mind my own business, I finally decided to get off my ass and get some things off my chest. I realize that it is only remotely analogous, but there was a time when I felt that things looked pretty hopeless—downright bleak—when I lost my arm and leg. But, with the help and support of my friends, I realized that life is short and life is for the *living*! If you're thinking of quitting law school, or worrying about returning because of some social stigma—you're selling your friends—*all of us*—short. Granted, it won't be easy but I've learned it's never half as bad as you think it's going to be. So please give it a try, or you'll kick yourself someday. It goes without saying that your family needs you now more than ever. Your resilience could be very heartening to them. Whatever you decide to do, I've got a closet full of booze and my f . . . ing door is always open . . .
>
> B.T.

GRADUATION

Six years ago, I was lying in a hospital in Vietnam.
I was in a lot of pain.
I believed I was dying and I was terribly afraid.

Santa Clara University Law School
Commencement Address, Class of 1973,

B.T. Collins

During his second year of law school, B.T. ran for President of the Student Bar Association. Legend has it that while other students ran on real issues, like the Vietnam War, B.T.'s slogan was, "Let's have more beer parties and put a little fun in our lives!" His campaign materials included mock *Playboy* centerfolds featuring a one legged candidate, hand and hook raised in the famous Nixon victory salute.

He won, of course, and the B.T. *reign of terror* began. For Santa Clara's Class of 1973, the years in law school became happily unforgettable. The only bad moment was when the student body voted to protest the bombing in Cambodia, an act which to B.T.'s mind sought to nullify the reason he left half his body another land.

In fact, his candidacy did have serious objectives: "I personally do not view law school as a competitive rat race, but rather as a difficult three years that could actually be made more palatable if students would help each other get through. To that end, I would like to see a volunteer tutorial society, composed of students willing to assist those with academic problems, and a list of students willing to lend their notes and/or books to those whose materials have been lost. The scope of SBA influence is limited, and I promise no unrealistic changes in the balance of power between students and the administration. The real strength of the SBA lies in the votes of the class representatives. It is the function, therefore, of the president, as chief administrator, to orchestrate these votes into meaningful programs. Yes, I would support more social functions. They do have a place in law school, and help make for a better relationship between students and between students and faculty."

It was the beginning of a life of public service, one in which he would treat the little guy and the big guy, and all those in between, the same. A blood drive was held on campus, and B.T. took charge. There was nearly 100% participation. Students who didn't give blood typed, gave out orange juice, and helped in some way. A reporter inquired about the unusually high number of people involved. "You don't understand," the interviewed students replied. "When B.T. Collins says, 'Do it,' you do it." It was easier to give in than listen to B.T.'s harangue. The Student Bar Association presented him with a bullwhip that remained proudly on display in every office he ever occupied.

B.T. was chosen to be the commencement speaker by acclamation. The privilege was normally reserved for the graduate with the highest academic average, for which he certainly didn't qualify. I was present for his performance. It began with a number of inside jokes. Somehow, he contrived to mention almost everyone in his class by name and trait or recognizable deed. His classmates roared. Even the seated Monsignors slapped their scarlet-covered thighs in glee. As he pounded the polished podium with his hook, I wondered why he hadn't mentioned the cause of his missing right hand. I should have known better.

There was a pregnant pause and people wiped their eyes and chuckled over remarks past. The pause grew longer. He had bowed his head. His mood had changed and people looked expectantly at him to continue. I knew what was coming. The line had been thrown, his hook sunk, and mercilessly, he would reel them in. They would never, ever forget this day.

"Six years ago," he cleared his throat, "Six years ago, I was lying in a hospital in Vietnam. I was in a lot of pain. I believed I was dying and I was terribly afraid."

The laughter died. The faces fell. The ensuing silence was broken only by the sound of paper programs flapping in a wandering breeze. The shock of an admission so personal drew us together in a knot of attentive compassion. He caught us in that steel-blue gaze. I looked down the row at my mother and watched her nervously lift her hand to her forehead. She, too, had seen it all before.

"A friend came to visit me," he continued, "and because I was so lonely and because the very sight of him was so welcome and so unexpected, I began to cry."

Purses snapped. Handkerchiefs were withdrawn. Grown men rested their foreheads on the steeples of clasped hands; children, sensing the sadness, turned their cheeks towards the reassuring warmth of an older arm nearby. He had us—body and soul. Like those men in the jungle, we would have followed him to hell and home again.

"My friend told me," he went on, "You have a right to cry. Get it out. This is really tough, and this is only the beginning. You have a long, hard row to hoe!" His voice was tight and we felt the fine line between the pain of these memories and his iron control.

Full eyes overflowed. I heard the errant, muffled sound of sorrow shared. Each one of us thought, *He speaks to me alone.* I winced at the memory of him in his hospital bed, hollowed eyes and ghost-like face, beaded yellow sweat forming on a brow creased in agony.

He paused again.

He was standing taller now. He voice was clear and strong. "But it has not been a long hard road," he declared, "It's been all the way up because of Dean Strong and Mary Emery and . . ." He named name after name after name, "because of you and you and you!" he thundered, gesturing toward his classmates with hook and hand.

I thought the crowd would rise as one. There was a cheer caught in every throat. But before it could burst forth clattering on that silent afternoon, he stopped again. Looking out at those tear-stained faces, he smiled. It was a broad smile, an almost wicked smile coupled with a wildly conspiratorial wink. And leaning across the podium, chin thrust forward, he asked with mock sarcasm, "Now—is everybody happy?"

The laughter rained. We'd been had, or had we? We had not. It was Ruben Garcia's story; Ruben, who had gone AWOL to find B.T. in the dark recesses of a Quonset hut; Ruben who had cried with B.T., just as those who listened had cried that day. The hook had been explained; the tears shed washed away. Pity replaced by admiration. Ties tied, never to be forgotten.

Five months before B.T. died, classmate Elliot Daum, a liberal Democrat, wrote to him, "You've been one of my heroes since that unforgettable graduation speech in 1973." Later, in an obituary, Daum proclaimed, "Like the blinded heroes of Greek mythology, B.T.'s loss of limbs had not diminished him but had caused him to grow beyond his destiny, to become larger than life. You made me cry that day, old friend," he added, "and now you've got me crying again. Farewell."

Daddy, too, was very proud.

June 4, 1973
Dear Butch,

That was some speech you made. I remember how, as a little boy, you were afraid of ants, yet socked the kid next door for hitting Marialis, how you willed yourself back to health by sheer courage. Your dogged determination to do things with one hand instead of two. The way you kept from having shots when the pain was so very severe. The one wish I would have for you is that you continue to keep your shield untarnished and your reputation for telling it like it is. Stay as you are! We love you for what you have shown yourself to be.

B.T. was also in charge of the graduation reception. The champagne flowed. The largest strawberries I have ever seen were heaped red in see-through bowls. Trailing behind him, I had the feel of following a Kennedy. He was surrounded, followed, halted, touched. Judges whispered, "When you're ready to work . . ." People of power slipped him notes. Everyone reached out to him, grandparents, children, siblings, husbands and wives in tow, "B.T., I just wanted you to meet . . . Mother, this is B.T. . . ."

After graduation, B.T. stayed at Santa Clara to work as its first Placement Director. To that point, there had been no official mechanism in place to connect and support alumni. B.T. created the position. He launched innovative programs to help students professionally. Relentlessly unorthodox, he took charge of a fellow lawyer who was a recovering heroin addict and bank robber and tried to get him a job with the very federal judge who had sentenced him to prison.

On the job, he was the picture of insubordination. His boss, Dean George Alexander, reported, "He didn't do what I asked or even vaguely approach the task in the way I had hoped, but he always accomplished it magnificently."

The Dean began to respond in kind to B.T.'s interminable missives, "Rest assured," he retorted at one point, "with respect to your personal comments, I will continue in every possible way to give you a hand . . . one finger at a time."

Judge Jim Wiederschall met B.T. in the Placement Office while he was a law student. During our interview, the judge began to cry. Somehow, B.T. had learned that Wiederschall had been in the Army, and called him in to chat. When Jim arrived for the appointment, B.T. unceremoniously shouted, "Wiederschall, get your fat ass in here!" Jim entered the office and immediately stood at attention. B.T., touched, barked, "At ease, soldier," in return.

Wiederschall's service had been in Alaska with the Army Band rather than in Vietnam. In front of B.T., he felt ashamed. But the two became friends, and eventually B.T. met and completely won over Jim's widowed mother and mentored his handicapped sister.

Wiederschall was humiliated when he failed the bar exam the first time, because he had graduated Magna cum Laude. "But B.T.," he explained, "was kind and sympathetic. He insisted, 'You are not a failure.'" He gave Jim the names of several well-known figures who had similarly failed and demanded that he contact them. Jim was touched and grateful. He knew about Sam Bird. "B.T. Collins," he confided to me, "was my Sam Bird, and I told him so. He seemed unable to reply. His silence told me at what level my remark had touched him, that this was the ultimate praise, a laurel of which he would forever feel himself unworthy."

Through some act of God, B.T. passed the California bar. The ceremony, which marked his admission, to the practice of law was vintage B.T. Collins. A transcript follows:

June 21, 1974

Judge Premo: Good afternoon, ladies and gentlemen. The Court welcomes all of you here for this happy and auspicious occasion of the acceptance of Brien T. Collins into the practice of law before the State Bar of California and all the courts of California. Some of you may not be as well acquainted—and I may risk a little embarrassment here—but some of you may not be well acquainted with the fact that he is one of the few people in the country who is able to be characterized as a military hero, in the sense that he has rendered extremely distinguished service to this country, for which all of us owe him a personal debt of gratitude. Mr. Collins served his country with great distinction and at very serious personal cost; however, after leaving the military service he went on to law school at Santa Clara University where, as I understand, he served with great distinction as well.

So in a few minutes, Mr. Collins, you will be walking out the door as Brien T. Collins, Attorney at Law, and you will be in a position that traditionally has been accorded great prestige and respect by the rest of society. You also assume your position at a time of great national convulsion. You may see now and in the future that your status as an attorney may depend in great measure on your ability to adhere to increased standards of professionalism and increased ethical standards as a citizen. So,

Casket in the Rotunda. Lying in State.
(Courtesy Sacramento Bee, Photo, Carolyn Cole)

Casket plus speakers "Brien We Hardly Knew Ye." Left to right John Banuelos,
Gayle Wilson, Governor Pete Wilson, Ann Cunningham, Maureen Collins Baker,
Stan Atkinson, Governor Jerry Brown. (Courtesy Ed Andersen/Office of Gov Pete Wilson)

The Collins kids.

The Family Collins.

B.T. and fans.

B.T. First Air Cavalry Vietnam, 1966.

B.T. accepting CIB plaque from Sam Bird, Vietnam, 1966.

Ruben Garcia, B.T., and unknown child,
Special Forces, Vietnam, 1967.

B.T. jumps on 50th birthday, 1990.

B.T. learns to ski while in Law School, 1972.

First swim with Dickie Erlich, 1968.

B.T. lectures Conservation Corps, "I'm going to work you to death!" (Courtesy, Robert Wilkins)

B.T. and Corps.
(Courtesy, National Wildlife, Mark Wexler)

B.T. drinking Malathion.
(Courtesy, California Conservation Corps)

B.T. and Sam Bird, Vietnam, 1966.

B.T. learning Vietnamese, 1987.

B.T. visiting Sam Bird's name on Wall. Washington, DC, 1987.

B.T., Governor Brown, and Jack Dugan.
(Courtesy, California Conservation Corps)

B.T. and Nora Romero.

B.T. and Sister Kathleen Horgan.

Marialis and B.T. on Election night.
(Photo, Brian Downey, deceased)

Saying Goodbye. Saluting soldiers.
(Courtesy, Sacramento Bee, Photo, Carolyn Cole)

along with the prestige and status, you have very serious responsibilities. I wish you success and fulfillment in your career as a lawyer. The Court is very pleased to have with us a former law professor of mine and of Mr. Collins', the venerable Associate Dean of the Law School at Santa Clara University, Dean George Strong who is going to make a few remarks at this time.

Dean Strong: Thank you, your Honor. I do have a few things to say. It is indeed with considerable incredulity and amazement—and, if I may say so, relief—that I move the admission of Brien T. Collins to the Bar of the State of California.

Born in White Plains, New York, forged in Gary, Indiana, and fabricated in Rochester, Minnesota, Mr. Collins overcame the obstacles of class preparation and attendance to earn the degree of Juris Doctor at the Santa Clara University School of Law, within the maximum time and the minimum unit requirements. His perseverance has demonstrated that he is a man of steel will . . . and foot . . . and leg . . . and arm . . . and hand.

In addition to his scholarly pursuits, Mr. Collins found time to serve as President of the Student Bar Association. During his reign, he was personally responsible for numerous outstanding accomplishments. He . . . he . . . I don't seem to have my list of numerous outstanding accomplishments with me but I'm sure I'll think of something. (Long pause.) Ah yes, the Class of 1973, Mr. Collins' class, had ninety cases of champagne at their graduation reception. A record not soon to be broken.

This is a time of growing legal specialization. Following the good advice and example of one of his many mentors, Mr. Collins has conducted an intensive search into the records and files of this court regarding equity action. Such research, Mr. Collins informs me, reveals not a single equity action suit filed in this Court. Having found the need, Mr. Collins intends to fill it. Consequently, he has decided to choose the much-misunderstood field of Municipal Court Equity as his special area. I am sure that Mr. Collins will have a brilliant future in equity; however, his sights are not limited, and if modesty permits, I believe I may say that I inspired him in this respect; Mr. Collins looks forward to becoming a judge *pro tempore*. I have just thought of another outstanding accomplishment. Mr. Collins had the lowest grade point average of any student to receive the Outstanding Graduate Award; another record not likely soon to be broken.

It is my honor and pleasure, therefore to present to the Court, Brien T. Collins, who has satisfied the requirements for admission to the State Bar of California.

Judge Premo: Thank you very much, Dean Strong. Lest there be some misunderstanding, I'm sure Dean Strong's remarks were made with great affection, and Mr. Collins' rebuttal will be reserved until after court—*outside* of court.

Mr. Collins, will you please stand and raise your right hand. "I do solemnly swear . . . So help me God." Thank you, Mr. Collins, and congratulations to you. You are now Brien T. Collins, Attorney at Law. Would you like to address the Court and your friends?

Mr. Collins: Thank you, your Honor. If it pleases the Court—that's how Owen Marshall always begins—when this ceremony was planned, I didn't realize, considering the international date line, that it would take place exactly seven years to the day that I was injured in Vietnam. At that time there was considerable doubt as to whether I would live to see the next day. Unfortunately for the standards of justice and the American taxpayer, I persevered. It means a great deal for all of you to be here, particularly since I have only known the majority among you since my arrival in California. I can assure you that I was much better looking seven years ago and far more humble. But again, I appreciate your coming, and let's go have a party. And, (referring to Dean Strong), special thanks to my grandfather here.

After B.T. left the University, he appointed himself the Class of
'73 Alumni Secretary. "Give back to the school!" he'd admonish.
"Give to your country!" He badgered, he whined, he coerced, in
letters and phone calls. Wherever he went, he got in touch. And
alumni, in turn, gave money and returned to the University for
reunions, roasts, and fund-raisers. He'd criticize them while asking
for favors and, individually, they'd respond in like manner; "Keep
well. I miss you, you crotchety old son-of-a-bitch."

"He convinced me to come all the way back to our reunion,"
Mitch Lyons, a classmate from Massachusetts recalled. "Every time
I got a letter from him, he'd add some insensitive, right-wing
comment that would make me laugh—like, "Who's going to
represent the knee-jerk liberal establishment from the People's
Republic of Massachusetts, if you're not there?"

He was the target of many roasts; a sure-fire marketing device to
guarantee maximum attendance at alumni events.

"When B.T. was brought in by medics from the Mekong Delta,"
Professor Poche announced at one, "they recorded his having no
vital signs. It was on that basis that Santa Clara University admitted
him. When I later managed to get him out of the employ of the
University, I received the Owens' Award for University Service."

Known for his biting wit, Dean Strong was asked to deliver the
final blow to a roast, hosted by the Santa Clara Law Society. "As
the clean-up speaker, and because of our long association," he began,
"I have been asked to say a few nice things about our honored guest
this evening." Long, long, pause. "Thank you very much!"

The burst of laughter that had become B.T.'s routine background
music filled the hall. B.T. responded by promising Dean Strong and
others to specialize in criminal law. He planned to wear only short
sleeved shirts and Bermuda shorts, and then if the jury didn't acquit
his clients, well, what kind of people were they anyway?

Classmate Pat O'Laughlin claimed to have first met B.T. in the
library, a place, he said, B.T. only entered to "collect money or see
if anyone owed him a beer." He described that initial encounter and
B.T.'s blood drive at still another roast:

"A lot of people hid out from him in there (the library). One day he stood in the door just glaring, and I'll admit, I was frightened. I'd heard stories about Vietnam, and I didn't know if this was exhibit A for an Agent Orange or what.

"And then I felt his hook in my shoulder blades and he growled, 'O'Laughlin. You give blood?'

"Not only had I never given blood, but I was unfamiliar with the whole concept.

"B.T. said, 'O'Laughlin, ya' ever look around this school? You haven't done anything for anyone. You're just a punk, right out of college and I'm rounding up everybody in the law school who is a communist or a socialist or who didn't register for the draft for this blood drive and you're going to be first!'

"And so, we gave blood. And afterwards I was feeling kind of lightheaded and B.T. says, 'You've got to replenish your system.'

"And I said, 'Right. Let's go have a lemonade or something.'

"So, B.T. gives me this withering look. 'O'Laughlin. D'ya drink?'

"And I said, 'Well, I've had a few beers and stuff.'

"And he said, 'O'Laughlin, someone like you, well, you don't have anything going for you, so the least you ought to be able to do with a name like yours is drink. Then instead of being a loser, at least people could say, that O'Laughlin sure can hold his hootch.'

"So we went to a bar and B.T. introduced me to Tanqueray. I think we were there for about two weeks."

Santa Clara decided to remember him officially. The University wanted to dedicate an office to him, but, in typical fashion, he preferred the almost unacceptable, something by which he would be remembered, but a memorial that would make the law students laugh. So, he chose a urinal, a memorial latrine. He called it a "latrine" because it was a military term, one that would upset the liberals.

He felt he'd made an appropriate choice. "My kind of student would never go into a technical service office. My kind of student will be studying late when he should have studied before. A last minute crammer, living on the edge, he'll go into the urinal, the B.T. Collins Memorial Latrine, and right above it there be one of my sayings: 'If it's not in Gilbert's (a legal outline cheat sheet) it's not common law. B.T. Collins, 1973.' And he'll be wondering, 'Who was that guy?' Now that's immortality."

True. How many students stop to ponder the origins of the name of a building, or the life story of the subject of a somber portrait on the library's walls? Ah, but a brass plaque above a urinal. That would indeed give one pause.

He would give a lot of people more than pause. In time, he would join the ranks of other high-profile Santa Clara graduates, but first, Judge Marc Poche would bring him to Sacramento, to the attention of one of the nation's most talked-about governors, Edmund G. (Jerry) Brown, also a Santa Clara alumnus. "Immortality," B.T.Collins' style, was on the horizon.

XII

B.T. AND BROWN

Dear Cosmopolitan,
I noticed you selected Governor Edmund G. Brown Jr.,
as one of the sexiest men in the world.
I work for the man. You couldn't be farther from the truth.

B.T. (Sour grapes) Collins.

In 1976, Marc Poche was working as Governor Brown's Legislative Secretary. There was an opening on his staff and, acting on a suggestion by Santa Clara University's Mary Emery, he decided to try to bring B.T. on board. It would be B.T.'s responsibility to run interference between the Governor and the Republican side of the state assembly.

B.T. responded to Poche's offer with characteristic candor; "I don't know the Governor; I've never been to Sacramento, and I'm a Republican."

Nevertheless, a first meeting followed, during which the Governor *reportedly* asked B.T. whether or not he had voted for him. To which, he *allegedly* responded, "I never vote for short ex-Jesuits." True or untrue, it made all the papers and my brother got the job.

Said one reporter, "This may be a fun year after all."

However unflappable he appeared to Poche, B.T. was genuinely excited.

Privately, he saw the job, whatever the Governor's politics, as an opportunity to serve. He called to tell me.

I said, "I haven't heard from you in weeks. What's going on?

"I'm moving."

"Moving? Where?"

"To Sacramento. I'm going to work for the Governor."

"*Brown?* Brien!"

An unforgettable era in California politics was about to begin. The double amputee Republican troubleshooter and his boss, the Democratic Governor of California, two Irishmen; the stereotypical, hard-drinking, silver-tongued orator who could charm the pants off a leprechaun and his pot o' gold out' the ground, and his apparent antithesis—the chaste, ever sober son of Erin who, nevertheless, understood Irish guilt, Irish temerity, Irish humor, Irish will, and, therefore, my brother.

"B.T. Collins and Jerry Brown," Carrie Dolan of the *Wall Street Journal* wrote, "like a bourbon chaser after a cup of herbal tea." Seen as California's political odd couple, they were more accurately a potential dream team. Brown the brilliant, scholarly philosopher; B.T. the intelligent, politically savvy pragmatist. The Governor and his best right—make that left—arm; the first led with his mind, which doubled as a sort of cerebral dump truck wherein ideas were thrown for eventual downloading; the other, with heart and mind inalterably interfaced.

Both men were wildly unconventional: Brown in his choice of political appointees, his administrative style and his lack of attention to political niceties; B.T., because he refused either to stand on ceremony or walk on eggshells. Brown slept on a mattress *sans* bed, called subordinates on the phone directly, and drove around in an old blue Plymouth. B.T. "told it like it was." Each, in his own way, said, "Take me as I am or not at all." B.T. was too passionate, too personal, too straightforward for politics' delicate digestion. Jerry Brown was too bright. There was no popular political precedent for intellect at his level.

His thinking was "light years ahead of its time," B.T. confided to me, which had earned Brown the ungrateful label, "Governor Moonbeam." He was not, the uninitiated believed, of their time and place, for which California and the nation can only be grateful:

solar energy, telecommunications, trade with the Pacific Rim, and attention to the environment, all in the 70's.

But if Brown lived in the future, B.T. looked equally to the past, his principles rooted in a time when honor was not the exception but the rule. Each man had his peccadillo. A governor can't appear consistently insensitive; his appointee can't use bad language indiscriminately. Colorful vocabulary aside, there was no question that B.T. had the chip that Brown was missing—an uncommon common touch.

Both men cared about causes.

Brown cared deeply about humanity, sometimes forgetting about being human. He saw people as a citizenry to be saved.

B.T., too, believed in causes and people as a means to their end. But if collectively people were a powerhouse, B.T. saw them first as individuals. He related to them on a very personal level. Like the good CO, he was always "on duty." Legislators knew where to find him, night and day.

The Governor, almost impossible to reach, could now be contacted through Collins. B.T. understood that people were the conduit through which ideas became actions. And he tried desperately to build the bridge that would transport Brown's vision to those who needed to know and understand it.

Both men had been raised Catholics. Both took issue with some of the tenets of the Church. If they had resolutely avoided structure as young men, they later turned to the most disciplined and exacting environments, for Jerry Brown, the Jesuit rule, and for B.T. Collins, the military.

In the seminary, Brown sought the contemplative company of the intellectual cream of the Catholic clergy. But the Jesuit's teachings were too far removed from the problems of the real world, so he fled from the Society of Jesus to anti-societal Berkley. B.T. ran from the real world to one surreal—the bloodied battlefields of Southeast Asia.

Both the seminary and Vietnam left their marks. If Brown seemed remote, he had been schooled to be. Religious life, particularly the Catholic variety, isolates. Relationships with anyone but God are eschewed in exchange for solitary reflection. Not the best practicum for one who seeks to lead.

If B.T. seemed inordinately in touch, he had been both sensitized and de-sensitized by a daily montage of man's inhumanity to man.

The training in the Church and the military made for dissimilar administrative styles as well. The scholar-priest dazzled by sheer intellect; the patriot-comic made you laugh and cry, and rubbed you ideal-raw. They processed information differently. Jesuit education requires endless, open-ended discussions focused on the gathering of thoughts and theories, which will lead not necessarily to resolution, but to ever more thoughts and theories. Brown collected facts and ideas in absentia from their human consequences. In the military, information received is productive only in proportion to the lives it protects. Fact-finding is mandatory; lengthy reflection can be life-threatening.

Knowing how to take care of his troops was not Brown's forte. Morale depends on small things: praise for performance, and an awareness of each person as a separate and important entity. Brown walked a higher wire, untouched by common necessities and the basics of daily interaction. Small things were B.T.'s stock in trade. Brown's men had none of the attributes of good soldiers. They were too individualistic to work as a team.

B.T. understood the urgency of working as a unit. He counted on connections, on cooperation, on multiple minds focused on a single mission. B.T. served a commander-in-chief; loyalty was the bottom line. Brown surrounded himself with apolitical types to whom true loyalty was unknown. B.T. operated under a chain-of-command. Brown preferred to go left and right at the same time. Yet, somehow he and B.T. moved ahead under a crossfire of ideas and actions. Brown constructed an in-house think-tank. And B.T., as reported in a 1982 *Wall Street Journal* article, ran his show like a "cross between a saloon and a platoon."

Both men were bachelors. Both apparently had first great loves, each of whom went off and married "the other guy." Both understood that politics and lifelong mates make uneasy bedfellows; that political wives and families must, of necessity, take second place, that the women in today's world who would accept such a role are few.

Both men were very attractive to women. Brown because he was so serious, B.T. because he was so merry; Brown because he looked so Wall-Street elegant when dressed in silk ties and pinstripes, B.T. because his pinstripes and paisley came with impeccable manners and dozens of endearing *petits déférences* when and where it counted. Brown was so mysterious; B.T. so un-committable. B.T. had a "reputation" with women. Brown had none.

It must be said, in the interest of objectivity as regards B.T.'s "reputation," that there were an extraordinary number of women in my brother's life; so many that even the most macho among his male friends sometimes shook their heads in disbelief. Little old ladies fluttered around him, and beautiful young ladies were similarly attentive—although the latter came and went with alarming alacrity.

Was there something to prove? That a one-armed, one legged man could more than hold his own? Or was the combination of good manners, (thanks to Mother), tenderness, (thanks to Daddy), and power, (at this point, thanks to Jerry Brown), too much to resist? In any case, he always told them after two dates that he never intended to marry . . . ever! Then he proceeded to be so attentive and charming, they figured he had changed his mind. Maybe it was simply that he required so much care and sacrifice which are a woman's forte.

Actually, both men needed a lot of mothering, a thankless and almost impossible task for anyone foolish enough to undertake it. Neither B.T. nor Brown took very good care of himself.

B.T. stayed out all night drinking, making and cementing relationships, thus adding to his already considerable background in life among the living. Brown stayed up all night thinking, questioning the quality of life, America's place on the planet, the nation's potential and, consequently, its responsibilities.

Their eating habits were unacceptable by any standard. Brown, perpetually hungry, was a fast-food man. Secretaries, thinking to

match his California image, would run out for bean sprout treats
and avocado things. Left to his own devices, the Governor
preferred sweets, fries, fried chicken and other coronary disasters.
In concert, B.T.'s *bon appetit* was measured by the amount of
Tabasco sauce any dish could sustain before totally disintegrating.
Brown routinely ate whatever he found, wherever he found it, to
whomever it belonged. B.T. would call out to the delight of reporters
and staff, "The Governor of California has taken a cheese sandwich
from a crippled veteran who got to work before he did and who
hasn't eaten all day! Put it back!"

Both men were raised to serve by different Irish fathers, but the
messages in each home were the same: Make a difference, and do
for others. Each "Da" presented a difficult model. Governor Pat
Brown was the gregarious, charismatic, archetypical politician the
younger governor could never be. Jerry Brown neither fully
understood nor approved of standard public political behavior. He
saw backslapping and glad-handing as artificial and insincere. He
couldn't have kissed a baby if his life depended upon it.

By contrast, B.T. believed in contact of every kind. He understood
that such was the stuff of which not only politics but life was made.
It wasn't enough to care—Brown cared—people needed to *know* you
cared. B.T. was no stranger to the healing power of human touch.
He had held, and been held in return. "It's all about relationships,
Governor. It's all about relationships," he would plead, as Brown
noted at B.T.'s funeral. The Governor's father, Pat Brown and B.T.
understood this and, therefore, each other. Yet Jerry Brown
understood B.T. too. He knew that above all else that B.T. was real.

Each of their fathers was a gladiator in his own arena, though
father Brown was well-to-do and father Collins, of necessity,
pennywise. B.T.'s more humble beginnings made him hungry. He
needed to succeed. He had worked extra shifts and more than one
job to do so. Brown's more sheltered upbringing would cost him.
There are those who resent a "silver spoon," and his lack of living
in the trenches or coming up hard set him apart from those he
needed most to reach. And so they grew up—B.T. quickly,

mercilessly, in the midst of men dying, Brown in the shadow of California's political coliseum and the bleaching sunlight of his father's legendary might.

Daddy was very proud of B.T.'s new position.

Dear Brien,

Naturally, both Mother and I are aglow with your latest accomplishment. Actually though, we are most proud of the way you have shown the way to those who have been held back because of their disabilities. I well remember your sweat-soaked shirt when you were determined to learn how to use your artificial hand—and you did! In truth, we are more proud of that than if you were elected governor. But of course we're proud of your job with the Governor—so darn proud it brings a lump to our throats.

So continue to conduct yourself that despite worldly criticism, men will say of you in Antony-like cadence, "*This* indeed is a *man*!" May you forever be as successful as you have been! May straight arrow follow you always!

Love, Dad

Neither B.T. nor Brown suffered fools lightly. Rule of thumb— have your facts accurate, ready, and aplenty. Neither could stand "yes men or women," so they surrounded themselves with types from whom they could learn. Brown's closest advisors consisted of a former Apollo 9 astronaut, a Buddhist priest, a former Christian Brother, a French film director, a tough talking former prison guard who worked his way up to Chief of California's prison system under the Reagan administration, the creator of *The Whole Earth Catalog*, and, a one-armed, one-legged, raving, conservative Republican who had voted for his opponent in the most recent election.

B.T.'s eclectic mix—bearded scholars, (communists, by his definition), Latinos, news anchors, writers, FBI agents, lawyers, veterans, army nurses, bankers, politicians and policemen of every ilk agreed neither with him nor with each other.

Brown seemed to have no friends by common definition. This worried B.T. He knew the value of those who had no other agenda than the bond between you. B.T. was happiest in the presence of other people, whether in the midst of the brouhaha of their conflicting views or simply silent by their side.

Brown needed solitude.

B.T. didn't like to be alone.

Brown was known for his austerity, B.T. for his generosity. Brown had plenty of money, but didn't spend it. Not that he was stingy; he just took money for granted. Both men understood its potential power when used for good intentions. Neither man spent on himself. B.T. gave his away. On one trip to Sacramento, he sent me off shopping to amuse myself while he worked. Before I left his office, he opened his wallet and dumped a pile of credit cards on the desk so that I would have enough money. The secretary in attendance gasped. B.T. laughed. "You don't know how safe this is. You don't know my sister!" But he remained a regular old lady regarding his personal expenditures. He refused, for example, to turn on the air conditioning in his own home even during the hottest Sacramento summers.

The walls of the Governor's simple apartment were markedly unadorned, his refrigerator usually bare.

B.T.'s refrigerator was full to overflowing, often growing insidious somethings he was nevertheless loath to throw away. The backseat of his car, an office on the road, was rife with similar antibiotics in progress. His walls groaned 'neath the weight of pictures of himself with other notables: B.T. and Omar Bradley, Jimmie Doolittle, General Westmoreland; B.T. and Carter, Ford, Reagan, Prince Charles, and Admiral Stockdale; B.T. and Bob Hope; B.T. and Willie Brown; B.T. and everybody else's children. Friends were called upon to help hang those pictures—there were hundreds of them—and to help him move. After several new addresses, they were close to mutiny. "Collins, I packed this jar of mayonnaise in '75 and again in '79. It's going out! And hang your own damn pictures!"

"I would," was the sardonic reply, "but I lost my arm and my leg in the war. Remember, while you guys were parading around with all those signs?"

It follows that B.T.'s office also contrasted with Brown's. B.T.'s looked more like a souvenir junction, an exhibition that immortalized the profane to the crushingly poignant. Every item in his office evoked a memory which made a human connection. A tee-shirt hung on the back wall proclaiming, "Kill a Commie for a Mommie," and beside it, the picture of B.T. as a bearded skeleton in an Army hospital. A yellow and black traffic sign cautioned, "No riding the hook." Giant sized jars of Midol, deliberately sexist, and aspirin were in plain view of whiners and complainers. An old electric shaver sat on top of a much-thumbed volume of *The Ho Chi Min Trail*; a battered toothbrush protruded from a Santa Clara mug. Yet, prominently placed midst the clutter was a business card holder bearing the date he was wounded and the inscription, "The golden thread of courage has no end."

Brown's office, if richly carpeted, was, like his living quarters, singularly spartan. "What will people think?" B.T. whined to the Governor. "Who's gonna believe in you with no legals, no diplomas, nothing?" This troubled B.T. to the point of doing the unthinkable. He went flea market shopping and found Brown some framed credibility. His collection contained things like notice of Mary O'Leary's first communion, Joe somebody's longest drive in the American Legion Golf Tournament, and various certificates for meritorious this and that, none of which pertained in any way to Brown. Then, with help, he hung his collection on the walls of the office of California's Governor. He led the Governor into his newly decorated office with a "Wadda ya think?" Brown never blinked. The story goes that he left it all there.

He worried in other ways about the Governor's image. Adriana Giranturco, Director of the state's Transportation Agency, dressed like a hippie. B.T. felt her clothes were inappropriate in a post at so important a level. "Listen, Babe, these rags have got to go!" he told her frankly. Unbelievably, she agreed. He took her to a department store. She came out of the dressing room modeling the various outfits he had selected. He gave his "yeas" or "nays." She complied.

The Governor's relationship with the legislature was antagonistic. In recommending B.T., Poche remembered how artfully he had made his Santa Clara classmates bend to his will. He hoped working with the Assembly would be a repeat performance. B.T.'s job as Assistant Deputy Legislative Secretary was to make the Governor and the legislature understand each other. One of his more onerous responsibilities was to bear the bad news of an impending gubernatorial veto. "They chose me for the job," he quipped, "Because nobody's going to hit a one-armed man."

At first, everyone thought he was just a giant put-on. "Better than psychotherapy and cheaper too," said one member of the Assembly.

B.T. laughingly called the Assembly an "adult day care center." And he was the only man in the Governor's office who could and did tell the grumbling Republican lawmakers, "Hey, don't blame me, I voted for the other guy." His sense of humor was a nice touch, but his need to tell the truth won them over. "I may be a lying, thieving dog, but I'm not going to lie to a legislator. You may get away with it once, but this is a regular Peyton Place, and lying will catch up with you."

His penchant for political incorrectness drew both legislative and media attention. In a world in which every word is watched and recorded, he made the science of irreverence an art. "Arguing with this guy," columnist, Jack Clifford wrote, "was like trying to get in the last word with an echo."

He strolled and he stroked, not just on the day of a crucial vote, but over the long haul. His method of stroking was unusual. He gave the legislators nicknames; "Garbage Mouth, Father Confessor, Mother Superior, Oreo Kid, Jar-Head."

In Norman Lear imitation, he introduced Alice Lytle, the black Director of State Consumer Services, as the Governor's "colored maid." He was publicly mocking still-held stereotypes. Lytle found him "absolutely charming." She explained that people were far more insulted if they hadn't been given a name. With good reason. These labels were reserved for those co-workers he liked best. In fairness, he referred to himself in similarly unflattering terms, as the "House

Nazi" and the "Gimp's Greatest Success Story." The message: "Lighten up. Take the problems of those you serve more seriously and yourself less so."

An article in the April, 1978 *Quarter Horse of the Pacific Coast* put it all into perspective.

"B.T. Collins would have made a great horse trader, because his powers of persuasion are unequalled in the hall of mirrors where persuasion is considered a great art. However, remembering the old proverb 'Horse traders have no friends,' I realized he wouldn't qualify because he lives by the creed, 'Never give a sucker a break, but don't cheat a friend.' Besides, he's liked by all the members of the California Legislature and you don't get in that position by sitting on your backside or being a phony."

There was something else. As Nora Romero reminded us at the funeral, B.T. kept track of personal dates. People in every position came to wait for his birthday call. They knew when things went well there would be praise, however crudely given or humorously phrased. They knew when something bad happened, B.T. would be there. They also knew that B.T. would put the best possible case to Brown when he was considering a bill. "Democrats and Republicans alike poured out their troubles to B.T.'s tolerant ears." Make that "ear." B.T. worked on making the Governor more accessible to legislators, constituents, and various other notables, among whom was Charles, Prince of Wales.

The capital newspapers, followed by the *New York Times*, the *International Herald Tribune* and several others took note.

Prince's Pauper Meal Prompts Aide to Sprout Off.

"There was the affable B.T. Collins, Jerry Brown's legislative aide, who had been put in charge of details for the October 29, visit of Britain's Prince Charles to the Governor's office, and a reporter wanted to know what was on the menu. "Bean sprout sandwiches or something just as simple," B.T. said. A plain-speaking man, B.T. went on to say how he'd like to get the Governor and the Prince off in a corner for a really good talk. "What you'll have here that day," Collins continued, "is a man who has been trained and educated all his life to become ruler of Britain talking with a guy who would like someday to be ruler of the US." The ink wasn't dry on the word "day," when the sprouts began hitting the fan. Cracks like 'loose lips sink ships' were winged at Collins. National TV picked up the quote. Letters to the editors started flowing in; *The London Daily News* went with the story—and B.T. went into seclusion where he penned the following response for whoever cared to read it:

I solemnly swear: No bean sprouts sandwiches; the word, "ruler" has been stricken from my vocabulary; if Governor Brown even thinks about going to Washington, I'll lock him in his room, and that recently purchased crown, scepter, and cloak will be returned forthwith."

When the Prince arrived, he was actually given a bean sprout sandwich in a brown paper bag. His Highness was not without a sense of humor. Noticing B.T.'s hook, he commented, "Ah, I see you've been dealing with the press."

After two years as the Deputy Legislative Secretary, B.T. was still not the main man. He had moved from Assistant Deputy Legislative Secretary to Deputy Secretary without the commensurate raise in pay. The reasons given were that he had a pension from the Army to supplement his income and that he was only at the beginning of his career—all of which was irrelevant. B.T. communicated this to Brown bluntly. Meanwhile, Saudi Arabia and big bucks beckoned . . . apparently not hard enough. He stayed, but not before he had allegedly written a letter of resignation and rescinded it. A capital column later carried part of the story:

The Sacramento Union, September 3, 1977

"Brown Outdraws Sheik," it began. "It's been an open secret around the State Capitol that B.T. Collins has been planning to leave for greener pastures. However the mercurial, witty Collins has agreed to stay on due to a little arm twisting by the Governor and some legislators and lobbyists who view Collins as the strongest part of Brown's legislative staff. In short, everybody thinks he is too valuable to let slip away."

May 13, 1977

Dear Governor Brown:

As we have discussed before, please consider my resignation effective as of October 1, 1977 or any earlier date should you so choose.

Sincerely,

B.T. Collins, Deputy Legislative Secretary

Memorandum

June 10, 1997

To: Edmund G. Brown Jr.

Rescind crybaby letter of resignation. Main reasons for the letter were the following:

See attached memo re: salary. Your rationale that I am making more money than I ever did before does nothing but infuriate me. Either I'm worth it or I'm not; if I have to put up with the abuse, and *I mean abuse* that these legislators hand out, I want to be compensated for it. Granted, I asked for it, having become the most visible and accessible member of your office.

Reasons for rescinding my resignation:

No one else would hire me; *David's* and the *Torch Club** have liens on my house and my car; the women in the Capitol feed my ego; everybody knows about my letter of resignation; consequently, bartenders, legislators, lobbyists, secretaries, consultants, sergeants-at-arms have been on my back not to leave; I have come to relish my role as hit-man and bearer of bad news. Therefore, if you want to make me happy, give me the raise I want and do it before the budget, in order that I may continue to rip off the taxpayers, albeit at a greater rate. Get everybody off my back who is operating under the delusion that it is such a fantastic opportunity to work for you, especially since you and I both know you are impossible.

---

* Local watering holes

Stop stroking me. I don't need it. It is unnecessary for me to be seen in public places with you. Besides, you just cramp my style. I appreciate what you are trying to do, but I'd like to maintain a respectful subordinate-superior relationship if for no other reason than it prevents one entertaining grandiose career plans. Furthermore, I am old fashioned enough to still believe in respect for the office. So I cannot address you as "Jerry" in our conversations or in those with others.

I came to this job with my eyes open, and I don't expect any rewards for sticking around. My main problem in years to come will be erasing the taint of having worked for you. Perhaps you could supply me with a prison record for the time I spent here. If I don't get the raise, I will go into a sulk and will badmouth you throughout the Capitol.

B.T.

Whether or not the resignation as written was ever sent to the Governor is a matter of conjecture. The in-house memo, written tongue-in-cheek, however, contained more than a modicum of truth. Jerry Brown was hard to work for. Aides and assistants at all levels were on demand 24 hours a day. It was not unusual for them to be called out of restaurants, movies, and even friends' houses because the Governor wanted to talk. B.T. joked about it:

"It'll never end. I'll be 75 and he'll be calling to say, "I've got this little job for you."

"But Governor, I'm on a respirator."

"Well, how soon can you make it?"

But B.T. added, "Hey, I owe him. Without him, I'd be a nobody."

As a Republican, B.T. was suspect because he worked for a Democratic governor, although he continued to support fellow Republicans. Many did not understand his willingness to serve in any administration.

In fact, despite his lifelong membership in the Republican Party, B.T. was in many ways non-political. He operated above the fray of party politics. It was patently obvious in his allegiances, in the speeches he gave, in the causes he supported, and the friends not forgotten, that what mattered most was what was good for the nation and the people of the State of California. Although he would eventually work under two Republican governors, neither gave him full reign nor appeared by their appointments to understand fully his potential. No question, Brown did.

B.T. got his pay raise but not the job of Legislative Secretary, much to the consternation of the legislators themselves. Jerry Brown had other plans for his most popular aide. He named B.T. Director of the then floundering California Conservation Corps.

Later, B.T. considered his work with the CCC his proudest achievement, but he was not immediately enthusiastic. "Hell, I thought the CCC was the California Coastal Commission," he joked. "I thought I'd get a car, sell all the land to developers, and then go live in Nicaragua. Actually, I have never managed anything but 26 Vietnamese," he commented wryly, "and, (waving his hook), I didn't do too well at that."

Reportedly, B.T. agreed to take over if the Governor would agree: 1) to give him *carte blanche* in running the beleaguered organization, and, 2) to remain uninvolved himself. A plaque on a rocking chair later given to B.T. by corpsmen bears witness to this arrangement: "EGB is not to sit in this chair! Signed, The Management."

Brown may never have been to war, but he knew a commander in chief when he saw one. He gave in, B.T. started out, and the show began.

XIII

THE CALIFORNIA
CONSERVATION CORPS

Don't tell me you were oppressed or disadvantaged.
I don't care.
I am not concerned about your happiness.
I'm going to work you to death.

> Inspirational Speech to members of the CCC
>
> B.T. Collins

First, there was the matter of leaving his current post. The Capital newspapers had some fun with his supposed letter of resignation:

> Office of the Governor, Sacramento, California, 12/19/78
>
> Governor Edmund Brown Jr. announced today that he has accepted the resignation of Deputy Legislative Secretary, B.T. Collins. Collins has served as the Governor's liaison, and was recently named Chief of Protocol for the Governor. The Governor praised Collins as a "two-fisted fighter. However, due to Collins' impending dementia and the rising cost of spare parts, he has accepted with regret Mr. Collins' resignation." Collins is a Republican. He will not be replaced.

B.T. had his work cut out for him. The Corps, initiated during the Reagan administration and re-constituted under Brown in 1976, had become a favorite target of the California Legislature. Viewed as Brown's political plaything, it was roundly, and perhaps justly, criticized for mismanagement and non-judicial use of state funds. It was not attaining its stated goals and was not cost-efficient. It had failed to improve employment opportunities for California's youth. It had not done enough to save the environment.

The Legislature was wrong on two counts. The California Conservation Corps was nobody's toy. Jerry Brown was fanatically committed to public service, as was his appointed director, and B.T., by his own admission, might joke, but he never "played." If he took himself lightly, he was dead serious about his responsibilities.

Basically, the Conservation Corps was built on the Roosevelt era organization of similar name and objectives. The C's, as it was called at the time of B.T.'s intervention, was composed of 1,600 men and women between the ages of 18-23, 35% of whom, B.T. discovered, could not read above third grade level. Corps members, housed in centers throughout California, were paid a monthly wage, part of which was returned to the state to cover board and room.

B.T.'s first task was to determine to what extent the picture drawn by the legislators was true. His second was to change the public and political perception of the CCC by re-making it in his own image. He went on a B.T.-style fact-finding mission. During his first week in office, he put on a field jacket, hired a bush pilot, and, at 3:00 A.M. headed for the most remote of the Corps' work centers. Arriving, he kicked a dorm door open, leaned against its frame and hollered, "O.K., everybody up!" The half-asleep corpsmen must have thought they were having a bad dream. For some, it was the beginning of a nightmare.

Attrition in the CCC was high, but B.T. was determined not to bend the rules to keep the kids. If anything, he made things harder. He told would-be corpsmen, "I dare you to join! This is going to be one miserable year out of your life." And to underline that thought, he created a new CCC motto: "Hard work, Low Pay, Miserable Working Conditions."

At the Sacramento's CCC headquarters, he posted a sign: "In this building work the toughest, meanest, most dedicated, civil servants in the state of California." Corps members would be required to rise at 5:00 A.M, and run two miles before breakfast. "Eighteen-year-olds," B.T. explained, "do not need sleep. They need structure and discipline."

Under Director Collins, they would be required to write in a journal every day, and to learn to read at a sixth grade level. They had to register for the draft and give blood. Before being accepted, they were forced to sign what he called his "nasty letter" in which they agreed to "no booze, no drugs, no violence, no destruction of state property, no refusal to work." They knew in advance they would do "dirty, backbreaking work without a thank-you, in intense heat, rain, high winds, mud, snow, and cold mountain streams."

"Do it my way or hit the highway," he threatened. And he meant it. "If you don't like what you hear, there's a bus leaving in the morning. Today is the first day of the rest of your life with me," he shouted. "Don't tell me where you came from. Don't tell me you were oppressed or disadvantaged. I don't care. *I do not care about you!* I am not concerned about your happiness. The only thing that matters to me is the expenditure of the California taxpayers' money. I am going to work you to death. You'll work, or I will fire you!"

Soon, there were 1,500 male applicants on the waiting list.

He wanted women too. According to B.T., "they worked harder; they took the initiative more often; they had more staying power."

He reached out to them, B.T. Collins style: "Women aged 18-23. Want equal rights? Equal blisters? Sore backs? Equal pay, responsibility, ulcers? Equal misery? Only 38% survive. Are you tough enough? Are you good enough? Dare to join!"

Like his boss, he was big on other minorities as well. B.T. made his position on discrimination very clear: Anyone who was caught using any kind of racial or ethnic slur was fired forthwith. "Tell me," he asked them directly, "did you ever think you would eat and sleep and work side by side with *those kinds* of people? Guess what? We're all those kinds of people."

Applications were open to the handicapped. A blind man ran the tool shop. He took care of, and distributed, all the axes, saws, hatchets, knives and scythes—by touch.

B.T. reminded the men and women in the Corps, "You owe your country and future generations of Californians. Years from now, you can tell your grandchildren you were there when it counted." He had said the same thing in Vietnam to the troops in the field. He said he would never thank them, but he did—by the look of amazement which flooded his face, and the sound of his voice wrung tight with emotion when he saw what they had done. In the end, when he appeared before them, bellowing, "I do not care about you!" they cheered.

They knew he cared, and so did I. He once asked me to accompany him to a meeting of some of his directors in the field, his "seconds-in command." I sensed that there was something to which he wanted me to bear witness. There was. The meeting took place in a nondescript room stocked with a standard lectern, a few tables, and a scattering of metal folding chairs. The men attending were standing in the back. They were tall, as I remember, broad shouldered, casually dressed, and joking as B.T. and I entered. As the sight of him, it was as if someone pulled a switch. All talking stopped. The chemistry between them was palpable; the tall stood taller, every eye was on him. He went to the front, and I followed, sitting on a chair beside him. He cautioned them to watch their language in front of me. They then presented him with a plaque from which a three dimensional brass horse's ass protruded. Beneath that shining derriere, a rude yet loving message was engraved. They watched for his reaction like kids. He was quiet for a moment and then grinned, a small grin, one that said "thank you" in a way no boisterous language could ever translate.

In August of 1981, the Mediterranean fruit fly threatened the whole of California's 14 billion dollar fruit industry. The only solution: Clear away the infected fruit, and kill the larvae by ground and air spraying with Malathion. Brown, a strict environmentalist, was against the widespread use of chemicals, but the situation was so desperate economically for the state that he had to allow it. Corpsmen, assigned the task of removing the fruit from treated areas, became increasingly anxious about their health. B.T. chose a highly unusual method of allaying their fears. He drank a glass of Malathion. He drank a glass of Malathion, diluted to same strength used for spraying. He drank a glass of Malathion in front of them, after assuring them that he would never put them in harm's way.

Soldiers understand: *Never ask your troops to do what you wouldn't do yourself.*

It was unpleasant but harmless.

Nora called my parents before it hit the news, to let them know that Brien was still alive.

The next day, 1,000 corpsmen began the month-long project of clearing 50 square miles of infested fruit. One of the backyards to be cleared belonged to Marialis. Watching the sweaty kids work nonstop, she offered them some iced tea. They refused. "It isn't allowed," they explained, "we'd get fired."

"But your boss is my brother; B.T. Collins is my brother," she protested.

"We can't. He'd kill us!" they replied.

B.T. was overjoyed.

Marialis, herself, generally kept B.T.'s celebrity status in perspective. He brought the Governor to Hewlett Packard, where she had worked for a number of years. Her fellow workers were astounded. "You never told us B.T. Collins was your brother!"

"I would have," Marialis replied, "but he's adopted."

Redheaded law professor Lillian Altry, of "purple sweater" fame, celebrated his latest accomplishments with a poem:

> *A Law Professors' Lament*
> *To quiet triumph of the mind*
> *We law professors are resigned,*
> *Content to lead our paper chases*
> *Instead of arguing actual cases.*
> *But yet, hope springs eternal*
> *Whenever we read the Wall Street Journal*
> *That there in boldest print will be*
> *A former student's name. (Let's see,*
> *Was he the one in Real Property*

Who seemed less keen on land than me?)
Surely he'll say in here he owes
Everything to me he knows.
Let's see . . . Let's see . . . Oh, here's finesse—
He's serving sprouts to his Royal Highness.
Instead of successful cases tried
They say he drinks insecticide!
Oh my God, what next then?
They say he's rising through the land of Zen.
Did I deserve this? Honestly,
"Fee simple," I said, not "simple be."
Well, farewell hopes of worldly fame.
(Now I'm glad I changed my name.)
And to my books I, chastened, flee
From the reflected glory of Ol' B.T.

Antics aside, he did convince the corps members of their own importance, and he did the same with the legislature. He had no choice. Upon acceptance of his role as director, he was given a year to save the CCC. So "he began working the corridors of power," in NBC's Garrett Utley's words, "like a fox in a chicken coop." In the end, 85 of 95 legislators co-authored a bill to extend the CCC's life and increase its budget by five million dollars in an otherwise austerity year.

It was no accident. He had conducted a fierce campaign to that end. He made surprise visits to the centers at all times of day and night, accompanied by lawmakers and reporters. He extended invitation after invitation to legislators to visit the centers. If they did not, he made sure that their constituents, fellow legislators, and the press knew about it. He had the CCC do conspicuous work in the districts of its most outspoken critics. Yet, when an article appeared about the rape of two corpswomen, he immediately had it copied and forwarded with his subsequent plan of action to every legislator.

He loaded lawmakers with information, but he knew when to keep it light. "Senator Jarvis, What were you doing on Christmas Eve when CCC workers were giving blood?" a Sacramento store window poster inquired. "In the last 40 days, Senator, they have worked 36,000 hours to fill nearly a half a million sandbags to shore up the levees. They were doing this while you were watching the Superbowl. And they take pride in it."

He told skeptical lawmakers, "Its most important benefits may not be felt for over twenty years. This is an investment in our future. These kids are going nowhere. We are keeping at least some of them out of the criminal justice system and off the welfare rolls. People who fight fires together are less likely to murder each other, or, for that matter, anyone else."

Sixty-eight percent of those who stayed the year went back to school, on to jobs, or into the military.

B.T.'s energetic defense of the CCC, and the philosophy on which it was built, resulted in several thousand print articles, hundreds of radio and television news stories, and three televised documentaries. *People Magazine* did a feature on him, as did NBC's *News Magazine* with David Brinkley. Articles appeared in the *Smithsonian*, in *Life*, in *Time*, and in *National Wildlife*. Thirty-nine states and fifteen other countries adopted similar environmental work programs. He spoke everywhere, to any group that would listen. The message of what really mattered never varied, though the accent and the language changed from New-York-Bronx to weary-public-servant; "It's not the foxiest lady, not the greatest dope, not the most expensive house, not the fanciest car. Is the world a better place because you were there?" And he repeated, "Is the world a better place because you were there?"

Behind all his rhetoric was the sincere belief that as a citizen, you owed your country and your fellow Americans. He was convinced that we had somehow lost our way; that the spirit of 30 years ago was gone and that we needed it back, and that a get-by attitude had spread like some deadly cancer to the backbone of the country. "Our pride," he said, "had been lulled to sleep, and we have begun to excel at mediocrity."

The aim of the CCC was not to make master carpenters or electricians. "What good did it do," he argued, "to hire a skilled worker who was late three days out of five to the job?"

B.T. Collins' California Conservation Corps was a work ethic program; its intent to make young Californians understand what it meant to be dependable on the job. Both B.T. and the Governor felt that people looked too often to the government to solve their problems, that they must help each other, and do so voluntarily, without expectation of remuneration.

My brother believed in mandatory national service. "I support national service as opposed to a straight military draft because I don't think the military is for everyone. However, there should be some form of national service for everyone, the disabled as well as the fit. No exemptions! Everyone should be given three choices: "The military, public service, no public service. An individual would still be given the chance to decline to serve—the spirit to serve cannot be manufactured—only this time, it would be a matter of official record. Hopefully, employers would place a great deal of importance on whether a youth volunteered to serve his or her country."

Exhilarated by the difference he was making, he was nevertheless exhausted. Visiting every center more than once, climbing in and out of small planes, dragging his leg over rough terrain, standing, day in and day out, to speak to groups of every size and composition, workdays that began and ended near dawn, and the emotional drain of pleading with individual legislators, left him mentally and physically done in.

One disbeliever had called him a socialist, and added, "B.T. has as much chance of having me co-author the bill to extend the life of the CCC as he has of convincing Jerry Brown to pose for a Penthouse centerfold." And he continued, "There was more chance of the latter." The legislator in question had underestimated B.T.'s powers of persuasion and had misread Brown completely. Meanwhile, the stump of his leg grew ominous, bleeding sores from almost constant abuse. He hurt. He really hurt. There was no time for repairs; no quick trips to the hospital would have sufficed. So he endured. The pain remained a private matter.

While still serving as CCC Director, B.T. was asked to be co-Chair of the state's anti-crime force. B.T.'s greatest concern was the condition of America's youth. "We can build more prisons and enforce stricter laws, but can we restore in our young a sense of responsibility and a respect for traditional values? Front page America is the tragic account of a civilized nation's disregard for human life. It is a society at war with itself, and it is a war without reason or honor. What we need most," he lamented, "is to re-kindle a respect for human dignity."

B.T.'s success with the California Conservation Corps and as a legislative aide convinced Brown to appoint him his Chief of Staff. The differences between B.T. and his predecessor were remarkable. B.T. was big. He consumed any space he occupied. Gray Davis was smaller, obviously corporate, and totally political. Intelligent, yet colorless, Davis was the model of sobriety, measured response, and a life in order. B.T. Collins was brash, candid, and forceful in the extreme. Eloquent when the occasion demanded, he nevertheless had a reservoir of irreverent language. "He ran things," to quote one source, "like a one-man-mob leading a cavalry charge." The mood of his first meeting with his new staff was uneasy. He was so clearly unlike any other politician, then Congresswoman (now Speaker of the House) Nancy Pelosi commented, "We were really shook up when we first heard about his appointment. But after ten minutes in his presence, we couldn't remember what all the fuss was about."

His choice of words and outlandish behavior often bothered me, but I became reconciled to what I referred to as "B.T.'s noise." I felt that he used it largely as a defense mechanism. I knew what he believed, so I heard the message, the passion, and yes, the longing beneath the language.

While Gray Davis had spoken for the Governor, B.T. made it very clear that the Governor would speak for himself. "I'm his first sergeant," he said. "He's the commander in chief. The Governor tackles the issues. I deal with the people."

B.T. liked the Governor to hear firsthand from those who disagreed with him. And Brown, listening, would watch B.T.'s eyes for an evaluation. Privately, B.T. tried to temper some of Brown's excesses and to re-build the Governor's "burned bridges."

He understood the power of perception and all the myopic misrepresentation it engendered. "We are a colonial nation, he argued. "We wanted to elect George Washington king. We like royalty, pomp and circumstance. You can only play that hair shirt and blue Plymouth thing so long." People couldn't relate to Brown because he didn't fit any known mold.

Neither did B.T. Nevertheless, legislators trusted him, and they openly complained to him of Brown's insensitivity. "Hey, B.T." they whined, "can't you take this guy out and get him laid?" So he took the Governor instead to eat in the Capitol cafeteria. The lawmakers loved it. "People need to know he eats lunch, drinks beer, and picks his nose like everyone else," B.T. commented.

He made Brown appear for appointments on schedule . . . more often. The Governor was so regularly late that the press had coined the term, "Brown-time." B.T. talked his boss into small, thoughtful deeds. The Governor wrote my father, enclosing a copy of his State-of-the-State message in which B.T. was mentioned. He called his press secretary's father on New Year's Eve on the stroke of midnight to wish him a Happy New Year. The Governor even called me.

"Merry Christmas!" he began. "Is your name really Maureen Reagan?"

"Yes." (It was at the time.) "It's Christmas Eve," I noted. "Shouldn't you be in church?"

"I'm just dragging your brother off to mass right now."

"Good. He could use a little supervising."

Their relationship was marked by an unusual candor and casualness. And then, overnight, it was almost all over.

B.T. had developed a tremendous rapport with the press. He was so outspoken, so quotable that reporters gave him ample print, and it was always good. He was coming off a public relations high, due to the CCC. He had attracted media attention nationally and in other parts of the world, attention which had served the state of California, himself, and the Governor well. So when he was asked by a reporter if she could follow him around for three days, the answer was, "yes." He trusted reporters and prided himself on being "street smart." No question he was cocky as well. He believed privately that no reporter would ever say anything bad about him. This reporter, however, was after the scoop of a lifetime and she would get it—six pages worth in a 1981 Sunday *Los Angeles Times*.

He was overconfident, foolishly naïve, and dangerously careless about what he said, how he said it, and the impression his remarks conveyed. She followed him day and into the night and beyond from bar to bar. She caught him in *flagrante politico*. B.T. complained about Brown, everything from his hair needing to be washed to his lack of understanding of the little people because he had never been to "a whorehouse or a war, nor had to pay a mortgage." He described the Governor as "out in Uranus," constantly reading and thinking instead of meeting with those standing in line to see him. It was the voice of someone who'd had way too much to drink, the thoughts of someone brought nearly to the breaking point of frustration. He so believed in the Governor's potential for greatness, a potential he thought was being destroyed. To those within the Capitol, there was little new here. In fact, the Governor, at one time or another, had already heard it all.

But the reporter bought into the language meant to keep the listener at a distance and B.T. in command. She never actually saw the man beneath; the loyal warrior whom those close to the Governor, as well as the Governor himself, knew. No matter. He spoke and she recorded. The effect was devastating. "Sometimes," he lamented, "I'd like to strangle him, (Brown), and other times, I'd follow him to hell and back." The reader was left with the former rather than the latter impression.

In a letter to the *Times* editor, B.T.'s friend Richard Steffen commented, "I've had my run-ins with B.T. Collins too. While other bureaucrats snickered at me as a hopeless refugee from academe, he gave me lessons in politics and lobbying. He got me to put up posters recruiting more women to the CCC's, and bugged me to hire inner city kids for government programs."

B.T. was sick. He had, in his own words, blindsided the Governor, the man to whom he owed so much. He called Brown to warn him. He offered an immediate resignation. The Governor wouldn't hear of it. He made fun of himself, saying that he had actually saved the state a lot of money on shampoo. To others he said, "B.T. is the Don Rickles of Sacramento. Irish humor is sardonic, ironic," he explained. "He's got a good heart, a good mind. He's sensitive to people. He's fun to work with."

Brown knew to be true what later appeared in Carrie Dolan's 1982 article in the *Wall Street Journal*, that "B.T. Collins did obnoxious things loudly and nice things quietly." That, plus the fact that he believed B.T. was both loyal and inspired loyalty was enough. The Governor's detractors applauded the article; his friends said it made him appear a lot more human. Insiders knew it was just more of B.T. Collins' hyperbole. Whatever lines B.T. had crossed, the reporter had crossed a few of her own.

It was one of B.T.'s darkest moments. It brought him down. He became for the first time the cripple he'd never been. Jerry Brown, however, took it upon himself to cheer up his crestfallen Chief of Staff. "We only allow long faces around here for forty-eight hours," he told him. And when B.T. didn't respond, he added, "Hey, I thought you were tougher than that."

Even years later, describing the Governor's unbelievable loyalty, B.T. was visibly moved. Finally, he had to face his staff. And they were ready for him. A huge cake had been ordered, replete with mocking detail. There was B.T., bellied up to a bar, cocktail in hand, foot in his mouth, all in sugary, iced perfection. They applauded. They'd been awfully worried about him. He nearly burst into tears.

So he rallied. "If the *Los Angeles Times* says you're a scumbag, you're a scumbag," he joked. He did not talk openly to reporters for a long time.

Nevertheless, they continued to talk about him. "It's Tuesday night and a former Green Beret is telling jokes in the California Capitol. He has a hook for a hand, a big mouth, and a lot of friends. Across the hall, his boss, Governor Edmund G. Brown, Jr. is intently watching a slide show on solar energy in Tibet." Carrie Dolan, in the *Wall Street Journal*.

The office antics began anew: "How about getting me some coffee," he'd call out to his assistants.

"Get it yourself!"

"Gee, I would, but I got my arm and leg blown off in the war."

The Governor ran for the US Senate. "If Governor Brown manages to become Senator Brown," the *San Diego Union* reported, "he wants to take Collins with him. They are a good team." The move to Washington never materialized. Brown lost the election. B.T. believed that, had he been on board a little longer, he could have made the crucial difference.

An era had ended. But for B.T. there were memories of substance. He had watched the spaceship Columbia land. He had been on the receiving end of a personal Linda Ronstadt serenade. The Governor of California had put on his shoe.

Governor Pat Brown had contacted B.T. in hopes that he would convince his son to attend a "Sons of Hibernia" dinner. "If you'll go, he'll go," he pleaded. B.T. and Brown had started out in casual clothes, changing into tuxedos on the way. Dressing at a motel along the route, B.T. couldn't get his good shoe on his right foot. Brown's aides all volunteered to help, but the Governor said simply to "throw over one of those hangers," which he proceeded to bend into the shape of a shoehorn. Kneeling, Brown pushed and shoved, makeshift tool in hand, his then-black hair falling over his forehead.

"This isn't necessary, Governor . . . really."

"Just hold still. I've almost got it."

"Let one of the guys do it, Governor."

"Can you bend your foot a little?

"Not much. Really . . .

"Ah! Got it."

"Jesus!' (under his breath) "Thank you, Governor. Thank you."

As to what B.T. would do next, an aide suggested that he might find a place in a Tibetan monastery, in the CIA, or even the KGB. B.T. laughed. He said he was through with politics; that he planned to run guns to the Falkland Islands. There were offers: lobbyist, talk show host, Deputy Mayor of San Francisco.

Mother reminded us that the most recent deputy mayor had been shot, and that someone would surely shoot Brien. He would have made a colorful pundit—earnest, hilarious, annoyingly truthful. But, instead, he chose the private sector and, for once, a salary of substance.

So in 1983 the Governor went off to reflect, B.T. to ply his influence in the world of high finance. Brown's biographer, Orville Schell, speculated that what the Governor needed most was for someone to bring him down off the mountain. B.T. Collins had, for the moment, brought him closer to earth. Actually, he saw the Governor through different eyes. "He's a fighter," B.T. said, "a man to go into the jungle with." Then he smiled. "Ah, but where's the next jungle?

XIV

LETTERS, HEROES,
MONUMENTS, MEMORIES

———·•·——

Mr. President:
You must not waver in your determination to bring us
through this madness. Forget about the popularity
of your decision. Just hang in there!
This American supports you.

Letter to Ronald Reagan, B.T. Collins

B.T.'s next jungle was in the California branch of a distinguished
Wall Street firm. However chaotic the financial world may seem to
outsiders, it didn't fit my brother's definition of either jungle or
battlefield. In political circles, even at the highest levels, there is
that back room, bar room, deals made, over-the-counter, under-
the-counter atmosphere. Now he entered the corporate quiet of the
button-down, look-out-for-yourself, forget-about-the-other-guy
world of boardrooms—and eventual boredom.

He was still B.T., but as a Vice President of Public Finance for
the distinguished and ultra-conservative Kidder Peabody, (now
UBS), he had to behave himself . . . well, a little. He played the role,
No more running into the office with his tie hanging from one
pocket and his toothbrush protruding from another. He even
enlarged his wardrobe, actually spending a little money on himself,
if only for clothing. He organized his belongings, or, rather, he talked
a teenage neighbor, Jon Walker, into doing it for him.

Jon was 13 years old when he met my brother. "Hey, kid," B.T. had called across his backyard pool. What are you doing this summer?" When Jon hesitated, B.T. set him straight. "You're painting my house." So, from his early teens to the time he went to college, this boy kept B.T. Collins' life in order . . . at least inside the house. The man who once left leftover sandwiches on the back seat of his car, now became positively anal about cleanliness and organization—one drawer for blue shirts; another for white. The faucets in the bathroom gleamed like military brass. The pool was clean, the cupboards filled. Young Jon became the California equivalent of a houseboy, and B.T. Collins became his friend and older—much older—brother.

Jon was not the first called into service. When it came to convincing others to help him, B.T. Collins was a con artist of extraordinary finesse. When he moved to Sacramento, he telephoned his Santa Clara classmate Dick Cunha to simply say, "Hello." During the course of the conversation, he invited Dick over to his apartment for a beer.

The rooms were crammed with boxes. "How are you going to unload all this stuff?" Cunha asked, innocently and mistakenly.

"Oh, I'll figure out something," B.T. replied. The boxes got unpacked and B.T. "pitched in" to get the job done.

Banker Dennis Carpenter recounted a similar experience. He first met B.T. in a well-known Capital Bar. The two hit it off immediately and Carpenter followed B.T. home for conversation and a "final drink." Entering his apartment, he couldn't believe the *ménage à morass* before him. The kitchen, particularly, was beyond belief. Dishes were stacked in the sink, and counter tops were caked with what had once been dinners.

B.T. excused it all with a wave of his hand. "My cleaning lady hasn't been here for a week."

Then Carpenter realized, "My God, this guy only has one arm and one leg!" So he put on an apron and did the dishes. "I don't do my own dishes," he admitted. But he had done B.T.'s. As to whether there had actually been a cleaning woman, only my brother knew for sure.

Charming manipulation could be construed as an asset on Wall Street. Otherwise, a brokerage house would not have seemed the likely choice for a personally penny-pinching, yet give-to-any-cause Lochinvar with a loud mouth and too many principles. He had made the political arena his own, and it seemed the one for which he was most ideally suited. There, wheeling and dealing meant changing lives and making a difference. In politics, he played for keeps; what he did, he did for love.

In the private sector, the name of the game was money. It no longer mattered what he stood for, but whom he knew—and my brother, B.T., prided himself on being well known. He had once received a letter addressed to "B.T. Collins, California." Marialis, had jokingly given him a pair of vanity license plates, embossed with "B.T. Who?" And I had this picture in my mind of crashing in a small plane in the jungle and, crawling out of the wreckage, finding myself surrounded by angry looking natives with spears. Then I would say, "B.T. Collins, B.T. Collins," and they would drop their weapons and, smiling and nodding, come over to shake my hand.

The opportunity to work in the rarefied air of the corporate community actually came about because of his political antics and the 1982 *Wall Street Journal* article that described them. The essence of Carrie Dolan's "Brown's Brash Aide Handles the People" became the *raison d'etre* for his position with Kidder. As the article made clear, his contacts of substance were diverse, of an unbelievable number, and geographically widespread. He obviously had the ability to establish, and even more important, to maintain relationships. He knew the inside machinations of government; what worked and what wouldn't, and how to interface the two. He would be an invaluable resource with regard to public policy. And so, when public finance investment schemes were hatched, he would advise and/or consent. An investment banker, however, he was not.

The final hiring process ran true to form—Collins' form. A Kidder executive, Mike Lambert, took B.T. to New York to meet Albert Gordon, then Chairman of the Board. Chairman Gordon was a formidable figure by any measure. A Harvard graduate and, at that time, an octogenarian marathon runner, he was the consummate old-world gentleman of investment banking. The least B.T. could have managed for their first meeting was to wear matching socks. One of the problems confronting a one-legged man is to remember to change the sock on your wooden foot when you put a clean sock on your real foot. In California, this problem was resolved when his office staff made him lift his trousers each morning for a routine check. No matter. Apparently, Albert Gordon was more impressed with B.T.'s yesteryear thinking than his footwear. Returning to California, Mike Lambert received the following call.

"Mike."

"Yes, Mr. Gordon?"

"What do you think your friend sent me?"

"Sir, sent you? I have no idea, Mr. Gordon."

"A hard hat! A yellow hard hat with CCC on it! And 'Al!' It says 'Al!'"

"It says . . . 'Al?'"

"Yes, 'Al.' I don't know whether I'm going to display it in my office or wear it. I think I'll put it on."

"Yes, Mr. Gordon. Right!"

Albert Gordon was not an "Al." Albert Gordon, starched crisp, cutting edge conservative Chairman of the Board in appearance and mindset, in a yellow hard hat marked "Al." It made a picture, one all the more marvelous when it's known that "Al" insisted that "Kennedy" Airport still be referred to by its original name, "Idlewild," and New York's "Roosevelt" Highway as the "East River Drive." He even refused to allow a "liberal rag" like the *New York Times* on the premises. Of course, B.T. was only cutting to the core of the man, showing the world and perhaps Al Gordon himself, that the Chairman of the Board was, at heart, a regular guy.

At Kidder, B.T. was already out of the element that excited him. Not that he was uneasy with corporate elegance. He'd been trained as a Collins in forks and dinner conversation. And he did meet lot of interesting, if financially driven, people. The problem stemmed from the fact that there was simply too little opportunity to do great things, and "great" in the corporate context did not translate as "good" in the larger sense—good for humankind, good for Americans, and good for the guy next door. With or without Kidder Peabody, the world was not necessarily a better place.

So, he spread his message through letters, interviews, and speeches, wherever and whenever his Wall Street responsibilities allowed. Walking in my father's footsteps, he had long written lots of letters. Now, denied access to the kind of action he most desired, his letters grew longer, more passionate, and more presumptuous. He reached out to the powerful and the powerless, to those who knew him, and to many who had never heard his name. He wrote President Ronald Reagan and the President wrote back.

Ronald Reagan was one of B.T.'s heroes, particularly because of what he did for Vietnam veterans and, generally, because of what he was doing for American pride. B.T. knew that even the best and most important among us still welcome encouragement, affirmation, and unconditional loyalty. The world's most powerful man was no exception, and Citizen Collins coached and encouraged the Chief Executive throughout his presidency. His letter after the Beirut bombing was the first in a series addressed to the popular president.

25 October 1983

Dear Mr. President,

If I may be so bold, I thought I'd pass along a few gratuitous thoughts. The next week will probably be the toughest one you have faced during your term. The TV will be showing the bodies, the mothers, the burials, over and over again. If you get a chance, review JFK's press conference in which he discusses the disgruntled reservists during the Berlin call-up. The main thrust was that life is essentially unfair.

Remember, we didn't elect you to be perfect, but to just do the best job you could in leading us, that is if we are capable of being led. You must not lose your resolve. You must not waver in your determination to bring the world through this madness. You and I don't count anymore. It's the grandchildren that are important. Don't weaken, don't falter, and forget about the popularity of your decision. That's part of being President. You'll be surprised how many people support your decision—regardless of what the press and Congress say. We are a fickle people. Yet, we are incredibly fortunate to live in this wonderful country. Our good fortune does not come without a price. We all have to pay our dues. For some of us, those dues are higher. Yes, it's unfair but that's life. I left an arm and a leg in Vietnam during my second tour of duty.

Hang in there, this American is behind you.

B.T. Collins

THE WHITE HOUSE
Washington, DC

November 21, 1983

Dear Mr. Collins:

As you can imagine, I receive a tremendous volume of mail. Two of the letters, however, will always stand out in my memory. Yours was one of them. Let me tell you about the other one. It came from the brother-in-law of a Marine who was killed in the Beirut bombing. When the letter was written, however, they had not received this word, and the writer told of the long hours of waiting and wondering. He told me he must share with me a letter from the young marine to his family. "John understood his purpose in Lebanon," he wrote, "and he also understood his mission on earth."

The Marine's letter was short—written on a single page. "Although we aren't making fast results," he wrote, "I believe our mission of peacekeeping has lessened the danger for Lebanon and slowed the spread of communism into this country. I am doing well and growing up like never before. All my love, John."

I am sure you understand, Mr. Collins, why I wanted to share some words from that letter. Shortly after I read it, we received word that "John" was among those who gave his life for his country in Beirut.

I am sure you know that one of the hardest decisions a President can make is to commit the people in our armed services to combat situations or dangerous missions. But as your letter so forcefully reminds us all, we must look not just to the present, but to the future.

"You and I don't count anymore—it's the grandchildren that are important. Don't weaken, don't falter and forget about the popularity of your decisions."

I will always, please God, be guided by these words of yours. They are words of wisdom—a wisdom hard-won through your own sacrifices in the service of our country.

Thank you for your wise counsel and your support. It means a great deal to me. God bless you.

Sincerely,
Ronald Reagan

When Reagan buried an Unknown Soldier from the Vietnam War at Arlington, he brought B.T. to his knees. B.T. wrote again, this time to praise the President for having given those who served in Vietnam the dignity they deserved. "All the Unknown Soldier ever really wanted was just for someone to say 'thanks and well done,'" he told the President. Due to Reagan's speech, B.T. added, "This soldier was no longer alone—nor were the others still alive. After the ceremonies," he confided, "I cried my eyes out. I never knew I had such bitterness stored up in me. Now he is at peace and so am I. Thanks for bringing him home."

The President was touched, and again responded personally.

THE WHITE HOUSE
Washington, DC

July 3, 1984
Dear Mr. Collins:

Thank you for your letter of May 28. I don't know when I have been so moved, unless it was at the ceremony itself, where I had trouble getting the words past the lump in my throat.

If I have done anything to help bring a proper focus on the noble purpose you all served so well, I'd be more than proud. You fought as bravely and as well as any American in our history, and literally with one arm tied behind you. Sometimes two. The tragedy—indeed the immorality—of those years was that for the first time in history our country and our government failed to match your heroic sacrifice. This must never happen again.

Again, thank you for writing as you did.

God bless you.

Sincerely,

Ronald Reagan

The letters continued, and, in writing, B.T. made Reagan aware of events to which he would not ordinarily have been privy. The night before the President's appearance at the memorial, B.T. was in a bar near Capitol Hill. The place was packed. In the middle of the crowd were four young paratroopers who had been in Grenada with the 82nd Airborne Division. Because B.T. had been in the 82nd in 1965, he tried to buy them a drink, but there were too many others with the same idea. He explained to these kids that fifteen years before, they would have been spit upon if they had worn their uniforms into a DC bar. "Just by your example," he told the President, "you have turned this country's attitude toward military service 180 degrees."

It was through Ed Rollins, a Reagan advisor, that B.T. knew his letters had reached the President and that Reagan had answered them personally. B.T.'s letters to Rollins were less flattering. He caught all Ed's public appearances and was quick to offer feedback. After seeing Ed in the back of a *New York Times* photo of the President at a Cabinet meeting, he wrote to comment that "Rollins obviously had a sick need to crash Cabinet pictures, that *Pravda* would have been a better front page for his puss. Nine out of ten of the last mass murders and child molesters," he continued, "were bald, wore thick glasses, and beards." Insults ignored, Rollins continued to feed B.T.'s letters to the Oval Office.

B.T. had other heroes: *Fields of Fire* author and former Secretary of the Navy James Webb, and Vietnam POW, Admiral James Stockdale, with whom he developed a copious correspondence. Although he differed strongly from Webb on the means to establish postwar relations with the Vietnamese, B.T. was an unabashed fan of the Secretary's writing and often quoted from it. When Webb appointed B.T. to be a member of the Board of Supervisors at the Naval Postgraduate School at Monterey, California, B.T. showed his appreciation in Brienese.

1988
Dear Jim:

   I am still missing a picture of you at your actual swearing-in, and one of you and me at your farewell. Since I am a flagrant name-dropper, I would like to have something on my wall that says that you appointed me to the Naval Postgraduate Board. By the way, I refuse to write a letter of recommendation for any students who want to apply to a service academy until they have read *A Sense of Honor*. So, please live up to your obligations and get those items to me. Before I forget, please keep in the back of your mind that you ought someday to run for office. Know that there are many of us who, although we think you're a pig-headed son of a bitch, will be lining up to walk precincts for you.

B.T.

The letters to Admiral Stockdale were very different in tone. The Admiral was one of the very few people to whom B.T. never wrote tongue-in-cheek. He was in awe of Stockdale, who had thwarted his Vietnamese captors' plans to use him for publicity purposes first by maiming himself with shards of glass, then by bashing himself with a broken chair leg. It was not just Stockdale's courage, but his beliefs, and the level of scholarship he used to express them, that made him a hero's hero. Theirs was a running dialogue about veterans and wars and sacrifice and duty.

   The Admiral responded informally, always in his own hand. The principles by which Stockdale lived were those of the generation B.T. so admired. "You are your brother's keeper. Life is not fair. Every man can be more than he is." He wrote the Admiral often to express his gratitude. "I can never give you back those lost years. I can't straighten your leg; I can't take the gray out of your hair. All

I can do is say, Thank you and well done! Well done! How soon we forget!"

B.T. was particularly sensitive to the wrongs perpetuated by history. The first step toward righting those wrongs was an admission of guilt. He wrote to Daniel Inouye, US Senator of Japanese descent, after watching the documentary, *The Code of Honor*, to thank him for what he had done for the next generation. "I know," he told the Senator, "that I can never assuage the pain that you, your family and your ancestors suffered due to the ignominy visited upon them by the government of the United States. I guess the only way we can truly express our gratitude is to make sure that it doesn't happen again, and to develop a greater awareness of those who have been the victims of thoughtless injustice."

Uppermost in his mind were the victims of injustice he knew best—the Vietnam veterans. He was delighted, therefore, by Michael Medved's 1980's article in the *Wall Street Journal* in which Medved noted that "a quick examination of the anti-war movement demonstrated beyond question the direct connection between draft calls and campus protests. By 1969, the all but unanimous anti-war sentiment among students and faculty at our elite universities had become so strong that it took far greater courage to defend our role in the war than it did to follow 10,000 others to a protest demonstration. Nixon," he continued, "effectively undermined the movement by committing the country to an all volunteer army in 1971."

Replying to Medved's article in a letter to the *Wall Street Journal's* editor, B.T. wrote:

> It was with unrestrained glee and smugness that I read Michael Medved's candid concession to the academic megalomania that dominated the campuses of this country during the 60's and 70's. I was always impressed with that generation and their obsession with 'love.' In response to the agonizing concern for the welfare of those 19-year-olds in Vietnam, this love manifested itself by pelting ambulances and spitting on people in uniform in wheelchairs. I never saw any of these young people visit GIs during

the 22 months I spent in seven military hospitals. Yet, those wounded were watching their contemporaries from their hospital beds as they rioted and plundered their way across the nation."

Jerry Brown was not one of B.T.'s heroes, but he owed the former Governor who first recognized and then supported his political potential. As thanks, B.T. continued to offer Brown gratuitous advice on how to conduct himself politically, to whom to speak, and what to and not to say. The advice was largely ignored. Yet, humor remained a hallmark of the relationship. On B.T.'s first "life day" after leaving office, Brown remembered in a telegram.

> June 20, 1983
> B.T.
>
> On this unusual occasion, I join a couple dozen miscellaneous Americans in congratulating you on your continued ability to exploit the sympathies of the general public and further your megalomaniacal goals in the world of finance. I am not unaware of the pathological effort you made to keep the ship of state afloat during our years in Sacramento—forcing helpless kids to sweat fear through the forest and keeping the office staff chasing chimeras during the midnight hours. For my own reputation, I am compelled to remain in the protective custody of Los Angeles, far from the marginal antics of your Sacramento cronies. My best wishes for a memorable evening, I remain ever in your debt.
>
> EGB

B.T.'s relationship with Jerry's father, former Governor Pat Brown, grew stronger with the passage of time. B.T. constantly sent news clippings, comments, and often suggestions to the former governor about how to correct his son's seemingly inept political behavior. The brief but meaningful replies arrived by return mail and always closed with personal requests for B.T.'s company. "If anything brings you to Southern California, please call me. I'd like very much to take you to lunch; I miss your stimulating remarks and handsome face. There is no one I enjoy talking with more than you. Maybe, in the days ahead we can do something constructive together; I assure you that the father of your former associate likes you very much." The letters, on the heavy law office letterhead, were signed simply, "Pat."

Meanwhile, for the first time in his life, B.T. was making real money. The heavy-duty income earned at Kidder allowed him to indulge in two of his favorite pastimes, spoiling those he loved, and helping everyone else. For a widowed, super-cultured aunt, there were season theater tickets. For Marialis, there were rounds of golf on the world's most famous courses. He sent Mother and Daddy to Paris, and through the Panama Canal. He lent money to friends on the strength of simple IOU's. He sent $500 to my father's faculty to "have a party," in thanks for the television sent to Valley Forge. He contributed to everyone from Cambodian refugees to his Catholic high school, to innumerable people running for office. The latter included a fair share of Democrats. And, as we learned at the time of his death, 10% of his salary went straight to Santa Clara University. I was not forgotten:

"Maureen . . . Maureen are you listening to me?"

I was going through a divorce, crying so hard I could hardly hear his voice on the other end of the line.

"Yes."

"Maureen!" he jerked me to attention. "Listen to me! Listen carefully! Whatever you need, *whatever* you need, I will take care of everything. Everything. Do you understand me?

"Brien?"

"What?"

"I love you." I had forgotten an unspoken rule. Never *say* "I love you."

"Hey Babe," he reminded me, "everybody loves me!"

"Right. I forgot. There's a banner over Main Street that says 'All the World Loves B.T.'"

"I know," he said, "I put it there."

He gave more than money. In the spring of 1985, Marialis had been diagnosed with bone cancer in her left wrist. A lifelong golfer, who lived to be on the links, she was facing the possibility of losing both her hand and wrist. We were struck by the irony of the possibility that two out of the three of us might be missing a hand.

B.T. had been counseling her, and early on the morning of her operation, he drove from Sacramento to the hospital in Palo Alto to be with her. As she was being wheeled toward the OR, the nurse guiding her gurney muttered, "Who's that jerk standing on the couch?"

"That jerk" was B.T., actually standing on the back of a couch in the adjoining waiting room. As they passed him, he unfurled a large sign that read: "Hey, if you don't make it, can I have your golf clubs?"

Happily, Marialis still has her hand, and she plays better golf than before. Brother B.T. went away empty-handed.

He liked giving but more than that he was happy . . . the happiest he had been for a long time. He had fallen in love . . . with my best friend. There had always been women in his life; the long-haired blond whose mother loved him, the savvy lobbyist, nurses, lawyers, and many others. But this one caught and held his attention in a way no one else had. She was beautiful: wide gray-green eyes in an Indiana co-ed's face complete with dimples, and honey colored skin all year round. She was very bright, a university professor and later, a dean. She was caring and extraordinarily kind. And she was fun.

Everyone crossed his fingers. B.T. even mentioned the word, "marry." But distance is a destroyer. There was a country and B.T.'s obligations to it between them. She would have made a home and had hot dinners waiting. He wouldn't have made it home to dinner. She needed and wanted to be loved. He knew he could never allow himself to love her enough. He didn't have the courage to admit his own need. He recovered . . . partially. For a long time, he wouldn't totally let her go, and she suffered mightily as a result.

Long after the relationship was officially over, however, B.T. continued to mentor her teenage daughter

> Dear Lisa,
> Mothers aren't perfect, you know. Nobody is. So just go to her and tell her that you love her, that you forgive her all her faults, whatever you may or may not believe them to be. Then

drop to your knees and pray to God that when you grow up you have her legs and her brains.

However difficult, B.T.'s choice not to marry was undoubtedly wise. His promise to pay back those left behind consumed him. He had a full-time job at Kidder, yet he worked equal hours trying to direct society's attention to state and national service. His efforts ate away what little of his energy remained. He now added the cause of building of the California Vietnam War Memorial to his other responsibilities.

California had sent 334,000 men into combat and lost 5,822—more than any other state in the Union. Among these were 28 Medal of Honor winners. Nearly 1,000,000 military veterans of the Vietnam era were living in California. All of which made it unthinkable that the state that had contributed the largest number of sons, fathers, and brothers had created no lasting memorial to their sacrifice. Herman Woods, a double amputee who had served in the First Air Cavalry, returned home from the dedication of the national Vietnam Memorial in Washington with the dream of a California memorial. It was a dream realized. The legislature established a commission to build its own Vietnam War Memorial, and B.T. was appointed one of its members.

An Army Communications Sergeant Linda McClenahan, and a POW, Medal of Honor recipient Leo Thorsness, were named Chair and Vice Chairpersons, respectively. McClenahan originally demurred at accepting the Chairmanship. B.T. insisted. He felt that it was terribly important that women's contribution to the war be formally recognized. He laughingly *demanded* that she accept the job, saying, "The only other place for you is as secretary," and that he refused to listen to all those 'screaming feminists' if that turned out to be the case.

He also knew the nature of McClenahan's service in the Army. Linda had spent her tour of duty keeping meticulous records of the mortally wounded. She was responsible for the on-paper body count—the name, date, age, rank, and site of injury; the why, where, and how of those killed. As she worked, helicopters landed at the nearby airfield depositing the litters holding the dying and the horribly wounded. She ate in the mess hall of an on-site evacuation hospital that specialized in burns and head injuries. So, after spending her day with the dead, she dined among the suffering and the walking disfigured.

The California Memorial would, in fact, be the first to honor the 15,000 women who had served in Vietnam—the first to honor POW's. At the monument's entrance, the seated bronze figure of an archetypical 19-year-old combat veteran would be reading a letter from home.

The letter was symbolic for B.T. "No matter how much this country sold us out or how little some people cared," B.T. told an audience, "there were those who kept writing, and we knew then that we were remembered."

When it was decided that the young soldier in bronze should be reading an actual letter, it was Linda who composed the text. She read it to B.T. over the phone. When she finished, she told me, "There was silence, absolute silence on the other end of the line. B.T.?" she asked, "B.T.?"

"Very good. It's very good," he replied tightly. Then he hung up without another word.

I had seen him similarly moved, many times. I know what his silence meant. Alone in his office, I imagined, he leaned back in his chair and with his remaining hand he pressed his eyes shut to stem the tears.

XV

THE RETURN

They were only kids, these boys we seek to honor:
dead kids, who if they stood side by side on this California soil
would make a line seven and one half miles long.
And you have forgotten them.

                                        B.T. Collins

B.T.'s dedication to the completion of the monument took on a new edge, and the pace of his efforts became unhealthily furious. In May of 1986, the *Los Angeles Times* noted his efforts with an article, "Quiet Battle Goes on For Vietnam Memorial: One Veteran Makes It His Personal Objective".

In fact, it became an obsession.

"A few reporters have told me that California would rather forget than remember, play golf rather than pay tribute to those who gave their lives more than a decade ago," he scolded. "That's crap! I have to believe that there are enough people in this state willing to forge a lasting tribute to these gallant men and women."

The monument was to be a citizens' memorial, paid for by the people, its goal to show the families of the fallen that the sacrifices of their own had not been forgotten. It would reflect the youth and camaraderie of those who died. The age of each man was to be carved beside his rank and hometown. A plaque at the monument's entrance would be inscribed with the words of Major Michael O'Donnell, written January 1, 1970, in Dak To, Vietnam:

> . . . *save one backward glance*
> *When you are leaving*

For the places they can no longer go.
And in that time
When men decide and feel safe
To call the war insane,
Take one moment to embrace those gentle heroes
You left behind.

The Major was killed in action three months later.

Every race would be represented. A giant bas-relief would reproduce the cover photo from the book *Bloods*, which celebrates the participation of Black Americans in Vietnam. The design included a place for artifacts, among which were Herman Wood's bronzed combat boots. He had left a pair at home between tours of duty. When he returned from the war, his feet were missing.

A time capsule was created to be opened in 150 years. Inside it, B.T. planned to put James Webb's *Fields of Fire* and a letter from Andy Anderson, his ever-faithful RTO.

Finally, this new responsibility added to stress endured under the Brown administration took its toll. Traveling alone one afternoon on the interstate, B.T. was forced to pull over because of severe chest pains. A former California Conservation Corpsman was there to help him. Driving by, he recognized the infamous, "B.T. Who?" plates, saw B.T., and took him to the nearest hospital. The facility also happened to be a well-known "drying out" spot for area alcoholics and drug addicts.

There he was, with no cigarettes, no booze, no fast food, and a possible heart attack. He called Mike Lambert at Kidder and *demanded* that he come to get him with an additional request and an admonition: "Bring me a pizza, and if you tell anybody where I am, I'll kill you." Luckily, although the incident later required a cardiac procedure, there was no heart attack. B.T. put his own spin on the event. It seems he was lying by the side of the road, looking at his watch thinking, "If someone doesn't come along soon, I won't even make the Six O'Clock News!"

There was no question that he needed a break.

He took his first real vacation in fifteen years. He returned to Vietnam. Traveling over 2,000 miles on rut-filled roads to the spot where a grenade had blown away half his body twenty years before might not seem like a vacation—but it was time away from the office. It was a pilgrimage he had to make. He was there to re-connect with a moment in time that had changed his life forever. More than once, the sights and sounds brought him close to tears.

He made the trip with his friend Stan Atkinson, the news anchor at Sacramento's NBC affiliate, KCRA, and the network's cameramen. Stan had been in Vietnam as early as 1961, as an adjunct to a fact-finding tour with CBS' Fred Friendly and Vice President Lyndon Johnson. Friendly and Atkinson had won the trip as a prize for their film documentaries. Atkinson, pitching B.T. as an American iconoclast and a war hero, convinced a top Vietnamese government liaison officer that the proposed visit would engender much positive publicity for both countries. KCRA's application was put at the top of the administrative heap and approved.

Their itinerary took them from Hanoi to Hue, to Da Nang, past An Khe, to Quinhon, to Saigon, now Ho Chi Minh City, then finally to Loan Toan in the Mekong Delta, the site of B.T.'s final mission. The two Russian-made vans promised for transport turned out to be one van and a near-ancient sedan. Travel on the highway was only slightly less hazardous than hand-to-hand combat. At night, escaping from the heat of their huts, the Vietnamese habitually sat out on the edge of the road. They kept their backs to the traffic, unseen until illuminated by the last-minute glare of headlights. In the daylight hours, military trucks careened from lane to lane, dodging poultry and wobbly bikes, water buffalo, and speeding Honda motorcycles. The Russian-made vehicle was loaded with gear, cans of extra gasoline for the trip, and B.T.'s *smoking* Vietnamese guides. Thus, their transport was actually a moving bomb in the making. "I've got this heart condition," B.T. quipped, "I'm not going to get excited. I'll just chew a lot of aspirin."

The diagnosis of "a bad heart" had been followed by the discovery of diabetes. The doctor was direct—stop smoking came with the first diagnosis, stop drinking with the second. B.T. did—on a dime, but not without the accompanying mood swings. So, when a bureaucratic snafu kept him from returning to the base for his beloved Bravo Company at An Khe, he went mute for two days. He simply could not believe that he had traveled so far only to be denied his destination. But he remembered the troops as he bypassed the base in the unrelenting rain.

"The men of Bravo Company," he began softly, "The men of Bravo Company," he was forced to start again, "were nothing like the men in Oliver Stone's *Platoon* . . . nothing. You cannot imagine the incredible love they had for each other."

Through the water-streaked van window, he imagined the troops standing at attention as he drove away, the wind and rain providing camouflage for the tears he had promised not to shed. Superimposed on the passing landscape, he watched Sam Bird, in nothing but skivvies and boots step out into an opaque sheet of water to dig a drainage ditch down the center of their camp. Sheepishly, each man in the company followed suit. He saw Sam dropping from a helicopter into a hot landing zone. All that promise shot to hell in a moment of insanity, he thought. He ached for his comrade, free at last from the rain and the pain in a grave in Wichita, Kansas.

They went on to the Vietnamese cemeteries. Among the markers, B.T. found the grave of a soldier who had died on his *life day*. Like so many young Americans, this young enemy had stopped living before he stopped growing. It brought to mind the story of another soldier, an American, whose hands B.T. held as the doctors treated the stumps of his legs. "I told him," he explained to Stan. "'Look at me. Hold on tight. Scream if it helps. Look at me.' This kid's legs had been sheared off at the knees, and I knew how badly he hurt. I asked him how old he was, and he said 20. In 1965, when it all began, this kid was only 12 years old. Then I knew the war had been going on a long, long time."

Some things made him angry. One of his guides, Colonel Bui Tin, of the North Vietnamese Army, who had accepted South Vietnam's surrender at the end of the war, had also been Jane Fonda's guide when she visited the North Vietnamese at the height of the conflict. Colonel Tin explained what Fonda's visit had meant to those fighting for the North. "We now understood there were two Americans; the ones who dropped bombs on us, and the ones who had sympathy for us."

"To the Vietnamese," B.T. said, "an American movie star was a representative of the American people. By her mere presence in the seat of a North Vietnamese anti-aircraft gunner, she said as an American, 'you may do whatever you want with those American pilots.' Whether she realized it or not, she gave her blessing to the torture of American prisoners of war." Her open fraternization with the enemy during wartime was, by his standards, treasonous.

It hurt him to see the wreckage of a decaying B-52 bomber sinking in a village pond. He thought of the men that had gone down with that plane, men the locals hastened to explain "had all had parachutes; airmen," they insisted, "who had not died as the plane fell from the sky to the water."

He relived the battle of Hue, standing on a now-quiet combat square. He pictured the tangle of men and arms; the human and mechanical cacophony of guns fired and lives lost in agony. "A lot of good men died right here," he explained quietly. "If you ever talk to someone who was at Hue, then you know he's really been through a lot. JFK said 'we will pay any price, bear any burden,' but after the Tet Offensive, we hedged our bets. There were more casualties than American mothers could bear. Our cause was just, our methods, at the very least, misguided. We were winning the war in Vietnam. We lost it in DC."

In the states, B.T. was tall. In Vietnam, he was a giant. Wherever he went the American captain with a hook for an arm and a wooden leg attracted attention. War amputees came out to admire his technological appendages. Vietnam's injured had not fared so well. Many made do without prostheses and others used makeshift means—old shell casings—to help them walk. The film crew recorded unforgettable images; the towering American in a baseball cap holding the shoulder of a tiny white-haired Vietnamese elder to make it down the steps; the fair skinned redhead squeezed among gaggles of hopping, skipping, brown children. He stood at their center two times the size of the tallest among them. Painstakingly, he practiced their language lessons, while they laughed and applauded his efforts. He was an event. Word spread from village to village that the "big American" with the magic arm and leg was on the way.

At last, the site of his injuries was at hand. They approached the canals, conduits to the Mekong, birthplace of B.T.'s most important memories. They descended from the van to find a hoard of workers, male and female, piling stone and throwing dirt to finish what was later to be known to KCRA and its crew as the "B.T. Collins Memorial Bridge." The van was traded for an old slatted bus that literally had to be "pushed" into going over the bridge and down the road. Finally, reaching the canal's edge, they transferred to a hollowed-out wooden motor boat and set out.

The day, like the one twenty years before, was hot and brutally humid. The handmade craft bobbed forward on the muddy waters. B.T. watched the moving shoreline and the old map before him alternately, conferring with his Vietcong guide. This guide, a captain in the North Vietnamese Army, had unbelievably been in the same general area as B.T. when he was injured. The spot they sought appeared. B.T. steadied himself on one of the Vietnamese and stepped from the boat. He cried out, caught off guard as his *right leg* hit the uneven ground. The trip had been an ordeal physically as well as emotionally. While others rose at dawn, he rose before them. To attach his multiple parts took time and patience. The jolting ride over thousands of miles of poor roads had pitted leather and plastic and wood against skin, and his flesh was not the winner. Sores rose along the strap of his prosthesis on his back. The stump of his leg was swollen and festering. Stan Atkinson confessed he had just never realized to what extent B.T.'s missing limbs were both an inconvenience and a source of daily suffering.

They pushed through the dense brush to the clearing beyond, where, so long ago, life for B.T. Collins began for the second time.

"There was June 20, 1967, and the rest of my life," he said softly. "I just can't believe it. I will never, ever forget that I got this chance. So many did not. You know, your only way out if you got hurt was to be carried by your own Vietnamese, and it took three or four of them to carry an American. We were so much bigger. I was lucky. I had saved one of their lives early on, and the word had spread. 'This guy won't run out on you.' But hey, I'm no hero. Another guy was saving somebody, and I just followed suit."

The North Vietnamese captain informed him he had known of the Americans' presence because he had seen their supplies air-dropped. And B.T. thought how much he wished he had moved on. The stump of his leg throbbed and sweat ran thick as syrup down the tired paste of his complexion. He recalled how sick he had been of the brackish river water, how mortally tired. He relived the confusion, the scramble of men, the shouts, the wind and shadows made by the hovering helicopter that took him away. He heard his own cries to the medic one more time, "T-burg, T-burg, am I going to die?"

Microphones picked up a single, deep sigh. He pulled off his cap. His fading red hair lay flat to his head in sweat-drenched whorls. He plucked his Special Forces pin from the cap's brim and, consulting the interpreter, he explained that he would like to present it to the Captain. It was the ultimate grand gesture, warrior to warrior. He said that he meant no disrespect to the captain's uniform, but that he would like him to have it as a symbol of the mutual sacrifice they had made. The two shook hands, the slender, shorter Vietnamese officer and the tall, now paunchy, pale American. "He had," B.T. smiled, "just one last question. Had anyone seen an arm . . . with a hand . . . five fingers?" Only the interpreter understood and laughed.

He was quiet on the trip downriver. He admitted that his thoughts were bittersweet. His most painful memory was of the treatment that he and others had received when they returned home. The most touching moment during the trip was the chance encounter with a South Vietnamese tourist, who wanted to "thank him for the sacrifice he had made for his country."

B.T. remarked that no one at home had ever expressed similar appreciation. But the picture that would remain in the minds of Atkinson and KCRA's crew was the sight as they came round the bend, of a pyramid of laughing, cheering children waiting on the mud brown bank. B.T. Collins was getting still another resounding "standing O."

"They must think we're the Russians," he joked.

The tape was edited, shown on Sacramento television in nightly segments, and eventually distributed, but not before a final sequence was added.

Three years before, fellow veterans Dean Parker and Dave Porreca had returned to Kansas with B.T. to bury Sam Bird. They sat watch at the undertaker's after making sure that Sam's uniform and multiple decorations were properly placed. They knew that his death was the direct result of his war injuries. He had never fully recovered from his wounds; it had simply taken him longer to give in to them. They and several others believed that Sam had a right to a place on the Wall in Washington. On Veterans' Day, 1987, their efforts bore fruit. Sam Bird's name appeared, inscribed on that towering surface. B.T.'s visit to The Wall was recorded.

It was a blustery day, cold for Californians, and slippery underfoot. The falling snow grew heavy. Using his cane, B.T. made his way cautiously. His Green Beret turned white; flat flakes stuck to his bushy, graying brows. He leaned forward to trace Sam's name in the polished stone. Wedged in the panel crease beside it was a weeping, near-frozen rose.

"When I get to be 85," B.T. said reverently, "I shall come here to this sacred place and say proudly, I served with this man." Then he turned to his friend, Stan Atkinson, put his head on his shoulder, and sobbed. Even the snow-padded ground could not muffle the bitter sound of that mourning. It rang out in that white silence, the lament of love and friendship lost, all the pride and sorrow stored for twenty years let loose in that hallowed air.

B.T. went back to work, physically exhausted from the rigors of his "vacation." Mentally, however, he was refreshed and more determined than ever to see California's Vietnam Memorial finished. He was in charge of raising the necessary money.

Corporations' contributions dribbled in, but donations from the people were light. Apparently, the California Vietnam War Memorial was the best-kept public secret in the state. He felt personally responsible for the lack of funds. He was terrified that the existing better feeling about Vietnam veterans would evaporate and that the monument would never be built, so he set his sights on a 1988 Veteran's Day dedication, dug in, and never looked back.

B.T. called in all his markers. He capitalized on his reputation, on his relationship with the press, on his ability to inspire. His early days began earlier; his late days lasted longer. In addition to his regular workload, he now gave from 20-30 speeches a month. He was a popular speaker and emcee. He spoke so often that an invitation to one affair read, "B.T. Collins is *not* the emcee for this evening." Those who organized an event knew his presence at the front of the room insured a good turnout. No matter to which group he spoke or what the assigned topic, he never failed to mention the Memorial or to ask for money.

He loosened their purse strings with Irish charm and with a healthy portion of guilt. He told his audiences that their treatment of returning Vietnam Veterans had been unconscionable, and that this was their chance to make up for the near irreparable harm they had done both to the troops and to the families who survived them. "It's too late to say thank you," he admonished. "It's too late to say you're sorry, but maybe, with this monument, you can make a different kind of statement.

"They were only kids," he reminded them, "these boys we seek to honor. Dead kids, who, if they stood side by side on this California soil, would make a line seven and one half miles long. And you have forgotten them. Over thirty states have erected living monuments to their Vietnam War dead. We who lost the most have not." Then he asked each person in the audience to take home two extra envelopes and give one to a neighbor on each side. "This is how it gets done," he closed.

He was hard to ignore. At the end of an evening, he would turn to whoever had accompanied him and "download," pulling crumpled checks and bills from back, side and breast pockets. It was an event. A veritable shower of currency pressed upon him during the evening tumbled from his hands and clothing. Within the family, it was understood that all birthday, Christmas, and any other gifts to Brien were to be in the form of checks made out to the California Vietnam War Memorial. Of course, the honoraria for the multiple speeches he made went either to the Memorial or the battered-women's shelter in which he also had a keen interest.

Donations ranged from two single dollar bills from a fixed-income widow, to a check for $988, exactly matching one veteran's house payment. A child raised $300 in pennies. B.T. requested that one donation be returned—a $100 check from Jane Fonda and Tom Hayden. It was not. Yet, despite every effort, the fund was still nearly a million short. So, he stepped up what was already a killing pace.

While he raised money for California's monument, he also worked to support the Washington Memorial for women who had served in Vietnam. He was particularly moved by a cover story in the 1988 September/October issue of the *California Nursing Review* titled, "Vietnam—A Legacy of Healing." The author wondered if she was right to have saved those she did. B.T. wrote to reassure her and any other nurses with similar doubts. His letter was published in the *Review's* next issue.

There are those, both in the press and in government, who say I have made a difference," he confided, "but I am the one who knows who really made a difference. It was those 19-20 year old nurses who held my one remaining hand and told me to 'hang on,' in 1967. Back in the states, they were there when we woke up screaming. They were there when our parents and our girls came to look at us for the first time. They were there when we took our first steps. They were there when we got our reality checks in front of an uncaring and unsympathetic public. They

were simply always, always there. Know that our lives were
irrevocably changed by the presence of those military nurses.
They did something nobody else could or would do. And I swear
that we who were there will never, ever, forget them.

This was not his first public acknowledgment of the nurses'
contribution. In a previous letter to the editor, "Love in the 60's",
which appeared in the *Wall Street Journal*, he had explained the
difference between "chicks and nurses."

June 10, 1986
"There was an odd sort of feminism in those days, particularly
in Chicago in 1968 when the password was "chicks up front."
I can only presume that these were the "chicks" who were so
proud of their liberated status that they bought posters that
proclaimed, "Girls say yes to boys that say no." These were the
women whose idea of an attractive male was one who converged
on armed forces recruiters with about fifty other brave souls to
harass them. These were not the 19-20 year old nurses who
witnessed every night more horror and bloodshed than any one
of us soldiers saw during our entire tour. These nurses were the
"chicks" who knew the real meaning of love.

Like the nurses he so admired, my brother regularly took care
of others. He scanned the newspapers and listened carefully to
the radio for any accounts of people severely injured. He then
went directly to the hospital to sit at their side, to listen, to comfort,
to advise. One young woman lost her leg in a horrific accident.
He wrote and called constantly to check on her progress. He
advised her on high heels, guys' reactions to her injuries, and life
without limbs in general. He offered to take the day off and
introduce her to his leg-man in San Francisco, who was just "the
best in the West."

"The choice of a leg-man," he explained, "was as important as
the man she would eventually marry."

He later wrote in much the same vein to the son of the *Reader's Digest* Bureau Chief, Ken Tomlinson. B.T. knew the father, but not the son.

July 30, 1991
Dear Wil,

I can only guess what is going through your mind as you get ready for surgery. After 29 operations, I can empathize with your fears. I do realize that this tumor stuff is terrifying. However, you have a whole new responsibility . . . your folks. They can't take away your pain. They can't go into the operating room with you. They are totally helpless. Now, that's real terror.

So, my friend, you are going to have to look your Mom in the eye and tell her you're going to be O.K. (cause you're 14 and you know it all) and then tell her to take care of your Dad, because he is a wreck worrying about his son. Mothers are tougher than Dads . . . that's the way it is. Then tell your brother what kind of pizza you want him to sneak in, O.K.? After all, priorities are priorities! Next week you and I will talk about the scars.

His caring was not restricted to the potential loss of limbs. When the State's Director of Health, Education and Welfare had a mastectomy, he wrote on the very day of her surgery to *comfort* her, "Don't let it bother you," he cautioned. "You would have made a lousy topless dancer, anyway."

While he worked on the memorials and fulfilled his corporate obligations, he also campaigned for his friend, Jack Dugan, a Democrat, who was running for a seat in the California State Assembly. A hit piece about Jack had been circulated in the mail which infuriated B.T., and to which he responded, point by point, in a multi-page, handwritten letter which began, "Dear Friend, my reason for writing is not just to support Jack, but to support a precious commodity—integrity—and to assault its enemy—half-truths. He and I learned the lessons of integrity in Officers Candidate School. There, half-truths were called 'quibbling.' In Vietnam, half-truths were called 'tragedy.' Think about it," he admonished, "and vote your conscience!"

His answer provoked an answer, an angry reply written in red across his original. Unbowed, B.T. not only replied to the reply but, incorrigibly, hit up the dissenter for a contribution to the California Vietnam Memorial.

"I guess we'll just have to put you in the 'maybe' column," he wrote sarcastically. "Just do me one favor. If you ever get to know Jack, and possibly even admire him, please have the guts to say so. In the meantime, I've enclosed some material on a project on which you and I could possibly agree. We're a long way from our goal of two million. How about it? Maybe there's more to you than I originally thought. *Semper Fi*, B.T."

CARRYING THE TORCH

We're so concerned with rights in this country,
we forget about obligations.
There is an American dream that you can do anything you want.
But you have to give back instead of constantly taking out.

B.T. Collins

The *Return to Vietnam* tape, including B.T.'s visit to the Wall, was finally distributed. It went out across the country to the service academies, to the Citadel, to those with whom he had served in Vietnam, to childhood friends, lawyers, policemen, journalists.

Dear B.T.,

I have watched the tape three times. You *are* an American hero, and you didn't get to be one by shaking the President's hand or by being on television. You became a hero when you put all your character and heart and humor into the task of re-creating your life after Vietnam. All of your friends admire you more than you will ever know for that heroic and successful effort. Only a fool would think of you as handicapped.

And, yes, thank you for the sacrifice that you made in Vietnam. The gratitude has been slow in coming because many of us were just plain ignorant about the war and what it meant to those who served. All those nightly broadcasts with footage of battles alternating with protest marches and two or three lines from someone who had stumbled into the public limelight were merely background noise in my own self-absorbed world.

I hope the country will rethink Vietnam many times. And in spite of all the mistakes that were made, we will, I believe, eventually take pride in the sacrifices which sincere people on both sides of the controversy made for their convictions.

Take care, B.T. and keep in touch.

Susan Martin (former Santa Clara classmate)

Sam Bird's Radioman, Joe Forgione, wrote him at 2:00 AM after having watched the tape 20 times. "I would," he said, "have given my ass to have gone with you. I'm probably one of the few still around who saw B.T. Collins in action. You've impressed the shit out of me, then and since. May you always carry the torch!"

Sacramento's KCRA followed the distribution with a telethon featuring the tape. The phones never stopped ringing. Workers stayed until long after midnight. Every pledge made was honored— a rarity in fundraising. Additional money came in from those who were not able to get through. The California Memorial was a secret no more.

The official dedication was finally held on December 10, 1988. B.T. was in charge. The sun shone. The band played. Flags waved. Dressed in camouflaged fatigues, the veterans cried. Gold star mothers wept. The white rose bushes planted in a protective ring around the Memorial offered a profusion of creamy, scented blossoms. Brigadier General George B. Price, wearing a confetti-like collection of ribbons, spoke of pride and sacrifice. John Grattan, B.T.'s favorite tenor, sang the *Star Spangled Banner*. The Governor, George Dukemejian, failed to maintain his composure and so, in spite of merciless self-control, did B.T. Collins.

There would be celebration after celebration on this spot, ceremony after ceremony on Veterans' Days and Memorial Days to come. Who in the crowd imagined how soon this special place would also mark the passing of the day's principal speaker? How soon, in spite of the gutsy, heavy laughter, everyone would also weep. This time, the favorite tenor would sing B.T.'s favorite, *Danny Boy*. This time, helicopters would fly in formation overhead, missing one, and a near silent, flag-draped caisson would roll sadly below.

But the present occasion was faultless, and B.T. felt a peace and a pride that had been a long time coming. The touching ceremony was not, however, without its "B.T. moments." While an interpreter was signing for the hearing impaired, B.T. raised both his arms above his head, showing the hook that replaced his right hand. "Good thing I'm not doing this," he mocked, "You'd only get every other word."

The following year, 1989, both our parents died; Daddy in June, and Mother in October. Her funeral mass was on B.T.'s 49th birthday. I had the sad task of collecting their ashes and storing them on a closet shelf. In the spring of 1990, the family gathered as our parents were laid together in Mother's hometown cemetery. Refusing to be maudlin, I had put the ashes in a box wrapped in the most beautiful paper the local drugstore had to offer, and tied it with real ribbon (Mother only used *real* ribbon) and a bunch of daises.

"You should have put your mother in a Lord n' Taylor box," quipped one of my favorite O'Brien cousins. "She *loved* Lord n' Taylor's."

Picking up her lead, B.T. continued, "Yes, it's a good thing, a good thing . . ." All the lowered eyes now lifted. All heads now turned in his direction. A good thing? "Daddy," he paused, "Daddy was finally out of the closet."

With Mother and Daddy gone, and the memorials built or going forward, he had time to rest, time to live high on the corporate hog, enjoy the fruits of notoriety, and spend the day a little less furiously. But he was bored, because what mattered most in life was not even marginally operative in Wall Street's rarefied air. So, in the fall of 1989, he left expense accounts and expensive gifts behind. Accepting a 70% cut in salary, he returned to government service under a Republican Governor, George Deukmejian, at the request of the State Treasurer and friend, Tom Hayes.

In George Deukmejian, B.T. saw a man of honor, a solid, honest American who loved his country and would serve her. He was inexorably grateful to him for the support he had given the California Memorial. "Every time I face a father or a mother of one of the

5,822," he told Deukmejian, "I realize this is one of the best things I ever did in my life. You obviously saw something in me that I didn't see in myself."

Compliments and gratitude aside, he teased this Governor as he had governors and presidents before him. As always, he offered unsolicited advice.

June 3, 1987
Dear Governor:
"Happy Birthday! In a few short years, you will be another parasite at the Social Security trough that I refuse to pay into. *Hang tough on the education issue.* In 1979, they wanted me to ease up in order to improve the attrition at the CCC. No dice. The rest is history. Hang in there—you're doing the right thing.
B.T.

The Governor laughed and "hung tough." It was rumored that Deukmejian did not originally understand how B.T. could serve two so different administrations with equal passion. He quickly learned that B.T.'s notion of public service was to make a difference— not a Republican or a Democrat difference—and that his passion was the people.

The Governor's wife was one of B.T.'s unabashed admirers. "He had 'old world' manners," she told me. "He rose when I arrived; he pulled out my chair. He wrote me hand-written notes." Mother would have been pleased. Yet, Gloria Deukmejian also confided, laughing, that he once introduced her to an audience by sharing with them that he knew things about her no one else knew . . . that tattoo, for instance. And he let it hang there.

Unlike the Governor, B.T.'s friend Tom Hayes was uncomfortable with politics under any label. Unlike B.T., he preferred invisibility. Brilliant and unassuming, his focus was getting the job done. When he asked B.T. to return to government as his Deputy Treasurer, the reply was delivered in a second. B.T.'s respect for Hayes' as a man of unquestionable integrity approached hero worship. He told others it was his chance to *walk with the angels.* And then, Tom Hayes was a Marine. Their professional time together was fruitful, if short lived.

Hayes was defeated by Jerry Brown's sister, Kathleen, in his race for re-election. B.T. would serve under yet another governor.

His letters and speeches continued. He never lacked for opinions, and expressed them with abandon publicly, or on re-cycled stationery with the logo, "I paid for this with my own money!" He wrote to Colin Powell about the inclusion of the "Bloods" bas-relief on the Memorial, and to donate money to the Buffalo Soldier Monument, in memory of a young black soldier who had died beside him in Vietnam. The latter monument, representing the sacrifice made by African-American soldiers from the Civil War to the present, was finally dedicated in 1992. "Don't get discouraged," he cautioned the General, "It took us six and a half years to raise the money and build our memorial."

When Colin Powell was appointed Chairman of the Joint Chiefs, B.T. sent him an unusual letter of congratulations:

> August 10, 1989
> General—
>
> Who gives a damn if you are the first black to head the JCS? I think it's great that we have a combat commander and a Vietnam vet with a CIB! Nice going, Sir!
>
> > > B.T. Collins

It's safe to say that the Chairman received no other letter like it. B.T. shared his enthusiasm for General Powell, and his sense of irony about the Chairman's race with one of the capital's newspapers:

> Editor
> The Sacramento Bee
> August 23, 1989
> Dear Editor,
>
> How ironic that the first black to be appointed Chairman of the Joint Chiefs of Staff rose from poverty in New York City, the son of immigrant Jamaican parents, through the ranks of the United States Army. This is the same Army that Jane Fonda, Tom Hayden and Donald Sutherland chose to trash some twenty plus years ago as they toured bases around the country with their group called "F— the Army!"

This same Army was integrated in 1948, long before the dining room in the US Senate of our nation's capitol. This is the same United States Army that fostered the climate that allowed the first woman Captain of the Corps of Cadets at West Point, a post previously held by none other than Douglas MacArthur and General Pete Dawkins.

B.T. was by now able to accept only one out of every three requests to speak. The honoraria continued to go to charity. Occasionally, however, he extracted some small treat for himself in payment for his presentation. At one event, he asked that he be able to ride in a stunt plane that was part of the day's program. The plane belonged to Frank Christensen, premier flyer and designer of hand-crafted acrobatic planes. The cockpit behind the pilot was, according to Christensen, about large enough to accommodate an 18-year-old gymnast. B.T. fit neither category—no amount of stuffing, pulling, or rearranging worked. His right "leg" just wasn't flexible enough to fit the space provided. So he dropped his pants next to the plane, took off his leg, and thrust it into the arms of a shocked woman bystander. Then they threw him into the cockpit and off he went.

Christensen recounts that many people who *think* they want to ride in a stunt plane are subsequently either sick or terrified when the ride actually begins. Not so B.T., who called out like a child, "Yes!" and "Wow!" and "Do it again!" When Christensen was told how B.T. had lost his arm and his leg, he was totally surprised. "You mean he's missing an arm, too?"

He continued to travel long distances to support a cause or to do a favor for a friend. No group was too unimportant, too small, or too far away. These were not photo ops. He was not running for election. He had a message: service, service, service, loyalty, ante up. And the message, delivered by an increasingly weary, limping double amputee, hit its mark. A subordinate, Mitch Stogner, remembers, "Once, he was so exhausted he asked if I would drive him. He slept the whole way there, then walked in the door and blew them away."

Actually, he didn't "give speeches," he "had conversations." Many a member of Congress had the same experience, over the years, during his after-hours sessions at *Bull Feathers* in Washington, DC. There, way into the morning light, he held court, capturing them with stories and ideas.

He caught the audience's attention early, and he kept it. He told a group of Rotarians, "I know most people start their speeches by saying how honored they are to be here. Forget it!" After the laughter died, he continued, "I'm here because I owe the Rotary. When the legislature was trying to shut down the CCC, the Rotary came to my aid. And now it's pay-back time."

His trademark was self-deprecation. He was known at Kidder as an *outside* trader. " I have never had an original thought. Everything I ever learned, I learned from somebody else. I make Joe Biden look like George Washington," he bragged. He was, by his own account, "only one step away from a known felon who had conned corporate America out of a huge salary. "I only managed to become an officer," he continued, "because in the Army, if you screw up, you move up. So I lost an arm and a leg? Big deal! Hell, I blew off my leg and arm with one of my own grenades!"

Of course, there were themes other than his ineptitude. Responsibility stood high on the list. "We're so concerned with rights in this country. We have no concern for obligations." (My father's words.) "There is an American dream, and the American dream is that you can do anything you want. All you've got to do is work at it. But you've got to give back instead of constantly taking out."

"Never lie!" he remonstrated. "The trouble with lies is that when they are told often enough they're accepted as truth. The press and truth," he continued, "are not always faithful companions. Because bureaucrats and politicians, the media's meat and potatoes, are so self-serving, and so on the defensive, they sometimes play with the truth. Good news, therefore, is no news and bad news is not like wine. It doesn't get better with time. So, when you tell the truth and people are looking for lies, it's unsettling. Of course, the problem is, if the press asked me, 'Didn't we once see you with a goat and a bottle of Jim Beam on the corner of 10th and G?' I'd have to say, 'No, actually, it was on the corner of 9th and G.'"

Most often, he spoke on patriotic themes. On one such occasion, California State Senator, Alfred Alquist and his first wife were at my table. She confided to me, laughing, that, "She was one of B.T.'s girls."

A priest had given an invocation and departed. B.T. began, "I am glad Father was unable to stay. Before I start to speak on leadership, I have to set straight a rumor that is circulating in the Capitol—a rumor that a clergyman might not understand." He paused. "It is said that I am Senator Alquist's illegitimate son." The audience waited. I held my breath. He paused again, then confessed, "I am!" Cautiously, I checked out the senator's wife. She laughed merrily. The last time I spoke to the senator, he was still chuckling.

The real subject of that evening's "conversation" was Sam Bird, and leadership as Sam's life defined it. Leadership, B.T. believed, was having a great deal of integrity, a little bit of courage, and a few drops of whatever it took to inspire. Sam Bird had possessed those qualities in abundance. When B.T. spoke of him, his voice grew hoarse and the room grew still. The event that began with a whoop of laughter ended in a misty-eyed silence.

B.T. finally told Sam's story in an article, "The Courage of Sam Bird," for a May, 1989 issue of *Reader's Digest*. For everyone who knew Sam Bird, there were a hundred others who had known someone like him. The letters came from all over—the neurosurgeon who saved Sam's life, the chaplain who prayed for him. Joe Forgione, who'd landed only moments after Sam had been so hideously wounded, was, as a result of the article, reunited with his Vietnam buddies. The memories and the thanks poured in, sometimes scribbled in pencil on scraps of soiled paper, sometimes on stationery embossed with the scarlet flag and snowy stars of two- and three-star generals. A Vietnamese refugee, who had been in America ten years, wrote to express her appreciation to all American veterans. "You and Captain Bird are a hero of the US and Vietnam too," she said, and added, "You are a wonderful storyteller. I wish one day I can write as good as you are."

People wrote from the backs of pickup trucks on lunch hours, from the waiting areas of emergency rooms, from the dorms and offices of the service academies. The Air Force ROTC wrote, and the West Point women wrote. The Senior Army Advisor to the 49th Military Police Brigade, California Army National Guard, recommended to the Commanding General that every commissioned and enlisted leader within the brigade read and internalize the lessons and wisdom found within "The Courage of Sam Bird." The Superintendent of West Point, David Palmer, advised the class of 1989, "Read this article and refer to it as you embark upon your military career."

Of course, B.T. had his favorites.

My Dear Mr. Collins:

Having been a career officer in the Army for over twenty-five years, I felt there was little if anything that would soften the heart of someone who had spent time as a prisoner of war, one who had seen hell from a front row seat. I was mistaken. After reading your article, I cried.

I was one of those field officers who commanded the battalions that were made up of bright young officers like Captain Sam Bird. I loved them all. My heart and the heart of this great country of ours bleeds from the loss of these unselfish young men who so gallantly laid down their lives for what they believed was a just and honorable cause. Your article is a glowing and loving tribute to them and to your fallen commander.

My eldest son, a graduate of the United States Military Academy, served in Vietnam as an Infantry Company Commander. The loss of your friend and commander will ease the pain from the loss of my son who was mortally wounded while defending a village in the Central Highlands.

Again, let me say how deeply moved I was after reading your article. May God bless you and give you peace.

                              Edwin D. Webb
                              Colonel, USA Retired
                              Palmer, Alaska

B.T. answered. He told Colonel Webb that he had forwarded his letter to Sam's father, who was then 86 and in a hospice in Kansas City. And he added, "I read your letter every day. It gives me perspective on what is real and important. One thing for sure—my life has been pricelessly enriched for having had the experience of serving with men who would have without question given up their lives for me, and for whom I would have done the same. Thank you for all your generation did for mine. We should do no less."

So Sam was laid to rest in print. There was a message in this public display; that Sam Bird was a model for the kind of American we need to be, and B.T. wanted everyone to know it. His father's son, he remembered "to speak up, speak out, and put it on paper," so there would be a record of what he believed and who he revered. There were many lessons and less and less time to teach them. And sometimes, after the laughter, he would look levelly at his audience and offer some serious advice:

"I can't impress enough upon you people how short life is; how incredibly short. So just go ahead and say, 'This is what I believe in' before it's too late."

XVII

POLITICS

*Winning in a war doesn't mean beating your opponent in a debate.
It means killing the other guy. And losing doesn't mean having to
give up your job. Losing means losing friends. It means coming
home minus an eye or a leg . . . or losing your life . . .
or even your country.*

B.T. Collins

December 1990

Time was short, shorter than even he realized. B.T. Collins was
out of work, and thereby minus an official, public forum. The
United States was on the verge of war. Protesters massed; pundits
parleyed. For B.T. it was a nightmare re-visited—old accusations
of engagement without purpose, the motives of the President
whom he admired questioned, the unwillingness of the citizenry
to stand by the country and its chosen leader. In his mind, there
was no need for debate—none. "The President," he said, "is the
chief architect of foreign policy. Only he has stood the test of the
entire electorate."

B.T. believed Americans were paying the price for their lack of
resolve 25 years before in Vietnam. "Saddam Hussein," in his words,
"was no dummy." He just played by a different set of rules. He had
seen how spineless our nation had been, and assumed the condition
was congenital. "Our goal," he stated, "should be the total eradication
of this madman. You must kill him, not wound him," he cautioned.
"You must cut the head off the viper!"

A coalition of California law enforcement associations, firefighters, and veterans, called "Operation America," organized a rally to support the troops in the Gulf. The gathering of nearly 5,000 supporters on the Capitol grounds made the papers, and the clippings were sent to the men in the field. This time, the troops would know that people were behind them. B.T. was touched and grateful. "I feel fortunate," he said, "to live in a time, in a state, and in a country that honors its military." It pleased him to have a former Marine as the new Governor of California. Privately, he also expressed his support for General Schwarzkopf, "Vietnam produced you," he wrote in his physician-like scrawl. "PFCs can spot a phony in a minute, and the troops know where your heart is. Your persona simply says to every mother in America, 'Your kid is going to be okay with me.'"

A man from Milwaukee's 21-year-old son had just been called to the Gulf. He wrote in anger to the *New York Times* accusing President Bush of wagering his son's life to save his political future. "While my son has written his last will and testament," he ranted, "the President has been "chasing golf balls and zipping around in his boat in Kennebunkport." The fathers this man knew were not "sufficiently well connected to call a general to keep their children out of harms' way. His son, he explained, had enlisted in order to earn money to go to college. Bush lacked the courage and the character to find a diplomatic solution to the [current] crisis.

He charged Bush with sending his boy off to war for something so unimportant as "cheap gas." He warned the President "If my son is killed, then God would have to forgive you because I, surely, will not."

B.T. was intensely loyal to those he considered "his own." Bush belonged in this category. He would not allow the President's service to his country or his honor to be questioned. He believed people didn't understand military service or the true nature of war. So, he responded harshly through the *Times* editor with an open letter to the father.

August 24, 1990

Obviously, you feel, in your own selfish way, that your son is the only man being sent to the Gulf. You say he joined the Marines to pay for a college education. I'm sure the Commandant of the Marine Corps and the American taxpayer will be pleased to hear that. People in the armed forces know exactly what their contractual responsibility is to their country: to wit, they are expected to lay down their lives for the rest of us. It's just that simple. It is explained to every recruit.

You whine about George Bush being on vacation during the crisis. Every other American knows exactly the image he seeks to portray. Plainly put, we are not going to let some two-bit Hitler dictate the schedule of the United States President. Your cheap shot about George Bush being the product of a privileged background totally denies his exemplary service in World War II. He could have used his powerful father, a US Senator, to keep him out of the service altogether, or to get him a cushy billet at the Navy Yard in DC. But he didn't lean on his dad. Instead, he became the youngest US Navy carrier pilot in history. By the time, he was your son's age he had been shot down in the Pacific twice.

So, I hope you realize that you have humiliated your son with your presumptuous threat not to forgive the President if he dies. Your son is a 21-year-old Marine. He's a warrior, not a boy, who will do the things he's been trained to do; break things and kill people. It's your son's forgiveness you should ask for.

"Break things and kill people." They were phrases he had used before. Of course, he was deliberately harsh, not so much to shock as to tell the truth. Soldiers are trained to protect and defend and in so doing they will kill or be killed, destroy or be destroyed. No one wants to kill, but members of the Armed Forces know it may be necessary.

This understanding of the military and war was central to his comments on "Larry King" during Desert Storm. He was interviewed with a woman who believed that no cause was worth fighting for. She further complained that the soldiers in the Gulf might get hurt or worse, killed. Where had she been when the "Lion of Juda" stared down Mussolini? he demanded, referring to the confrontation between Hailie Selassie, Emperor of Ethiopia, and the Italian dictator during World War II. The issue was having the courage to stand up for what you believed.

B.T. detested the *prettying up* of war, the making believe that it was all some glorious game in which those who were victorious were actually winners. He simply could not understand how someone would sign up for the Armed Forces and think he or she would face neither danger nor the possibility of getting hurt, nor even of dying.

"When I hear people use war metaphors to describe politics," he reflected, "I can only be thankful that most Americans don't know what real combat is. Winning in a war doesn't mean beating your opponent in a debate. It means killing the other guy. And losing doesn't mean having to give up your job. Losing means losing friends. It means coming home minus an eye or a leg . . . or losing your life . . . or even your country."

And yet, had this man's son been hurt, B.T. would have sat at his bedside and held his hand. He would have soothed and explained and shared his pain. He would have *been there* for the family, for the boy, not just at that moment, but ever after. For inside this old soldier was someone who hurt, someone who cared, a man-boy who one June day had changed his priorities forever.

War, as the ultimate nightmare, was something he was never able to forget. Pictures lay in his subconscious, and shared memories were always there to make them surface.

20 February, 1967
B.T.

Received your note last night. I wrote you a letter on 1 Feb. with all the details on Captain Bird. He's in Japan. At latest word, he is blind in his left eye, paralyzed on his left side. He was hit in the head and in his left leg on his birthday, at LZ Dog, north of Bong Son. We had three KIA and 14 WIA on the 12th. On the 14th, we had five WIA and one MIA plus one

KIA . . . Reese, third platoon. We found him four days later and they had tortured him and cut out his tongue—on the 16th, we had seven more WIA. Simmons was hit in the hand on the 27th but is back now. Fred was hit—head, stomach, and legs, with fragments. He is also back now. Patterson hit in the groin but will pull through. Riddle got it in the leg and is in Japan. Ray Jones got hit in the head and is in pretty bad shape. The skipper is dead. Died on the 31st. H/6 completely blew him apart. Sorry this letter can't be more cheerful but I'm sure you will understand. I'm beginning to think there is no God in the Highlands.

Take care, Dean

Sam Bird, brain bulging out of that clean-shaven Kansas head. Sam, seemingly at attention while lying in bed, the shoes that would never again fit on walking feet polished to inspection-level sheen, side by side, on the floor below. Yes, B.T. Collins knew about real war. And he remembered that coming home to ingratitude and disrespect was almost as bad as being in combat. So, in March 1991, he wrote an article, "When They Come Home," urging a warm welcome for troops returning from Desert Storm. It filled a page, via the *Reader's Digest*, in the *New York Times*. In it, he passionately described the service of the men and the women who served in the Gulf war:

"They didn't indulge in debates about whether or not this war was 'just about oil.' They reported for duty, and they did so with an intuition about history and human nature, a kind of street-smart understanding about the Hitlers and Husseins who turn up to remind us that some things are worth dying for . . . While politicians talked, they boresighted their guns. While protesters shouted, they kept the watch . . . They did all the dirty, dangerous jobs people have to do to break a despot's grip and re-teach the world the lesson it never seems to learn—that peace is worth fighting for."

He urged citizens not to repeat the travesty of the treatment received by the veterans of the Vietnam War. The soldiers of Desert Storm, he believed, ". . . had paid another installment on a great debt that will never be erased as long as there is tyranny in the world. And like their predecessors, they paid in time, in effort, and . . . in blood." He asked that ". . . there be parades"; that, "[we] step forward . . . and shake their hands. Stand up America, and cheer them. Raise your voice, America, and honor them." This time, of course, we did. This time, his message was less necessary.

In May, nearly 90,000 people appeared at Sacramento's McClellan Air Force Base for a "Yellow Ribbon Day," a spectacular salute to the troops returning from the Persian Gulf. Bands played anthems against a backdrop of Old Glories rippling in the California breeze. Earlier, services at the Vietnam Memorial had honored the 11 men who had given their lives in this latest conflict. B.T. had spoken with reverence of the flag that covered their returning coffins and decried those who would burn this American symbol. "You will not shoot my country down," he declared. You will not burn that sacred blanket that says to these men, 'your country has not forgotten you.'"

In the end, B.T. was not long unemployed. "The Marine," as B.T. referred to Governor Pete Wilson, appointed him Director of the California Youth Authority, where he was in charge of the state's 8,642 young criminal offenders, and all those who worked to rehabilitate them.

B.T. had only been part of Wilson's administration for two months when he created a ruckus of national proportion. The day he took office his desk was stacked with waiting written complaints from the state's young wards—complaints he read with difficulty because of their deplorable spelling and grammar. He was appalled to learn, as well, that these wards, like the majority of those confined to the CYA, could barely read. B.T. let it be known through an official directive that he would no longer attend to complaints not written in proper English. The letters received were then returned accompanied by a letter of his own in which he encouraged the kids to use the facilities available to them—libraries, dictionaries, teachers—and to try again.

"What about emergencies?" the worried worried.

Truly serious problems, he argued, were handled on site. He was well aware of the wards' complaints. How did he know the letters were so poorly written? He had read them! Educators were, predictably, up in arms. In a world of inventive spelling, rife with the belief that any writing, no matter how poor, is better than no writing, B.T. Collins instantly became the caring community's pariah. Unfazed, he fueled their fire, adding, "Next, I think I'll have them write a paper and give a speech every week in front of their peers."

Much as he had in the CCC, he intended to hold everyone to a higher standard. He believed these kids' chance to succeed was directly related to their ability to express themselves clearly and correctly. He refused to buy into cultural stereotypes—that Chicanos couldn't be interested in calculus; that people of color were destined to go to jail; that minorities wouldn't care about ecology. Those who opposed him, he thought, were actually saying that these kids were too dumb to learn. He disagreed. His long-range goal was to send a message to inmates that the CYA took the matter of their education and their future very seriously.

Maybe these kids, whom he sarcastically described as "8,600 of the most vicious people he'd ever seen outside of the state legislature," could understand that there were ways other than holding up a store or beating someone to death to get a thrill out of life.

Actually, there were 8,642 wards, 5,000 employees, 10 institutions, 4 camps, and 22 parole officers. According to Don Novey, when B.T.'s appointment was announced, the California Correctional Officers listening literally cheered.

If he had said simply that he wanted to make education the focus of his administration or that he was going to make literacy top priority, he would have received accolades.

He and the problem would also have been soon forgotten.

He understood that conservative statements of policy already heard from every corner end up in the proverbial dustbin, with the rest of the non-specific recommendations. New movements start with revolutions, battles with an assault, and combat was B.T. Collins' game. He knew there would be one hell of a flap, but he didn't care. What mattered was whether the kids under his watch increased their chances of becoming productive members of society. "I'm not," he announced, "going to be another MacDonald's." To his mind, the food chain had given up by turning to pictures in place of words on its cash registers, making the job easier while impeding real progress in the process.

The press and the public should have recognized his well-intentioned hyperbole and zeroed in on the issue rather than the issuer. With the exception of one or two journalists, they did not. He had stepped on everybody's toes—the Prisoner's Rights Union, those who supported non-English speakers, and of course, the ACLU. The latter he taunted, saying, "I hope the ACLU sues me for depriving these kids of their right to be ignorant." They did.

Some argued that if these inmates had known how to read and to write, they would not have been incarcerated in the first place. This defense only proved B.T.'s point of the importance of doing things properly early on.

"What if they *had learned* young?" he challenged. The thought went unnoticed.

"Throwing the Book at Them," one headline blared. The article beneath it cautioned, "He, (B.T.), better think twice before he becomes known statewide as the man with the red pencil who loves to play holier-than-thou with other people's mistakes. If that's the reputation he wants, he should be very careful about editing his own memos. An error might slip by and that would be embarrassing to say the least."

It was. But it was not a printed mistake that caught the red-penciler red-handed but one spoken, before a television audience of millions, in a broadcast segment that dealt specifically with his CYA edict.

The furor finally attracted the attention of ABC television in 1990, and earned him a spot on the evening news with Peter Jennings. B.T.'s position was amply explained and then, to the delight of those who dislike the ACLU, a letter from its lawyers was shown on camera in which the word, "grammatical" was misspelled. The interview closed with B.T.'s parting salvo.

"Just between you and I," he confided to the reporter, "I will not be responsible for underwriting these kids' illiteracy."

"Ah," cooed the interviewer in return, "Wouldn't that be 'just between you and *me?*'"

Actually, he had been "editing" others for a long time. During the Brown administration, he had returned letters to legislators with misspellings circled in red. And reporters had for years received notice of mistakes and typos, not to mention round criticism of their views and the theories that supported them. They loved it and fired back, thus establishing a long-term, love-hate relationship.

"The first time I met B.T. Collins," wrote *Los Angeles Times* reporter George Skelton, "we were sitting at a bar and he was threatening to run his hook up my nose. He was drinking and not smiling. It was something about my being a reporter . . . a 'scumbag.' I said I'd get a lawyer and it would cost him his hook and his artificial leg. We sat there for a long while sizing each other up, boozing, yakking, surrounded by Capital cohorts. And we began a 16-year friendship. Later, he delivered a moving eulogy for my former wife, also a reporter. And through the years, he corresponded with our daughters, although they were rarely on his side of the political fence."

Jim Trotter then at the *San Jose Mercury News* added, "Ours was a contentious relationship, conducted through the mail. When he didn't like a column, his protest soon followed; a furious scrawl reminiscent of a man taking a hoe to hard dirt. After he had pointed out the flaws, the errors, the plain soft-headedness in whatever I had written, he would conclude, 'no reply necessary, B.T.' He once took particular umbrage at a column I wrote which suggested that one of his directives as Chief of the California Youth Authority was unconstitutional. He came to the paper to express his displeasure to my bosses. Later, when he had fallen under attack from the religious right during his race for the legislature, I wrote a column in his defense. Ultimately, because I lived in his district, I had the unique experience of voting for the man who tried to have me fired."

Among those indignant many were a few who took the reaction to his edict a little less seriously. "If only your spelling had spilled over to your penmanship," teased Del Spurbock of the *Los Angeles Daily News*. "You write the greatest notes . . . I think."

B.T.'s handwriting was indeed like a "hoe taken to hard dirt." Always terrible, it had become increasingly illegible when he learned to write with his left hand. The reader's goal was to get the gist. Decoding every word was a virtual impossibility.

Another letter, which was not returned, despite its orthographic inconsistencies read:

> June 10, 1991
> Dear B.T.
>
> Kungratulashuns on ure nu job! Red about it in the *Kronickle* today—ain't no better place fore you—giv em hel!
>
> Luv, Nadjia

While Nadjia Krylov's spelling may have been deliberately less than *de rigeur*, she knew what she was talking about. The State of California stood to have another model institution, one much like the CCC, one that would receive international recognition, not to mention change lives and better society in the bargain. For B.T., it represented still another battle to be won, troops to command, and a mission to accomplish. He had once been a quasi-delinquent himself, yet he had grown up to be totally committed to tough love, to law, and to order. As in the CCC, he would have given no quarter.

Inmates would have soon recognized that here was no sissy administrator. He'd so obviously "been there," if not to their urban ghetto, to some dark equally dangerous hole. He was someone they couldn't bullshit, someone that cared little about their pasts and everything about their future. No one had ever expected these young hoodlums to give, to do, or to be responsible for their own actions. Of course, this hard line only worked if the kids knew you cared. He cared. They knew it. Then, there was the question of power. As the head of a state agency with a sizable budget, he had the power to begin a process of constructive change. Give my brother a telephone and a bit of clout, and he could have had Mother Teresa coaching the *Follies Bergère*.

Inexplicably to some, the Governor had other plans.

XVIII

THE ELECTIONS

------·•·------

The common political currency is fear
—fear that the wrong statement will end a political career,
that the risky vote will exact too high a price.
Those who live by caution and doubt
I honestly believe will live to regret it.

B.T. Collins

A member of the California State Assembly had left to run for the State Senate. Wilson personally asked B.T. to enter the race for the vacated 5th District seat. In truth, B.T. had thought about elective office for a long time. Friends were constantly encouraging him to move in this direction, thinking, based on their own feelings about him, that he *had it made.* His liberal law school classmate, Elliot Daum had closed every letter for years with, "Run for Governor! It will be the only Republican vote I ever cast." At the height of his name recognition under Brown, he had given it serious consideration. But running for office is more than a popularity contest and a good set of contacts. There are rules within the system and B.T. regularly broke the rules. His loyalty to a Democratic governor would have hurt him among Republicans, although he remained a fervent supporter of Republicans and Republican causes.

Of course, neither had he come up through the ranks; he had been appointed, rather than elected, to positions of increasing influence and authority. He did discuss running with political advisors he trusted; those who understood the perfidy of the game to be played. They concluded that B.T. didn't have the fire-in-the-belly. As it turned out, he did not. The primaries and subsequent races for the California Assembly took a toll never to be recovered.

Once, he had worried that his youthful misdeeds, his drinking, and his early failure as a student would keep him from being elected, or that the resultant publicity would somehow embarrass Mother and Daddy. But Mother and Daddy were gone. Publicly, his past was not an issue, for over time little information about him was left to the imagination. Every time a new article appeared, he claimed to have flunked out of still another school . . . part of the bad boy image he so delighted in embellishing. Years before, when a candidate for the Supreme Court had failed to pass muster because he might have smoked marijuana, reporters flocked to B.T., "Had he . . .?" The question was never completed. He held up his hook for silence. He looked each man and woman in the eye and, in a manner unfamiliar to too many politicians then and now, he suggested, "Everything you can ever think of and then some . . . the answer is, 'Yes.'"

"When B.T. was about to run for the State Assembly, I told him he'd have no problem, Nancy Pelosi recalled. "He told me 'my only problem would be if they ever figured out I gave a contribution to a left-wing, San Francisco, pinko Democrat like you!'" He had given her money. He knew, absolutely, that she wasn't a communist.

"My word is my bond," he said seriously to the audience at a Capitol Press Conference, we learned from the *Sacramento Union* in July of 1991. "The way to get things done as a legislator is to be honest. Otherwise," he added, "you get the reputation for being a dirt bag. Then, the only career open to you is to be a reporter."

His answer to Wilson was also finally a "Yes."

"When the Governor of California says, 'Hey Pal, step up to the plate,' what else can you do?"

Our father would not have been pleased. Daddy had praised Brien's positions within government while warning him to "*stay away from politics!* It was," our father warned, "a '*dirty' business*," an admonition B.T. shared laughingly with his friends.

"What does he think I do, anyway?" he joked.

Daddy's definition of politics was undoubtedly contingent on the act of running for office. In any case, the son did not heed the father. Those in B.T.'s inner circle pleaded with him to think of the consequences to his health and his finances. Constantly accepting reductions in his salary and giving to multiple causes had played havoc with his resources. But the Governor was a Marine, the Governor was his CO, and, the Governor needed him. B.T. was incapable of turning him down.

Much was made of that military metaphor: B.T. responding to his company commander—the mandatory loyalty of those who serve. Yet, friends who understood B.T. still questioned the Governor's judgment, as well as B.T.'s. Wouldn't B.T. better serve the state of California as Director of the Youth Authority? What *about* his heart condition and diabetes, at best a lethal combination? Had Wilson crossed the line in asking for this kind of physical sacrifice? Also, it was well known that while B.T. could talk a nun out of her rosary for a good cause, he would deplore, absolutely deplore, asking for money for himself. Had Wilson missed the core of the man, his vulnerability, his thin skin, the emotional cost of going hat-in-hand, of facing the personal attacks brought on by a governor's interference in party politics?

In this instance, the soldier's sword cut both ways. Wilson was himself a commander besieged. There was a hill to be taken, and so he chose the best combatant he had. The analogy is still under examination. One might argue that under B.T.'s command, the men would have come first, the taking of the hill second. There was no question that were the situation reversed, Wilson would have answered B.T.'s call. The question was rather, knowing all the facts, if B.T. would have made it.

For B.T., Wilson was, like Brown, "a man to go into the jungle with." Only this time, given Wilson's service background, the description was more apt. As he had admired Brown's superior intellect, he now admired Wilson's unfailing honesty and workaholic habits. Like the Governor, B.T. had the courage to support unpopular positions and stick by them for the good of the state. He liked Wilson personally. He was the eat-nails-for-breakfast kind of guy that made B.T. say under his breath, "There, by God, is a man!" Both men were steeped in military tradition. Both men read heavily of history and the biographies of those who made it. Both men had learned the rules of engagement and public service from their fathers during nightly dinner debates.

Neither was easy to label. B.T., like Wilson, took a hard line on defense, crime, and taxes. Wilson, like B.T., was tough minded and realistic. But Pete Wilson was inalterably sober and singular of purpose, whereas B.T.'s allegiances and causes were widespread. Wilson was a man "who prized discipline over passion" while B.T. Collins' entire being was passionate born and passionate bred. He had spent a lifetime trying to keep his intensity under control—unsuccessfully. And if Wilson's youth were remarkably without escapades, the record of B.T.'s shenanigans read like the rap sheet at an Irish police station.

Having lived on the edge of the political arena for years, B.T. should have been hardened to the hypocrisy and the passions that politics engender. He was not. One of his great weaknesses, yet the quality that made him so attractive to so many, was his *naiveté*, his basic belief in human goodness. He had built a wealth of support that he believed would hold him in good stead. It did. It helped him win the election, but it could not protect him from the picayune or the quasi-informed or the viciousness of the righteous.

Some of the vitriol to which he was exposed appeared to stem from the deliberately provocative remark he made about being an atheist. But first, he had to get by the fact that he had entered the race literally at the zero hour, lived outside his district, and had been hand-picked by the Governor, which in the eyes of many put him in Wilson's pocket.

For the Assembly seat, B.T. was the Governor's most logical choice. His vast experience far outweighed that of any other candidate. A team player, he knew the system. And he had been lionized in the media as "a tough-talking, straight-shooting no-

nonsense patriot," traits apparently lost on those who were not Wilson supporters.

Charges were made that B.T. was "Just a pimp for that whore of a governor, Wilson." "How disappointed I am!" an irate woman shouted on paper. "You walked out on the youth of California. You were going to teach them to talk and to write a letter. Did you follow through? No! Shame on you! You're a patsy to Wilson and Willie Brown, (Democratic Speaker of the California Assembly, later Mayor of San Francisco), the most hateful and wrong men in the offices they hold!"

His most serious opponent stated firmly that "she believed in God whereas B.T. believed in the Governor."

B.T. did believe in Wilson.

"Wouldn't he owe the Governor?" the opposition taunted.

"Owe him?" B.T. mocked in return, "Owe him for taking a 50% pay cut and allowing people to use and abuse me? I'd say it was the other way around."

In a sense it was. Wilson faced an increasingly fractious Republican minority in the State Assembly. His own party squabbled so regularly that it was common knowledge that he could not mount the support needed for his own agenda. Only 16 of the 31 Assembly Republicans were considered moderates. Eight Republicans and one Libertarian had already entered the race for the open seat. Wilson didn't simply need a Republican, he needed a different kind of Republican, someone who would cut through the bull, build enduring relationships, and, if nothing else, make the legislators behave.

Because there were multiple Republican candidates, there was a primary. B.T. did not get a clear majority, so there was a runoff, followed by the actual election, in which he defeated the Libertarian. A year later, there was still another election because the seat had been vacated mid-term. Within a year and a half, he campaigned and ran four times.

When he entered the first primary, some of the signatures on his petition for candidacy were disallowed—those who signed were Democrats. His petition was refused. A judge then reversed the order. In a special election, party affiliation was not a legal issue; the petition was re-instated. In fact, among his supporters there were a number of Democrats. Our sister, Marialis, was one of them, although living in Silicon Valley, she could not vote for him.

B.T.'s 1992 campaign paralleled the race for President. Marialis had to file an absentee ballot before driving to Sacramento to walk the districts for B.T.

"Who in the hell did you vote for," he demanded, Archie Bunker in the body of an older brother.

"Voting is a private matter," she answered, primly, which could only mean that she had voted for Clinton.

To his unprintable response, he added the admonition that she was not to say a word about it to anyone! Not *one* word!" Yet, arriving at B.T.'s campaign headquarters, she was greeted with hugs and congratulations. "Hey, we hear you voted for Clinton!" they chorused. Wide-eyed and incredulous, B.T. had ignored his own demand and told absolutely everyone, "My God! My sister voted for Clinton!"

They were delighted that she had the nerve to depart politically from *the Great One*. B.T. closed the midnight meeting with words of thanks and encouragement to his campaign workers: "I just hope your parole officers know where you are tonight," he cracked. "Should you be apprehended by the authorities, I will disavow any knowledge of you."

By the time he first ran for office, he had lived and worked in Sacramento for 17 years of 16-18 hour days for the citizens of California. But, just prior to the election, he had bought a condo that was a mile outside the district represented by the Assembly seat. So, for those for whom the letter of the law was more important than the quality of government, this became an issue of some proportion. "He had," his opponents complained, "corrupted the political process, making a mockery out of state election laws."

Congressional Medal of Honor recipients, among them Vice Admiral James Stockdale, circulated an endorsement for him. One letter of support was returned. Written across it in large red letters was the proclamation: "Our vote will go to Barbara Alby," (B.T.'s opponent.) A hasty postscript of explanation was added in black for contrast: "We do not vote for sneaks!"

The feelings of one man were expressed with even greater outrage. B.T. had broken the law, as had the Governor and the judge who re-instated his candidacy. "It is appropriate to say that in conniving at your unlawful candidacy, you trusted public servants have pissed on yourselves and every citizen in the State of California. And you will never again be able to urinate without reflecting that the once respected B.T. Collins has forever soiled himself."

Outwardly unmoved, B.T. changed his residence and borrowed the opposition's own vocabulary, forever, thereafter, introducing himself as "The fire-breathing carpetbagger from hell."

Privately, such statements hurt and angered him. He knew what he had done for the state and for its citizens in general, and at what cost, physically and emotionally. While he routinely portrayed himself as inordinately cavalier—immune to criticism and to unexpressed pity, he was sensitive in the extreme. And while such experiences never caused him to change his behavior, they left within him a residue of disappointment in the values and behavior of the electorate. He ruminated and worried, sick at the lack of awareness, if only by a handful of people, of who he was, and what he had long been trying to do. He called to share these thoughts, something he rarely did.

"I have to tell you," he sighed. "It really gets me down. The things they say and do. Unbelievable, unbelievable. After all I've done and tried to do. I just . . . and the money, Maureen. This costs so much money. I've had to raise almost two million dollars. Do you realize the good I could have done with that money?"

I did. It made me sick.

His lack of religion, however, far outdistanced his address as an issue of his opponent's crusade. A letter circulated by the lead Republican running against him read: "Anti-Christian forces dominate the [California] political system. And the only way to stop this evil, this outrage [perpetrated] by the Governor and B.T. Collins is to fight back."

The candidate, backed by two pastors and, presumably, any honorable Christians, was an active member of the congregation of the Capital Christian Center, a 6,000-member fundamentalist Evangelical church in Sacramento. "She was," in the pastors' words, "up against a self-proclaimed atheist who had worked hard for abortion on demand and homosexual rights," a collection of finagled truths used to fan the flames of the righteous electorate. B.T. had indeed claimed atheism, an admission apparently not taken too seriously by either Sacramento's Bishop Quinn or Rabbi Frazin, not to mention Sacramento's Dublin-based Sisters of Mercy.

As to the issue of his support for homosexuals, he condoned neither intolerance nor the illegal treatment of any group. He had never worked for abortion on demand. He was pro-choice, but believed in the need for parental consent—if a kid needed a permission slip to go on a field trip, he reasoned, she needed something to get an abortion.

As an added bonus, the Christians included a copy of a letter written by former State Senator H.L. Richardson during the Brown era. The Senator was known for his acerbic evaluations of B.T. at the time of the reinstitution of the California Conservation Corps. Undaunted by Richardson's ringing criticism, B.T. had later written to hit him up for a fat contribution to the California Vietnam War Memorial. He assured the former Senator that were such contribution to be made, he would forgive him all his sins. Richardson wrote:

> July 7, 1982
>
> Times are tough in Sacramento but not for B.T. Collins pet adult care center. Over drinks at the Torch Club and steaks at Frank Fats, the CCC has become the best known agency of the state government as seen through the twinkling eyes of B.T. Collins whose Irish ancestors cornered the controlling interest in the Blarney Stone. B.T. Collins is absolutely terrific and to top it all off, he is a disabled war hero. Getting angry at B.T. is

like insulting Mother Superior. Merit, logic, and cost effectiveness have given way to bologna, bull-pucky, bourbon and B.T. His bureaucratic expertise and legislative slick has been rewarded by moving into the number one spot in the Brown administration while his bureaucratic offspring, the CCC, grows merrily in size and scope.

Not to disappoint, Richardson, in conjunction with the pastors, continued to give the CCC, and its former director, now candidate, an additional verbal heave-ho:

> June 19, 1991
>
> B.T., with his affable manner, has been able to ooze from one administration to another. He has backslapped his way into the hearts of governmental insiders on both sides of the aisle. B.T. is not only a member of this exclusive cult. He is the symbol, the idol, the Mecca of what every aspiring bureaucrat wants to be . . . employed!
>
> I fondly remember the days when B.T. was trying to get me to vote for funds for the agency he headed, the CCC. This highly hyped boondoggle, this resurrected, regurgitated refuse from the depression era was B.T.'s darling. My "no" vote became a challenge to this Irish charmer and for months he sent me little notes or dropped by the office to chat. It was during one of these meetings that I got a good look under the blarney trappings. B.T. is a raw-bone atheist, a red-in-the-face, flashing eyed non-believer on the subject of an all-powerful God.

The "raw-boned, atheist" reminded California voters, "America was founded by men and women who deeply believed that an individual's religious convictions were a private matter. We're campaigning," B.T. explained, "to represent all the people of this district, not just one congregation." He couldn't resist adding an east-coast slam, "Even people with a California education should know that the first colonists were fleeing religious persecution. We should be judged on our commitment, on our experience, on our ability to bring the people of this community together—not to drive them apart."

Religion or its lack was not B.T.'s only problem. "Collins," according to candidate Alby, "was a 'good ole boy' and big spender. He got his money from 'cigar-smoking' inside bosses, and therefore opposed decency and family values."

Of course B.T. personally had strong family ties. He deplored the tendency in some circles to regard children as status symbols and not to consider marriage as a pre-requisite to family. He did enjoy a wide base of support, and he received a considerable amount of money from Democrats. This, naturally, raised a few Republican eyebrows. "I'm a tax fighter and he's a tax spender," Alby continued. "You can love him," she chortled, "you just can't afford him."

In fact, B.T. was long known for his fiscal conservatism and for being scrupulously honest. He had voluntarily cut his own salary at the Youth Authority by 10%, an act unparalleled in that political arena. It was also common knowledge in the Capital that he had left a six-figure salary behind when he agreed to re-enter public service as Deputy Treasurer. In that post, he had actually regularly submitted a check to the Treasurer's office *in advance* of any personal expenses he might incur while doing the government's business in order to avoid even the suggestion of the slightest impropriety.

He did refuse to promise that he would never vote for an increase in taxes once elected. Any candidate who would do so was, to his mind, just currying favor. He knew that he might not be able to deliver on this issue, and B.T. Collins didn't make promises he knowingly couldn't keep. He had apparently forgiven George Bush senior that lamentable error.

He fought the opposition through the mail. Some flyers directly attempted to correct misinformation about his record. Others described him personally. "B.T., A Man of Enormous Heart and Courage" was one opening line. A picture of B.T. as a young soldier was on the cover, and another as an older soldier was inside. He was using a cane, as was necessary when marching in any kind of parade. The copy gave a brief biography, and highlighted his work with the

California Youth Organization and the CCC. Again, some mailers were returned. On one, his cane and hook had been circled in anger. The handwritten message written read, "This mailing will *never* get an affirmative vote from me. There are absolutely no commitments to anything here, just an appeal to people's sympathies. I'll never vote for an unknown political philosophy or political alignment. Your attempt to cash in on the sympathy and decency of people in order to attain a political position is contemptible!"

Someone, it was reported in an August, 1991 *San Diego Daily*, had gone so far as to suggest that sympathy of any kind was irrelevant because "he had never actually served in Vietnam, and his wounds were self inflicted."

Still another claimed that he cared nothing about the mothers and fathers of those who had given their lives in Vietnam and had worked on the Memorial only for his own aggrandizement. Even those who knew him and had heretofore supported him voiced their objections. They said they were, ". . . embarrassed for him. His career had to that point been stellar." He had in their words, "Allowed himself to be manipulated to run, a choice which reeked with dishonesty and lack of integrity—two traits they thought he possessed before he had permitted Pete Wilson to coerce him." Due to the circumstances of his entry into the race, these former supporters would be voting for his opponent.

The issue was not how fine it might be to have someone of B.T.'s character or proven record of service as a member of the state's main governing body. No, better to have someone less qualified in whom the Governor had expressed no particular interest, underscoring B.T.'s belief that people get the government they deserve.

But he did have his supporters. Eighty-year-old Eleanor Walsh wrote a letter to the editor of the *Sacramento Bee*. "Every time B.T. Collins opens his mouth, he speaks my mind." She lambasted one of his female critics who had referred to him as a "vicious, arrogant, pity-seeking, cunning politician." This octogenarian wondered in print, "What's the matter? Did she (the critic) get dumped by B.T.? Most distressing," she added, "was the fact that so few people voted." B.T. seconded that. She added warmly, in a personal letter, "I love you," but cautioned him, "(Don't get all excited. I mean as a mother.)"

Another Republican confessed that the "great atheist debate, had caused her a personal dilemma, but that what she had seen of his public life was worthy of respect. What she knew of him as a Vietnam Veteran was above reproach. She was aware that other veterans respected what he had done for them and for the country. She was not the only Christian who could see beyond labels . . . even those that were self-imposed. "God bless you and prosper you," she closed.

Did she suspect that he was never as tough as he pretended?

> Midnight
> October, 26, 1992
> Dear Joanna,
> You don't have a clue what you have done for my morale. How thoughtful, how kind, how generous! The CCC and the Memorial are two efforts of which I am immensely proud. About the Memorial, I cannot forget that I lived. Those kids died. I have had 26 more years—great years—they had nothing. Writing this to you brings me to tears. I think of them every day and they are always 19, skinny, scared, brave, kind to each other—beyond description.

The *Sacramento Bee* agreed with Joanna Wilson, "Truth be known," wrote columnist William Endicott, in his July 1991 column, "there is more love and tolerance in the heart of B.T. Collins than in those who classify themselves as Christians. Underneath that gruff exterior is a real softy."

Sacramento's other major newspaper, the *Union*, praised him as well. "If your writing is half as articulate, insightful, and provocative as your public speaking, please consider doing a weekly column for the *Sacramento Union*. Give the idea serious consideration. You're the greatest," pleaded the Union's editor.

However, once B.T. entered the race, the *Union* took a somewhat dimmer view of his greatness and endorsed his opponent. Strong, if less serious support, was found in the voice of Peter H. King of the *Los Angles Times* who claimed, "This town needs every character it can muster, even one-legged, foul-mouthed vets with diabetes and bad hearts. If the state government isn't going to be important, let it at least be fun!"

He was, actually, very clear on where he stood on the issues and why. "This country wasn't built on selfishness, but on generosity. That's why my friends gave their lives. That's why my father's generation went off in '41. It's called paying back. I don't believe in single-issue politics," he insisted. "I have to vote my conscience whether you agree with me or not. I will not tell you what you want to hear. I'm nobody's boy."

When voters tried to bend him to their way of thinking, he responded by telling them, "Hey, I'm not your candidate. You need to sign up for the other guy," adding that while they might disagree with him, he would fight to the death for their right to do so. "You cannot demand loyalty," he argued, "You have to earn it." He believed he had.

This same brand of honesty was operative during the 1992 presidential campaign. People expected, given his strong views on national service, that he would be extremely critical of any of those running for office who had managed to avoid going to Vietnam. In a lead May 31, 1992 article in *USA Today*, he aimed his severest criticism instead at regular Army officers who drew combat pay without ever coming under fire. "To be a professional soldier, you have to make a contract with your country. If called upon, I will fight a war twenty-four hours a day, seven days a week, for twenty years. I take issue with those Saigon warriors who lived in air-conditioned trailers with clean sheets and cold beers and pretended they were at war."

At the end of the piece, he said that he had no regrets about his own service. He would always be able to look the previous generation in the eye and say he did his best—that he'd do it again "in a heartbeat."

This final phrase earned him warm praise from Mark Helprin, a contributing editor at the *Wall Street Journal*. It was not so much B.T.'s service but the "defiance, the courage and the strength" of those last words. "You, my friend are the real item," Helprin wrote, "and God bless you for it. Are you sure you're not the re-incarnation of Theodore Roosevelt or George Patton?"

During the same period, B.T. was called upon to defend Jerry Brown. His defense of a Democrat presented a political risk. Nevertheless, he made clear in a number of newspapers and on national television that his former boss was not guilty of the drug charges leveled against him in the media. B.T. gave the former Governor a somewhat unusual vote of confidence. "The story," he said, "was ludicrous because, 1) this guy was too cheap to ever hold any parties and, 2) who would come to a party he hosted? Besides that, 3) Brown didn't have enough forks and there was no TV in the house. And the police," he joked, "do not like Brown, but they like me. They would have said something, and I would have put a stop to it."

Whatever Brown's faults, B.T. knew the Governor was no phony. The real issue in this election was hypocrisy. And B.T. hated hypocrisy in any form. Lying was not just saying you did something in June when you did it in January. Lying was the denigration of honor. Lying was pretending you were one kind of person when, in truth, you were another. The fact that Al Gore served during Vietnam as a reporter for the *Stars and Stripes* was in no way reprehensible. Using a picture of himself with an M-16 to suggest that he was a combat soldier made him suspect.

Joining the ROTC or the Peace Corps were acceptable alternatives to enlistment or the draft. Finagling notices of "Greetings" from one's Selective Service Board, then publicly protesting national policy outside one's country during wartime cast a totally different shadow.

XIX

THE POLITICIAN

———•••———

It's downright awful.
The rooms are full of ego-driven people who do nothing but talk.
The problems are enormous, the phone calls nasty,
and nobody is in charge of anything.
It's the arrogance of power.

The California State Assembly, B.T. Collins

B.T. won his election, but not without cost. Selfishly, some of those closest to him, I among them, had privately wished he would lose. The final price tag was greater than a number of dollars and his mental health. Between elections, he developed a bleeding ulcer and a hiatal hernia. He was treated for anemia and lectured about monitoring his diabetes more carefully. Standing for hours, running from speech to speech, he had reduced the stump of his leg to pulp. It required involved surgery, after which he was told not to wear his prosthesis for three weeks. Seven days later, he appeared, as promised, at a Republican fund-raiser—no wheelchair, no crutches, in agony. "No one," he explained, "had ever seen him in public without his leg and he wasn't going to start now!" The leg healed—eventually. His general health began a downward spiral.

The campaign had played havoc with his diabetes. His staff made a heroic attempt to prepare proper food, but the schedule was too tight and too frenetic to allow for evenly spaced, healthy meals. It was also hard for him to find time to check his sugar and to take his insulin. The first task required that he prick his fingers four times a day, and he only had one hand. Everyone near him learned to give insulin injections. If he dated a woman more than once, he would unceremoniously drop his pants, hand her a needle and say, "This is part of the deal, Babe."

The more Nora Romero, his chief of staff, and others tried to help, the more the campaign and B.T. himself, seemed to thwart their efforts. There had to be some small treat in the midst of this nightmare. He went on binges, eating chili dogs and various other coronary disasters, raising his sugar and clogging his arteries. His willpower had run dry.

In November of 1992, he was admitted to Walter Reed, in DC because of severe chest pains. He checked himself out to return to the less prestigious Mercy General in Sacramento for surgery. He knew his health was unstable. The thought of dying was forever in the back of his mind. Dying away from home meant dying alone. It was something he truly feared. While staying in a hotel in San Francisco, angina had awakened him from a sound sleep. He had driven home alone in the middle of the night. He didn't want to die in San Francisco. He confessed to Ann Cunningham that the front door of his house stuck, and he was afraid that if he needed help, the emergency squad might not be able to get in.

He told me he was fine. He explained the state of his health to his constituents in the following letter:

December 15, 1992

Thank you for all the phone calls and notes wishing me well during my stay in the hospital. I see from the numerous messages that many of you were worried that all of the money you invested in my campaign may have gone to waste. As many of you know, my initial visit to Walter Reed Hospital in Washington resulted in a very successful angioplasty performed at Mercy General here in Sacramento. The good news is that the two arteries that were cleaned out in '86 are still open. The bad news is that another artery has two blockages. The joys of elective office!

Now, I feel great. I have been told by my doctor, as well as by several others, that this trauma to my heart is a direct result of my many years of heavy smoking, hard liquor, and sneaking out to Jimboy's Tacos to pork down the daily special. It's hard to believe that what used to be a lean, healthy, 25-year-old mass of muscle has turned into a droopy, 52-year-old body. I guess I'll have to slow down. But regardless of the other changes, the killer blues and great buns are still the same.

The atheist then added, in his own hand, "Don't pray for me. It's bad for my image."

His health on hold, he turned his attention to the enormous amount of money he still owed for his multiple campaigns. Part of his debt was retired with the help of Rush Limbaugh who made good on a promise to come to Sacramento for that purpose. The Limbaugh fund-raiser, described by one journalist as a "schmoozefest extraordinaire," upset both liberal and conservative Republicans. B.T. and Rush were in the same party, but not always the same camp. Sign-bearing protesters crowded the entrance to the affair, but inside there was no political agenda. Both men "made nice" and, for once, played by the rules. B.T. jokingly called Limbaugh "Balloon Belly." Limbaugh later eulogized B.T. as a "Damn Yankee . . . the American literally everyone should have known."

Now that the election was over, B.T. thanked his supporters publicly and his friends privately, listing all the numbers, his home phone included, at which he could be reached. He assured his constituents that his actions in office would not be predicated on getting re-elected, that he didn't care about their party affiliation or whether or not they had voted for him—that he would represent all of them faithfully. To his attorney and law school classmate Dick Cunha, he wrote more informally:

November 3, 1992
Dear Richard,

The overwhelming mandate I received in my election leads me to believe that I can solve all the problems of the world. Please call me if you have any. My machine takes calls 24 hours a day. If you will send me $5,000, I will include you in my daily prayers. Although election law states that cash is not to be received, I can fix it. Twenties would be appreciated, and in one lump sum, if you please. If you can't come through with the dough, I will take your first-born instead and teach him how to be a politician.

God Bless You and God Bless America!

B.T. Collins
Assemblyman, 5th District
A fine American, I might add!

"A fine American" in Brienspeak meant just the opposite. He always referred to society's worst, to the reprobates and reprehensibles of the world, (he included himself in that category), as "fine Americans."

Humor aside, he was scrupulously honest. Once elected, he had a sign made and posted in his office that read, "Please do not discuss campaign contributions in front of me or my staff. It will save us both a lot of time in the slammer." In 1992, when the state budget failed to pass on schedule, he received a paycheck. He called the comptroller's office to inquire how he could be paid when there was no money. It was explained that Assemblymen and women were paid anyway. He refused to accept the check.

"But I must issue you a check," the exasperated clerk replied.

"Then issue it with zero funds," he answered.

His request was honored.

B.T. then tackled those who had been less than kind, less than supportive, downright miserable. In a manner unprecedented in politics, he invited his critics by personal letter and in the newspapers to come to an open meeting, in essence to *let him have it* . . . to take a free punch." There was a caveat. The meeting was open only to those who had been to the polls. "If they had not voted at all—they were neither to call nor write. Nor were they to trespass through the gates of Arlington Cemetery, and, certainly, never to look a Gold Star mother in the eye!"

The invitation was blunt. He had hoped, he explained, to respond individually to all the nasty and vituperative notes that were sent to him during his recent campaign but the sheer number made this virtually impossible. He invited them, therefore, to attend a meeting at which "no supporters—only those who wanted to criticize, belittle, or insult me would be allowed. People generally feel better," he added maliciously, "if they can taunt a candidate when they are surrounded by people of like animosity. Remember, no ringers— only negative questions will be addressed. Why not test the courage of your convictions in an open forum?" Journalists had a field day. A significant number of people came, and if all his answers didn't satisfy, at least his detractors had their say.

He began his first full term full of contradictions. After asking for the electorate's vote, he reminded them constantly that he had run to help the Governor, not out of personal desire, that he did not truly want to be in the Assembly, that he might not run again. His theory—better to be a reluctant warrior than a desperate candidate. Desperate people will do and say anything. His remarks caused some consternation in the press and certainly among those who had voted for him.

There was one constituent, however, who seemed to understand and cared enough to put it in writing. "Although you indicated an original reluctance to run for office and a lack of strong desire for re-election," wrote supporter Dean Ross, "it is precisely your type of leadership that we most need today. Unfortunately, most of the good people will not run for office, consequently we get the rest."

B.T. agreed.

Uncharacteristically, he made no speeches from the Assembly floor. He introduced no bills. He sat in the back and listened. He took copious notes. Slowly, he built relationships, remembering each ally made and each vote cast. He listened for the merit of the message, no matter the messenger. He kept track of every favor. He admitted that the legislators knew what he was doing, that they understood a bill would be forthcoming, and that they would owe him. To those who wondered what was going on, he suggested he was practicing Irish politics. He drew ample fire from his detractors for his behavior.

He watched his fellow legislators' interaction somewhat scornfully. He announced at a roast for a local businessman that because he had been on the wagon for a number of years, he could no longer, with impunity, tell racist, sexist, or homophobic jokes. "What I'm telling you basically," he paused, "is that I can no longer talk about the California Legislature." He said for print, "It's down right awful. The rooms are full of ego-driven people who do nothing but talk. The problems are enormous, the phone calls nasty, and nobody is in charge of anything. I don't know what the people in the balconies think. Here they are visiting the Capitol for the first time and they see nothing but bad manners. How do you explain that to sixth graders? It's the arrogance of power."

Those who were familiar with his sarcasm accepted his remarks as such. He wasn't kidding. While there were legislators whom he greatly admired, he was appalled at the pettiness of too many others, and the paucity of the ideas and agendas that consumed them. "The real reason I'm not wild about being a legislator," he complained, "is that *I'm* not in charge of anything." He wasn't.

Nevertheless, as was reported in dozens of interviews and news articles, he remained the master tactician, a carryover from his days in the military. He approached each problem in terms of "this is where we are and this is where we need to be." He was a methodical thinker who also had a keen eye for marketing. He cut to the core of the issue, setting aside the things that didn't matter. He was unique in that he stayed pure while operating within an impure system. He had no personal ax to grind. He could be trusted absolutely to explain the merits of another legislator's proposal honestly to the Governor. He could make the inflexible flex. While some felt that he was wasted in the Assembly, others felt that had he lived and the political balance of the legislature shifted, he would have become Speaker.

Fellow politician Mike Antonovich, claimed, "He could have been placed in any number of government positions—transportation, water, the judiciary—and things would have changed dramatically for the better."

Former San Francisco Mayor Art Agnos, Collinsesque in his desire to do the right thing no matter the cost, had schooled B.T. in the art of the improper, encouraging him to speak his mind, however outrageously. "He could get away with it," the Mayor explained, "because he had the charm to match his irreverence."

The inner workings of the Capitol, B.T. believed, revolved around the human side of politics rather than the issues. He told audiences, "If you can build a consensus, if you can put your ego at the door, it's amazing how much you can get done. If I can set that kind of example, I can do the same thing that I did with the CCC, where I believe I made 'bureaucrat' an honorable word. This all sounds so self-serving . . . but I firmly believe we're in this thing together. We'd get a lot more done if we'd just give the other guy the credit."

Bills or no bills, he had strong opinions regarding law, order, and education. Inmates should be required to learn to read and write before release. There should be tougher sentences for drug dealers, especially for those who sold drugs to children. Gang members and other violent juveniles should be treated in the courts as adults. There should be immediate, permanent expulsion for any student caught in school with a gun. The best thing parents could do for teachers was to get out of their way. His ideas on education were my father's, save perhaps for the particular slant he had on the Academe. Leadership within the universities, he believed, was at the heart of California's educational problems. These institutions seemed unaware that there was no more money. If all university presidents had taken a 15% reduction in salary when the State University's budget was cut, everyone might start thinking, "How can *I* save more?" It was what he himself had done.

Because our mother and father had both been public school teachers, he was strongly pro public education. Education, further, was not an entitlement, but a privilege of a democratic society that should come at some personal sacrifice. The idea that students appeared to have more rights than their teachers confounded him. He actually thought students should play a meaningful role in their own education; that it was *their* responsibility to learn as much as it was the teacher's to teach. Parents, he believed, should go to school board meetings, not to complain about teachers, but to give them their support. The teachers, not parents, should decide when a student should be retained. And the latter action should be used with all students who failed to attain skills at standard grade level.

He made a vow to visit every school in his assembly district while in office. He wanted the children to understand government. He wanted to talk to them in person. He felt it was critical for them to meet a real live politician. Knowing politics' reputation, he felt it important that they understood that integrity and public service were not an oil and water mix. There were messages to deliver about making something of yourself and the importance of continuous learning; that anything was possible if they worked hard and had goals. He was the living proof. There were admonitions about how to live and how not to. After his heart surgery, he wrote one school to tell the children, "See, this is what happens to you if you smoke. Don't do it!"

He also participated in Read-a-Thons at the local public libraries on Saturdays, the only day when he conceivably might have had some time to himself. A local librarian recounted his reading of a time-honored classic: "I was annoyed because the book from which he read was in such terrible shape. As long as he was going to read why hadn't he chosen one of the new, beautifully crafted editions? When he finished, he said to the children, 'you may have noticed my book is kind of banged up. That's because I've read it so many times; you don't need a new book to have a really good story.'"

Whatever he did for the children was returned a hundred-fold. The lack of luster, of purpose, and commitment in the legislature depressed him, and he was increasingly sick and tired. When he visited the schools, he came alive; he relaxed. He needed the stroking these young people provided. Their youthful enthusiasm was a balm to his battered soul, and in them he saw promise and a lingering hope for the future of the nation.

He spoke regularly at funerals and fund-raisers for the widows and orphans of fallen police officers. He was particularly supportive of the California Correctional Peace Officers, among whom there were a large number of veterans. The president of the organization, Don Novey, had also served in Vietnam, and the Peace Officers had been the first public employees to give money to the Vietnam Memorial. He owed them. In his opinion, they had the toughest beat in the state. He couldn't imagine any worse job. What kind of reward was there? Police officers saw criminals apprehended and even convicted. Police officers got a rush from their own good deeds, from the lives they saved. "Where was the rush," he wondered out loud, "for the Correctional Officer? What made him or her want to get up in the morning? Motivation may not count when you're 23," he explained, "but when you're 46—it matters."

His support for law and order did not prevent him for giving advice to some famous law enforcement officers. After the Los Angeles' riots, he wrote Chief Daryl Gates, reminding him that he was responsible for everything his troops did or did not do.

> March 22, 1991
> Chief Gates:
>
> Call a press conference. Say that you will stay as long as they have questions. Point out the things in your forty-two years that are clear evidence that you don't tolerate the type of conduct under discussion. Be dispassionate, calm. Take your lumps, accept *total* responsibility, and stay in their face! Then, after they've had their say, tell them you do not intend to desert your men in their hour of need.

There is no record of any reply from the besieged Chief of Police.

Of course, education and law enforcement were not his only causes. In addition to his substantial commitment to DC's Women's Memorial and to his alma mater, Santa Clara University, he worked for Big Brothers-Big Sisters, for Volunteers in Victim Assistance, for "People Reaching Out," and a host of others. He was overgenerous with time, considering his physical condition and his meager assemblyman's salary, minus a lucrative law practice. Many assemblymen practiced law on the side. B.T.'s decision not to practice law was deliberate. He saw the combination of lawyering and holding elected office as walking too fine a line between honesty and the misuse of influence.

He admired women. He wrote to a woman midshipman after she'd been appointed brigade commander at the US Naval Academy, to commend her for her promotion and her poise, "Better than some admirals I've seen."

He wrote to a woman staff writer at the *San Francisco Examiner* who had done a piece on men's fascination with big breasts and breast implants. "You're right on the money. Phony is phony," he told her, and then recounted how he had long ago thrown away his prosthesis.

There's an event I remember—Brien sitting on the living room couch while I unpacked his clothes after he was discharged from Valley Forge; socks, socks, socks, underwear, tee shirt—and a hand. I jumped. "For God's sake, Brien!"

"Throw it over here," he told me, and reaching out, he caught the disconnected, five-fingered plastic form with his flesh and blood counterpart in mid-air. He left it on the coffee table until my mother found a place for it.

But the organization to which B.T. had long been the most committed was WEAVE, an acronym for Women Escaping a Violent Environment. His dedication could be traced in some measure to my drinking grandfather's behavior toward my grandmother and my father, but it went beyond that. He was, in an old fashioned way, a great protector of women. Of course, he teased female friends unmercifully, in a manner that mocked sexism; "Your contribution to my campaign would be greatly appreciated. Or you could sleep with me. You've got the greatest body, I think." Yet his record with women in the workplace was unblemished.

After the completion of the Vietnam Memorial, WEAVE received all his honoraria. He served on their board and became their chief fund-raiser, but not before he had commented on them publicly. "When I first ran into WEAVE," he said, "it was nothing but a bunch of Birkenstocks. I said you've got to get some Republican women, some circle pins; you've got to get some pleated skirts; and you've got to shave those legs!" He emceed their auctions, at which he sold his ties, himself, and sometimes his used parts. The last so disgusted some of Sacramento's society women they almost stopped contributing. The operative word was "almost."

On his 50th birthday, he had thrown a party. He charged his guests $50 a head, gave them practically nothing to eat, and raised $53,000 for a WEAVE children's center. Actually, the party was a little after his birthday, on which date he had parachuted out of a plane at 8,500 feet strapped to fellow Special Forces veteran, Ruben Garcia.

Friends came to wish him well from all over the states. There were tables designated for special guests, bimbos and old girlfriends. As in years past, Nora Romero had invited all the current and former women in his life to birthday celebrations. The table for "Hanoi Jane" was littered with leftover prostheses. Ms. Fonda did not attend. However, Admiral James Stockdale, the former POW, and his wife did, and received a standing ovation. There was a printed program for the evening replete with ads and congratulations, among which was Nancy Pelosi's half page which read, "If you were a Democrat, I would have taken out a whole page." The Los Angeles City Council sent a resolution praising B.T. for single-handedly making government fun again.

He continued to honor the memory of those soldiers he'd left behind. A group of 100 black men in Sacramento had chosen as its mission the mentoring of young Afro-Americans. When their focus was announced, B.T. decided to honor a young man he had had on his mind for twenty-five years; a soldier seared into his subconscious during the battle at Crazy Horse, a 19-year-old kid he barely knew. His name was Randolph Scott. It was for Randolph he had wept, hallucinating in agony, that day in the Fort Dix, New Jersey Army Hospital.

The memory dated from Brien's first tour. His rifle company came under a vicious attack—the firing so intense and so low he tried to make himself one with the ground beneath him. Late on the second day, he began to realize that everyone who composed his minuscule left flank was gone—either dead or badly wounded. He heard a groan and glancing up in horror, he saw a young black soldier, only inches away. The boy had his poncho over his ears, protection against a driving rain that hammered on the rubber hood blotting out the sound of surrounding fire. He hadn't heard the enemy. He looked at Brien wide-eyed, unable to speak. Then his hood fell back, and blood burst from the side of his head. He dropped, lifeless, to the mud. Randolph Scott had been directly in front of him. B.T. would ask himself forever if this terrified kid had taken his bullet.

All those years he remembered the date of Scott's dying. Every November, he traced the pale outline of this kid's name on Washington's somber granite. Inspired by the 100 Black Men, Brien remembered Randolph, this time, with a scholarship that bore the boy's name. He gave money and the 100 Black men matched it. When news of the scholarship's first winner appeared in the paper, he sent a copy of the clipping with the following short memo to the members of the California Legislature's Black Caucus:

1. My money, not campaign money.
2. My commitment is for five years.
3. I am a wonderful human being.

B.T. generally did not single out minorities. Whatever someone's color or nationality, he preferred to see him or her simply as a fellow traveler. He disliked the scarcity of minorities in the Republican Party and he had commented sarcastically as the emcee at a fund-raiser, "I don't know about the rest of you, but I see entirely too many white faces in this room."

These were not loyalties polished up and put in the limelight for political gain. As a high school senior, Brien had applied for a merit scholarship. The application required an essay and he wrote about one John Maloney, a man for whom he had worked as a soda jerk while a teenager. When John retired, Brien was invited to the celebration. Unable to attend, he wrote a long letter praising him for the lessons he had taught him; lessons Brien believed had influenced him all the rest of his life. The letter included a $500 check for the United Negro College Fund.

He spoke at the first fund-raiser for Matt Fong, who later became State Treasurer. Fong recalled, "He educated me with regard to the State economy and the relationships within the Capitol. He taught me something I have never forgotten. As a speaker, he was an enormous draw. Whatever the event, he was making a major contribution just by being there. Yet, when he believed in something, he demonstrated his commitment 100%. He always paid his own way. I have followed his example. Now I, too, always bring a check with me, even when I am the keynote speaker."

Jerry Chong, a Sacramento lawyer and former Marine, is one of three sons of Chinese parents, all of whom have served in some branch of the Armed Forces. B.T. constantly invited Jerry and his wife to join him at charity events. Eventually Jerry realized that this was a deliberate attempt on Brien's part to draw him into Sacramento's political inner circle.

He had first seen B.T. in action at a dinner for 800 people honoring a retiring judge. He was appalled. Brien was in rare form insulting all the prior speakers and claiming at one point that the honoree's son was born as a result of artificial insemination. "Somebody should stand up to this guy," he thought.

Later, Chong became President of the California Asian Pacific Bar Association. At the association's Chinese New Year celebration, B.T. was the principal speaker and Jerry was asked to introduce him. During dinner, B.T. reached over the lap of the man next to him and, using his hook, artfully stole the guest's napkin. "My God," Chong thought, "We're going to have to fight our way out of here. Not to worry. Brien smiled at his neighbor on the dais and, unbelievably, asked, "You don't mind, do you? I'm a wounded veteran. I don't have a napkin and I'm missing my arm and my leg," all as if there were some possible connection between the facts and his behavior.

Brien's intense loyalty to the other Marine, Pete Wilson, did not prevent him from offering the Governor gratuitous advice:

October 16, 1991
Governor,

Stay in touch with the people. Please learn from the Bush debacle. Too often people think Republicans are aloof, insensitive and rich. Best thing I do is return phone calls—even three a day would blow them away. Stop all travel and conferences—symbolic, but so important. Don't tell a soul, but give back the $35 K raise. Set the example. Why not contribute it to WEAVE? That's right, all $35K, and don't say a word about it. It will show up on your tax returns in '92. Otherwise, this money will be a millstone around your neck, especially when you have to start laying off people. Think about it. The $2K you sent me for the Memorial has been repaid in speech after speech. I, of course, will receive the credit for your enlightened generosity. Remember the best friends are the ones who will tell you the truth. I'm stuck with you, so don't screw it up!

When Joel Kotkin, liberal Californian academician, took to the national press to make what B.T. considered a vicious personal attack on Wilson, B.T. responded with an attack of his own. "It was simply deceitful," he roared, "for Kotkin to portray the Governor as a dour pessimist who took the state's economic depression too seriously. What California needed," B.T. continued, "was not smarmy salesmanship, but a leader who was willing to risk his approval rating to get the necessary reforms." After praising and defending every Wilson policy, from protesting the cost of illegal immigrants to the budget crisis, to child care, to down-sized government initiatives, he delivered his final salvo, "I think I know something about political and physical courage. I know what it takes to lead and this Governor's got it. Joel Kotkin isn't fit to carry his lunch!" Privately, he had referred to Wilson's tremendous political courage less politely. "This guy," he cracked, "must have a jock strap as big as a wheelbarrow."

Not content with Brien's real life antics, the media concocted their own. At the time of the State's 1991 budget crisis, *Sacramento Union* Bureau chief Daniel C. Carson had offered the following solution in his article, *Wilson team could seize solution for the budget, but it's a gamble.*

"Ladies and gentlemen," declares the Governor, "we have still another budget problem. Tom, (Tom Hayes, Finance Director), why don't you explain?

"It's really pretty simple." Tom sums it up, "We're flat broke."

"The real question," continues Wilson, "is what do we do now?"

B.T. Collins, feisty, irreverent director of the California Youth Authority leans forward. "Put me in charge of the California National Guard and in three days, I'll solve the state's budget shortfall forever. I've been thinking gambling might just be the answer to our prayers."

"We already have lotto and horse racing and bingo," Wilson says.

"Just petty cash," Collins responds and he bounds over to a large wall map and picks up a pointer. "As you can see, Las Vegas is just over the state line and Reno and Tahoe are even closer. It could all be over in a matter of hours."

"Wait a minute," says Wilson, "Are you suggesting we annex part of Nevada?"

"Not annex," replies Collins, "Invade."

Passion is expensive. It costs—physically, emotionally, as does doing too much for too many for too long. Thankfully, there was an important woman in his life. A Californian. Tall and lithe, she is as at home in a designer gown as she is in faded denims and bare feet. She has high cheekbones and the greenest eyes I've ever seen. Her skin is sprinkled with tiny freckles; my mother had freckles. And her hair is a deep red. When she enters a room, her height and beauty immediately catch your attention. She laughs often and has a wicked sense of humor. Working in government for most of her life, she knows all too well the pound of flesh it demands from the most dedicated. She knew about the midnight hours, dinners on the run, listening to the same speech a hundred times, and holding your own at any official party. Most important, she knew the drill: never *say*, "I love you." She gave him peace and acceptance when he needed it most.

Privately, Brien's greatest fear was that he would run out of time. The gift of life is a debt neither easily nor quickly repaid, and B.T. Collins owed. And so, he worked harder. In late December, 1992, following a November angioplasty, he experienced familiar frightening symptoms. At the beginning of January, 1993 he was admitted to the hospital with recurrent, vague chest pains. The next day, the cardiologist performed an angiogram, which indicated some irregularities but generally no cause for alarm. Nevertheless, two days later, there was another angioplasty. Although the procedure was successful, his doctor explained that an area remained, albeit small, that was diseased and not amenable to surgical correction.

The new year, 1993, was only one week old. In the distance, a piper played . . . a piper who would be paid. My younger brother, Brien, the family's "Butch," was dying. And I, on the great one's protective orders, was kept in the dark on all but the most general details.

He spoke often enough of his own departing this earth to let attentive listeners know both that he, himself, was worried and that perhaps they should be as well. He mentioned more than once that Mother's brother, John O'Brien, had died at 52 of diabetes and heart trouble and that he expected a similar fate. He confided to a friend that he dreamed that he had died—that Marialis, and I stood at his bedside, inconsolable. He questioned Tom Hayes about Nora Romero's status if something should happen to him. Tom assured him that she would be taken care of. Yet he was as deep in denial as were those who knew and loved him. We had been badly scared so many times. And then, he was simply too alive to die—too loud, too powerful, too annoying. And if he should die, a part of each of us would too. And we had neither the plans nor the patience for that.

He now wore rather than swallowed his nitroglycerin. He was light-headed—dizzy. His upper arms ached without reprieve. He was subject to recurrent episodes of cardiac arrhythmia—an irregular heart beat. He maintained his killer schedule.

In mid-February, he was seen again, this time for a dull ache that began in the chest and radiated down his arms. Frightened, he had called his doctor at home. He wasn't ready to die. Dr. Louis Vismara had been treating my brother since the onset of his heart trouble in 1986. Brien trusted him implicitly. He was as soft as Brien was loud, as introspective, and seriously reflective as B.T. was afraid to be. Vismara, therefore, understood B.T. as perhaps he had never taken the time nor had the tools to understand himself. Doctors survive by being detached. Remaining unaffected by B.T. Collins was about as possible as being in the middle of a combat zone and not noticing the bullets fly by.

Brien was an incorrigible patient. Once, as Vismara lectured him about his unhealthy habits, he read a newspaper and asked the friend, who had accompanied him, to get him a pizza. He was kidding. The real problem was the uncovering of a challenge he couldn't meet— a dilemma not solved easily by money, caring, or clout. Vismara understood that after Vietnam B.T. had developed a disregard for his physical being that allowed him the time and focus to make everything else in his life much more important. He valued neither his own body nor physical things. But the mind and body are inalterably attached, and the regular denial of his feelings, and lack of personal emotional outlet, were as lethal as his diet, his smoking and drinking.

On March 9th, he was again seen—this time for swelling in his remaining leg. His medication was adjusted. On March 9th Jack Dugan died. There were no pills for that. Dugan and Brien were together warriors, Irish, one-time Catholics, and New Yorkers. They communicated with that in-your-face, eye-to-eye honesty that is the Empire state's hallmark. Ten days later, B.T. Collins, too, was gone.

He left without a struggle, though those who loved him fought mightily in his stead. In truth, he went down easy. And there is a God in heaven, for there was no time for him to be afraid, to acknowledge that these were his final moments. He didn't die alone, but in a place he knew, within earshot of one of the nation's most respected soldiers.

That he never regained consciousness was indisputable.

The nurse who immediately gave him mouth-to-mouth resuscitation was a 5 foot 8 inch tall, honey-skinned California beauty. A yard of molasses-colored hair slid down the middle of her back. He liked long hair. The medics came in minutes. The CPR continued manually, and later, by machine. Machines made him breathe. Machines made his heart beat. They moved him from one hospital to another; they did an emergency angioplasty. It was successful. Attempts to re-start his heart were not. He died. He just died—and left us all. The announcement made, the TV cameras and lights went out. Those waiting turned and left in disbelief to weep.

He was always in a hurry, so much to do, too much to do. Saving the world took time, and he had known there'd never be enough. "Gotta go," he'd announce, too soon after he'd arrived. "Gotta go, gotta go."

We never thought he meant forever.

EPILOGUE

I am of the opinion that my life belongs to the community, and as long as I live, it is my privilege to do for it whatever I can. I want to be thoroughly used up when I die, for the harder I work, the more I live. Life is no brief candle to me. It is a sort of splendid torch which I've got hold of for the moment, and I want to make it burn as brightly as possible before handing it on to future generations.

George Bernard Shaw

Former Sergeant Linda McClenahan, whom B.T. bullied into accepting the Chair of the California Vietnam War Memorial Commission, is now a nun. She did not travel from Wisconsin to my brother's funeral. She could hear him in that New York gangster voice saying, "Ya gonna waste $400 dollars to fly to California when you could give it to the poor?"

So, she and her fellow sisters gathered balloons in hand, to celebrate the man he'd been and to pray for the Almighty in the hopes that He or She was equal to the challenge to come. Then they went outside to let their colored missives loose. She said they headed west.

Lisa Bleich, whom B.T. hoped would have her mother's brains and legs, has both. A super student, who could have succeeded in any number of fields, she has chosen law. Her first job was with the Manhattan, New York DA. As an attorney, she has a special interest in domestic violence. As a college student, she regularly manned hotlines and worked in shelters for battered women.

"He taught me that one person actually can make a difference," she explains. He has remained a role model, mentor, and father-figure even in death. "Be a survivor," she hears him say. "Do it yourself! Get off your butt! Send in the application!" How she longs to have him know her as an adult. "How often I have wished I could just call and say, 'Hey I won my first case today. I got the fellowship. I hope you're going to be at my graduation.'"

He didn't live to see her graduate from American University Law School, but he had been at her high school graduation. He had given her $50 with the admonition that she only spend it having fun . . . that she, in my father's words, "waste it."

Marialis and I have been left to spoil ourselves. There'll be no more new stories to tell, one more outrageous than the other, no turning on the tube to catch him calling others to task. Marialis, now retired from Hewlett Packard, volunteers her time as a literacy tutor and works as a Child Advocate for victims of abuse. And I write a book about a hero so the nation will understand the stuff of which heroes are made

The California Vietnam War Memorial now bears the New York hero's name. It stands alone—white etching on a black stone block: *Captain Brien Thomas Collins, US Army*. Brien would be upset to be singled out in such a manner. Facing the monument, his friends have placed a bench, a place to sit and think about brave men and B.T. My parents would be proud. The Women's Vietnam Memorial was dedicated in November of the year B.T. died. His letter to the nurses was re-printed in the program. His friend, Ann Cunningham, wore his field jacket in the parade; the standing figure of the nurse in the monument will wear it in perpetuity. It was used to make the bronze casting for her uniform.

The new California Conservation Corps' Sacramento Headquarters has become the B.T. Collins Headquarters. The side of the building in which it was formerly housed still flaunts the painted mural of the Corps in action, and B.T.'s motto: *Hard Work, Low Pay, Miserable Working Conditions*. In a light-hearted ceremony, the dedication of the new building and its war room were made to Brien and his friend, Jack Dugan, respectively. "Malathion" punch was served in memory of B.T.'s stunt.

On his anniversary each year, friends gather at the cemetery to share remembered insults, and talk about the days when they opened a newspaper to see what he'd gone and done this time. They've planted myrtle round his grave. Sadly, the remains of Stan Atkinson's 34-year-old son now lie buried near by, as does the young wife of one of B.T.'s closest friends, Richard Steffen. Friend and fellow veteran, Mark Hite, has left his Vietnam combat ribbon nestled in the surrounding greenery. RTO Andy Anderson leaves a letter each year on the anniversary of the battle of "Crazy Horse:"

> May 17, 1994
>
> B.T., twenty-eight years ago today you and I and two under-strength platoons assaulted up a hill called "766" in "Happy Valley." You were twenty-six, a Second Lieutenant. I was twenty-one and a Spec-Four. For four days, we battled a full company of P.A.V.N.* We came close to death . . . oh, so close. Not a day goes by, I don't think about you. I miss you old friend. Things are dull here without you. I told people on your anniversary that you were my best friend, but I think it goes beyond best friends. We were part of each other, our lives bonded in the heat of battle.
>
> Andy—Concrete 37 India** No Regrets

House-boy, now man, Jon Walker has contributed a cased-in-plastic diary of his nine years with B.T. Collins, a poignant story of the morning calls to wake him for flights, and get him ready, urging Brien's prosthesis onto the bleeding stump of his leg; the tale of the hilarious shopping sprees: 50 cans of soup, 25 of Spam, 4 jars each of peanut butter and jelly, 48 rolls of toilet paper. "Why so much soup and toilet paper?" Jon would ask, unloading. "You never know,"

---

* People's Army of North Vietnam
** Andy's radio call sign

B.T. would reply, "there might be another war. There can always be another war."

Close friend Jan Young has faced breast cancer with B.T. bravado. "I know what he would say," she told friends imitating his sarcastic whine. "You've got one. You don't need two. You don't sit on it. You don't eat with it. What's the big deal?" She didn't think it was right to complain; he hadn't.

The city of Folsom, California has dedicated a wide and wonderful space, a "field of dreams" covered with flowers, to his memory and named it, aptly, "The B.T. Collins Memorial Park." The Sacramento Valley Vietnam Veterans' Chapter #500 Scholarship for university-bound children of veterans now bears his name.

And his alma mater, Santa Clara University, has established a new fund, "The Captain Hook Scholarship" for entering law students. Aspiring applicants must explain why B.T. would have wanted them to receive the financial aid, and demonstrate an understanding of, and a commitment to, public service. "He was blind to limitations," one wrote. "He would want me to get the scholarship because every word in my application has been spelled correctly," wrote another. One young woman told of meeting him, of telling him that she had truly tried to model her life after his own. "He must have been having a really bad day," she said, "because he just got very quiet. I had the feeling that I'd touched him deeply."

His high school, Archbishop Stepinac in White Plains, New York now offers a high school scholarship in his name as well. Brien would be pleased to know that one recipient has gone to one of the service academies. Another, a young athlete, contracted a rare disease while at hockey camp and has lost both arms and legs as a result.

The California Youth Authority's Sacramento Juvenile Facility has been re-named, "The B.T. Collins Juvenile Center." Within, a huge smiling picture of him looks down upon officers and offenders, and a photographic montage of his public service circles the entrance.

"B.T.'s commitment is every day of the year," California Correctional Peace Officers Union President, Don Novey remembers.

"There are others that have great heart. He has both heart and brain, and he uses them collectively to help the people. You'll notice," he added, "that I never speak of him in the past tense. He's the 'gift that keeps on giving.'"

Journalists have had their say as well. "There's a novelty in a witheringly honest politician," Robert Norse of the *San Francisco Examiner* comments. "In a self-pitying age when many Americans nurture their victimhood, Collins celebrated the possible. Sadly, San Francisco will never have a B.T. Collins—a boozing, womanizing, outrageously funny, kind, truth-telling, Jerry Brown side-kick Republican patriot, an atheist Christian warrior whose favorite cause, next to the Vietnam Memorial, was the support of battered women. San Francisco would never be able to deal with such seeming contradictions. And if B.T. were alive to read this column," Norse concludes, "I would be condemned as a 'whiny, mushy, liberal.'"

Brien's "life days" come and go and reporters note their passing. "Two years ago a hook-handed, one-legged, leather-lunged, flag-waving legislator dropped dead. But the truly unique thing about Brien T. Collins wasn't any of that stuff. It was his honesty, a *rare* and precious trait in any field, but especially in politics." Steve Wiegand, *San Jose Mercury*.

"Some called him arrogant," California publisher Winnie Comstock, reminds us, "but only those who never saw him weep. Rather than sink into despair, he lifted the despairing up. Often I was appalled at his outrageous spontaneity, while secretly I wished to have more of that quality myself."

In a touch of irony, only days after the murder of Nicole Brown Simpson, WEAVE opened its newly renovated 20,000-square-foot offices dedicated to the survivors and victims of violence and sexual assault. The new building was named the B.T. Collins Memorial Center, twenty seven years to the day after Brien was injured. The week before he died, Brien had promised to raise the money needed to complete the renovation. Before his funeral was over, every cent of that sum had been pledged. Coming in on weekends and at night, over 200 union laborers and Sacramento city employees, as well as members of the California Conservation Corps, eventually donated $350,000 in labor and materials to the project.

On Veterans Day, 1999, The Captain B.T. Collins US Army Reserve Training Center was dedicated in Sacramento. It is the largest, most technologically advanced facility of its type in existence. The pipes played. A garrison flag was unfurled. Rabbi Frazin, now retired, flew in from Arizona to deliver the invocation:

"Think me not irreverent, but B.T. would have loved this. Large leprechaun he, grinning gleefully at his people, the troops arrayed with the colors of the nation he loved. For you he would have died. For you he gave his limbs. For you he bore the pain. Listen, B.T. speaks," Frazin continued, "Live and love and laugh, and raise your eyes to hope. You were born to give, not take. Swear loyalty to those who ask only your best and return in kind. I am here among you. See me here, at your side, always."

John Grattan sang "Danny Boy." Marialis unveiled a large bronze bust of Brien sculpted by Garr Ulgalde. The pedestal beneath it is inscribed with four of B.T.'s favorite sayings: "The best friend, the one that will never let you down is integrity. You take the heat. You stand up for your own people. You dig your own foxhole."

I read one of his letters written while at the Officers Training School at Fort Sill, Oklahoma. At the end of the ceremony, a man in civilian clothes appeared before me. He began to talk about how much B.T. meant to veterans—half sentences that signaled his distress. I reached across the dais to hold this total stranger and he hugged me in return, his tears falling on my shoulder. Behind him, I spotted Joe Forgione, tanned from his native Florida, wearing the Silver Star he earned the day Sam Bird was hit.

In the tiny town of Stonington, Connecticut, the 4th of July parade begins. As it passes, the onlookers fall in line. The honor guard, dressed in colonial garb, looks old enough to have participated in the original event. Every man, woman, and child carries an American flag. Every man, woman, and child wears red, white, and blue—a

"Norman Rockwell" come to life. There are no bands. No high-stepping majorettes throw batons into the summer air. We walk to the town-square and there, circle around a revolutionary canon, and a group of citizens from eight to eighty alternately read The Declaration of Independence out loud. My eyes are too bright and I see my brother's face before me. His arms, flesh and plastic, are folded across his chest. He's wearing one of his "looks," the one that said, "Wonder." This is too much the generation to which he owed everything. We are together touched.

I sit in a darkened theater. On the screen, the terrified kids hit the beach. I am upset, if not destroyed, by all the bloodied water and flying, floating body parts. It is war as I have always believed it to be, chaotic, unpredictable—undiluted horror. I have read it all in Stephan Ambrose's *Citizen Soldiers*, and I think, *These brave young men, my God, what courage!* It is only later when those in search of Private Ryan die that I begin to lose control. I feel the bonds between Ryan and his men and I remember the biting humor that kept Brien and his friends from falling apart in each other's presence.

The doorbell rings on a gray Chicago day. The deliveryman hides behind a heap of flowers. It's not my birthday; it's my daughter's. I read the card: To Mother, Thanks for giving me life. I love you, Erin."

On election day in Maine, everyone is urged to vote. From pundits to politicians, faces on the television and voices on the radio stop short only of bribing Americans to exercise their constitutional right. Brien would be angry. This need to plead that one participate in the political process would disgust him. My husband and I approach the polls. Ahead of us, a rickety man pauses to catch his breath. He's ninety, if a day, and wherever he's going, we wonder if he'll make the journey. My husband reaches out to steady him.

"Looks like you could use some help" he suggests. "Where are you going?"

"To vote," the old man wheezes. "Got to vote. Always vote, you know."

This man's "always" has been a long, long time. I see Brien take his other arm.

"Hey, young fella. It's a great day to be an American," Brien growls, his "New York" cutting through the New England air.

"Eya," the man answers with a Mainer's "yes." "Eya, always great to be an American."

I wonder if the rickety man knows what he's done to keep my brother's dreams alive. I remember Rabbi Frazin's words, "[B.T.] believed in small things: a simple stripe of white, a smooth slash of red, a star-lit field blazoned with blue, *and you and you and you* . . ."

The best of B.T. Collins? That he burned Shaw's "splendid torch" so brightly; that he left a legacy of obligation to future generations. He understood what it meant to be an American, and the payback that privilege engendered. We who remain would do well to seize the torch, remember the man, and live his message: *Is the world a better place because you are there? Is the world a better place because you are there?*

In the end beneath the hoopla and hurrah, beyond the warrior, inside the hero, he was only human.

"I hope," he confided, near the last of his days, to the only friend to whom such a confession was possible, "I just hope they won't forget me."

Never.

ACKNOWLEDGEMENTS

Over the past 14 years I have conducted hundreds of interviews and reviewed stacks of articles, letters, speeches and videotapes about or created by my brother. This book would not have been possible without the encouragement and assistance of B.T.'s many friends and supporters. If I've forgotten anyone, my sincere apologies. Thank you!

Alma Acala, Linda Adams, Art Agnos, Dean George Alexander (Santa Clara School of Law), Linda Allen, Professor Lillian Bevier Altry (Santa Clara School of Law), Bill (Andy) Anderson, Mike Antonovich, Stan Atkinson, Mercedes Azar, Judy Balmain, John Balzar, John Banuelos, Chuck Barry, William Bennett, Lynn Bennish-Hester, Rodger Bergmann, Annette Bird, Linda Bleich, Margaret Bohl, Jost Braun, Patrick Brosnan, Edmund G. (Jerry) Brown, Timothy Buckley, Jug Burkett, Jim Burton, John Caffrey, Bruce Carpenter, Dennis Carpenter, Peggy Carretta, Jerry Chong, Bill Choquette, Robert Christensen, George Christopher, Thomas Close, Henry Cook, Milton Cooper, Sheriff Glen Craig, Dick Cunha, Ann Cunningham, Eliot Daum, Joseph DeBriyn, Ernest DeGasparis, George and Gloria Deukmejian, James Diepenbrock, Norma Dillon, Carrie Dolan, Lisa Dowdswell, Patricia Dugan, Dick Ehrlich, Judge Frank Elia, Michael Elliot, Professor Mary Emery (Santa Clara School of Law), Gary Ethan, Jerri Ewen, Vic Fazio, Rhonda Fisher, Franklin Flocks, Matt Fong, Joe Forgione, Rabbi Lester Frazin, Steven Galef, Joseph Galloway, Ruben Garcia, Professor George Giacomini (Santa Clara University), Reverend Paul Goda (Santa

Clara Law School), Tom Griffin, Adriana Guiranturco, Tom Hayes, Christine Hayes, Edwin Heafry, Mark Helprin, Betsy and Mark Hite, Sister Kathleen Horgan, S.M., Peter Hubert, Gail Jones, Joe and Mari Kalashian, Professor Jerry Kasner (Santa Clara University), Michael Kelley, Michael Lambert, Susie Lang, Mary Jo Levinger, Sidney Levitsky, M.D., Susanne Levitsky, Linda Lezotte, Rosalie Long, Kerry McDonnell, Mitch Lyons, Susan Martin, Barbara Metzger, Linda McClenahan, Dennis Nino, Don Novey, Victor O'Beirne, Professor Timothy O'Keefe, Pat O'Laughlin, John Orr, Dean Parker, John Philp, Professor Marc Poche, Dave Porreca, Judge Gene Premo, Bishop Francis Quinn, Stephan Quinn, Dixie Reid, Mike and Judy Reid, Susan Roach, Robert Rocha, Ed Rollins, Nora Romero, Ginger Rutland, James Sargent, M.D., Deborah Saunders, Alan Schnazi, Linda Seramur, Bob Simpson, George Skelton, Katherine Sprinkles, Richard Steffen, Richard Stewart, M.D., Vice Admiral James Stockdale, Mitch Stogner, Associate Dean George Strong (Santa Clara School of Law), Richard Sullivan, M.D., Reverend Thomas D. Terry, S.J. (Santa Clara University), Bambi Tidwell, Peg Tomilson, Ken Tomlinson, J.P. Tremblay, Jim Trotter, Dean Gerald Uelman (Santa Clara School of Law), Brian Van de Camp, Louis Vismara, M.D., Jon Walker, Eleanor Walsh, Dan Walters, Richard Watters, Senator James Webb, Barry Weissman, Thomas Welch, M.D., Judge James Wiederschall, Pete and Gayle Wilson, Sylvan Wincour, Jan Young, Jerome Young.

AUTHOR NOTES

Chapter I The Wake

Chapter II The Funeral

15   *He Believed in Small Things* reprinted with permission of Rabbi Lester Frazin.

17-23   Eulogies from speakers were recorded on tape and reviewed by the author. Remarks by both Governor Wilson and former Governor Brown were quoted and excerpted in the *Sacramento Bee*.

21   Former Army nurse Ann C. Cunningham, a beloved Vietnam veteran served as the California and Virginia coordinator for the Vietnam Women's Memorial Project. She died unexpectedly in September 2007 while attending a veterans' reunion in Kentucky. Ann will be remembered as family to the author and her sister. She is one of the "Annies" mentioned in the dedication.

25   Reprinted with permission of Gayle Wilson.

Chapter III The Family: Growing Up Collins

33   Letters from J.J. Collins to students and parents are in the author's collection.

Chapter IV The Family: Act II

44   An account of Brien's speech to the 1989 graduates of The State University of New York's Potsdam College appeared in Potsdam's *Daily Courier-Observer*, "Collins: You Have No Right to Waste Your Life, May 9, 1993.

46   "Aunt Kathy stories" recounted by the author's friend Linda Seramur and Katherine's son, Dr. Thomas Welch, respectively.

Chapter V Vietnam

53   Brien's quote about going back appeared in "Vietnam Vet Has Answer to Hypocrisy," *Army Times*, June 1, 1992.

56...   Excerpts from 150 letters from Brien during his military service have been edited and sequenced for the Vietnam chapters.

60   Brien's initial attempts to make the Army send him to Vietnam are described in a March 26, 1992 *USA Today* article, "I have no quarrel with the draft dodgers."

61   The descriptions of Camp Radcliffe and An Khe come from "So Proudly He Served: The Sam Bird Story," Annette Bird and Tim Prouty, Okarche Books, Wichita, Kansas, 1993 which was dedicated to Brien.

Chapter VI Sam Bird

68   B.T. had talked about Sam Bird throughout his life to audiences of family, friends, veterans groups, the CCC, and supporters. The descriptions of their first meeting, their relationship, their differences, and the respect B.T. had for Sam's courage and leadership has been told and retold. In 1989, B.T. authored an article for the *Readers Digest* recounting his memories of Sam Bird.

69   Dave Porreca also supplied specific information on the role of a forward observer, the 1st Air Cavalry, and the two phases of the Vietnam war.

69 Valuable information about the life of a combat soldier and the specific phases of the war came from Michael Kelley, a Vietnam War artist based in Sacramento. Henry Cook and Dave Porreca who served with B.T. in Special Forces made clear the differences between life with the First Air Cavalry and the responsibilities of Special Forces teams.

71 The battle, "Crazy Horse," is described in "Battles In The Monsoon," by S.L. A. Marshall, William Morrow and Company, Inc., New York, 1967. A two hour audio-tape of a first hand account of that battle was recorded by Andy Anderson for the author.

75 "Courage of Sam Bird," B.T. Collins, © *Reader's Digest*, May 1989. Reprinted with permission.

81 Letter to Sam Bird's parents is included in "So Proudly He Served . . ." op cit.

Chapter VII Special Forces

83 Repeated interviews with those who served with him in the First Air Cavalry and Special Forces provided both personal and general accounts of B.T.'s in-country experiences. These include Dean Parker (deceased 2007), Joe Forgione, Dave Porreca, Henry Cook, Andy Anderson, Ruben Garcia and Gary Ethan.

95 All attempts to interview and thank "T-burg" have been unsuccessful. If you know of his whereabouts, please contact the publisher.

Chapter VIII Valley Forge

97 A phone interview with author, now Senator James Webb made clear the refusal by the troops to honor the Special Forces policy concerning the transport of troops too severely injured to be moved.

100 A transcript of B.T.'s entire medical records provided by the Army were explained in detail by former Army nurse Anne Cunningham. Ann supplied information on the Army field hospitals and general medical care. The author also interviewed the surgeon who amputated B.T.'s leg, Dr. Sidney Levitsky, at The Harvard Medical School, where he was Chief of Cardiothoracic Surgery at Boston's Deaconess Hospital at the time of the interview.

102 The nurse who took care of B.T. initially in Vietnam, Julia Gilje, met him several years later in Hawaii. This interview was taped.

103 Ruben Garcia provided a written account of his search for Brien and their time together in the evacuation hospital.

107 Drs. James Sargent, Richard Sullivan, and William Stewart provided written details of B.T.'s care and their experiences with him.

111 Patient, Patrick Brosnan was the source for what the patients endured including information on prostheses.

112 Stories about John Philp came from B.T., from John's letters which B.T. saved, and later letters to this author.

112 B.T.'s ability to cheer other patients was described in *The Valley Forge Hospital Newsletter*, "Numbah One at VFGH: Good Example Set by Officer Patient Here," Fall, 1967.

Chapter IX Mending

114 Surgery story supplied by Drs. Sullivan and Sargent.

116 Text of B.T.'s letter to Dr. Sargent's wife was supplied to the author.

118-119 The description of the two shows put on for the patients by Brien's friends: "Just What the Doctor Ordered for Vets," Theo Wilson, the *New York Daily News*, December 1, 1967 and "Troupers & Readers In Really Big Show," Theo Wilson, the *New York Daily News*, December 18, 1967. "Girls Give Show for Maimed Veteran," appeared simultaneously in the *Reporter Dispatch*, White Plains, New York.

122 The story about Brien's childhood friend, Dick Ehrlich, first appeared in the *Wall Street Journal*, November 11, 1987, "In Praise of a Comrade Back Home," and was later reprinted in *Reader's Digest*, titled, "My Friend in Need," April, 1988.

Chapter X Santa Clara

125 A description of B.T.'s feelings about Santa Clara is noted in "The Outrageous B.T.—Brown's Strong Left Arm," Cynthia Roberts, the *California Journal*, December 1977.

127 Background re Santa Clara University was provided by the University Alumni Relations Office.

129-140 Details of B.T.'s life as an undergraduate and law student at Santa Clara as well as life on campus during the "anti-war" sixties came from interviews and correspondence with classmates, professors, and deans.

130 Professor Mary Emery was one of B.T.'s supporters and later friends. It was she who suggested B.T. to Marc Poche for a position on Governor Jerry Brown's staff.

130 Professor George Giocomini supplied a copy of his letter to this author.

133 This story was supplied by Barry Weissman.

133 Professor Lillian Bevier is now at the University of Virginia Law School.

134 Pat O'Laughlin, who told the "blood donor" story at a B.T. fundraising roast, later served as Mayor of Los Gatos, California.

134 Professor Marc Poche is the source of this B.T. story.

135 The "broken leg" incident was recounted by a number of law students when asked for their favorite B.T. story.

Chapter XI Graduation

139 B.T.'s work as President of the SBA is described in "S.B.A. Board Tackles Budget," *University of Santa Clara School of Law Newsletter*, September 19, 1972.

144-146   The complete transcript of the swearing in ceremony is in the author's file. The ceremony was also described in a June 1994 *San Jose Post-Record* article, "He Raised His Right Hook And Was Admitted to Practice Law."

Chapter XII B.T. and Brown

150   *Cosmopolitan* had included Governor Brown in its listing of "The 35 Sexiest Men in the World" in an April 1977 issue. B.T.'s letter to the editor was printed in its July 1977 issue.

151   "Bourbon chaser after a cup of herbal tea . . ." comment is from "Brash B.T. Collins Handles People for Brown Camp," Carrie Dolan, the *Wall Street Journal*, July 19, 1982.

151-164   Interviews with a number of personnel from Governor Jerry Brown's office and B.T.'s office staff and friends provided the background for this chapter.

160   "Racing Room," Jack Clifford, *Quarter Horse of the Pacific Coast*, April 1978.

160   Prince Charles' visit was covered in many newspapers including the International Herald Tribune. The author's favorite is the *Sacramento Bee* account.

163   The "respirator story" was included in "Advice from B.T. to New Chief of Staff," *California Journal*, 1982.

Chapter XIII The California Conservation Corps

165-178   Note: Over 400 articles written about the California Conservation Corps were reviewed by the author for this chapter. Susan Levitsky was especially helpful tracking down information.

169   B.T.'s swallow of malathion was widely reported in California and national media. See "A Toast to Malathion," the *San Francisco Chronicle*, July 16, 1981.

169   *A Law Professor's Lament* reprinted with permission of Professor Lillian Bevier.

171   "A Viet Vet Fights to make Gov. Brown's work corps a success," *People*, May 1981; "B.T. and The CCC," Mark Wexler, *National Wildlife*, February 1982; "Not Too Hot to Handle," Jan Mason, *Life*, November 1982; "The Fire Season," Dru & Associates, documentary, 1982.

175   "Brown's New Staff Chief Has No Love for the Boss," Bella Stumbo, the *Los Angeles Times*, November 1, 1981.

177   "Brash B.T. Collins Handles the People for the Brown Camp," op cit.

Chapter XIV Letters, Heroes, Monuments, Memories

179-193   Much information on this time came from B.T. and his family. Additional sources: his close personal friends Dick Cunha, Stan Atkinson; fellow brokers at Kidder Peabody (now UBS) Mike Lambert and James

Diepenbrock; Dennis Carpenter, Linda McClenahan, Jan Young, Linda Seramur and daughter Lisa Bleich, Ed Rollins, and James Webb.

180 Jon Walker additionally left a story documenting his years with B.T. at his gravesite.

181 "Brown's Brash Aide Handles the People . . . ," Carrie Dolan, op cit.

183-186 B.T.'s letters to Ronald Reagan are cataloged at the Reagan Presidential Library.

188 "60's Generation Shouldn't Be So Smug," Michael Medved, the *Wall Street Journal*, April 28, 1986.

Chapter XV The Return

196-201 *The Return to Vietnam* was filmed in June 1987 by KCRA, an NBC affiliate based in Sacramento. B.T. was accompanied by news anchor Stan Atkinson and a team of photographers. A day-to-day commentary of their time in Vietnam was provided in writing and in person by Stan Atkinson. The films of the trip were divided into nightly segments and initially shown on California television. After including B.T.'s trip to The Wall, video tapes were produced and distributed throughout the country to raise funds for the California Vietnam War Memorial. An in-depth account of Brien's visit to The Wall was provided by Congressman Vic Fazio.

204 "Love in the 60's: Chicks and Nurses," B.T. Collins, the *Wall Street Journal*, letter to the editor, June 10, 1986.

Chapter XVI Carrying the Torch

207 Source of chapter quote: "Vietnam Taught Collins to Manage by Example," Joyce Terhaar, *Sacramento Bee*, February 10, 1989.

208 The Memorial dedication was filmed by KCRA, Sacramento. Approximately 350 articles were written about the dedication, more about the Memorial itself. Stan Atkinson was especially helpful in contacting information sources for the author.

212... Information on fund raising events and speeches contributed by: Stan Atkinson, Ann Cunningham, Jan Young, Alma Acala, and Nora Romero.

209 B.T.'s remarks to former governor George Deukmejian were recounted in a letter forwarded to the author.

210 Gloria Deukmejian supplied the "tattoo" story in an interview with the author.

212 Mitch Stogner and Frank Christensen described the stunt plane incident.

213 The Bull Feathers' late nights with members of Congress came from Dean Parker who had served with B.T. in the 1st Air Cavalry.

213 Re the "Joe Biden" and "goat and bottle of Jim Beam comments. "B.T. Collins: The Man Behind the Mouth," Trinda Pasquet, *Sacramento Union*, June 4, 1989.

Chapter XVII Politics

217 Source of chapter quote: "A Veterans' Day Message, B.T Collins, *Wilson Weekly California Report*, November 9, 1991.

217 Re the "Saddam Hussein comment. "What They're Saying Here About the Gulf Crisis," J.B. Lasica, *Sacramento Bee*, December 16, 1990.

218 "If My Marine Son Is Killed . . ." Alex Molnar, the *New York Times*, letter to the editor, August 2, 1990.

219 Larry King show, circa 1991.

221 "When They Come Home," © *Readers Digest*, March 1991. Portions reprinted with permission. This article was reprinted as a full page in the *New York Times* and *USA Today*, March 7, 1991.

224 Re McDonalds comment: "Collins Demands Literacy at CYA," Jim Trotter, *Sacramento Bee*, April 19, 1991.

224 *"Throwing the Book at Them,"* Editorial, Daily News, Woodland Hills, CA, April 21, 1991.

225 *ABC Evening News with Peter Jennings*, 1990.

225 Phone interview with George Skelton.

225 "Collins Demands Literacy at CYA," op cit.

Chapter XVIII The Elections

228-241 Background information sources for this chapter: B.T. Collins, Tom Griffin, Stan Atkinson, Tom Hayes, Richard Steffen, Norma Romero, Alma Acala, Jan Young, John Banuelos, Judy Balmain, Linda Seramur, Elliot Daum, and Dick Cunha. Dick Cunha later served as the Executor of B.T.'s estate and stored B.T.'s papers and memorabilia for several years as did Judy Balmain so that they could be reviewed by the author in preparation for writing this book.

229 Nancy Pelosi's comment was included in the Congressional Record.

232 Source for comment "pimp for that whore . . .": "Candidate Collins: He's a Wilson Loyalist and He's Proud of It," *San Diego Evening Tribune*, August 23, 1991.

232 Quote "How Disappointed . . ." included in letter to the editor, *Carmichael Times*, 1992.

234 Campaign literature circulated by supporters of Barbara Alby.

235-236 Richardson's original letter was dated July 7, 1982 while B.T. was in charge of the CCC.

235 "Pastors for Alby," letter containing H.L. Richardson's letter was circulated by religious right during the campaign.

238 These letters are in the author's personal file.

239 "Behind the Lines with B.T. Collins," Peter H. King, the *Los Angeles Times*, May 31, 1992.

241 Defending Jerry Brown: "Brown Aides, Police Deny Party Drugs," Steven A. Capps and Tupper Hull, the *Los Angeles Times*, 1992; "Brown Denies

Drugs Used at His Home," Thomas B. Rosenstiel and Melissa Healy, the *Los Angeles Times*, 1992. Also comments on Brown: "Who Is Jerry Brown? Voices from Past Show Why Man Is an Enigma," Robert Reinhold, the *Los Angeles Times* and the *New York Times*, April 2, 1992.

Chapter XIX The Politician

242 Source of the chapter quote: "Leadership: The Essential Need to Establish Integrity,' Mark Simon, the *Peninsula Times-Tribune* April 29, 1992.

242-259 Background for this chapter: Nora Romero, Alma Acala, Richard Steffens, Jim Burton, Sheriff Glenn Craig, Gayle Wilson, Don Novey, Mike Antonovich, Ron Texiera, Bill Shanley, Ann Cunningham, Judy Balmain, Stan Atkinson, Tom Griffin, Gail Jones, Sister Kathleen Horgan, Susie Lang, Jan Young, Peg Tomilison, Tom Flanagan, Christine Hayes, Patricia Dugan, Ken Tomlinson.

243 B.T. later wrote a letter to General Ronald R. Blanck, Commander, Walter Reed Army Medical Center, thanking him for the care he had received and apologizing for having tied up the switchboards when Rush Limbaugh announced on national radio that B.T. was a patient there.

247 "B.T. Learns to Adjusts to Life As a State Assemblyman," Jon Matthews, *Sacramento Bee*, January 17, 1993.

250 Don Novey, former President of the California Correctional Officers Association.

251 Source of the "Birkenstocks" comment: "Capt. Hook: Life of party," Michael Ackley, the *Sacramento Union*, December 5, 1990.

252 B.T.'s birthday booklet was titled "I'm Hooked on a Dream" and contained greetings from many supporters including: Congresswoman Nancy Pelosi, Governor George Deukmejian, KCRA, Congressman Robert T. Matsui, reporters at the *Los Angeles Times*, The Vietnam Women's Memorial Project, Santa Clara University, The California Correctional Peace Officers Association, etc. Also see, "Collins Flying Leap Marks Event," Michael Ackley, the *Sacramento Union*, October 10, 1990.

255 B.T.'s response to Joel Kotkin's attack on Wilson was not published.

258 Dr. Luis Vismara, B.T.'s personal cardiologist talked with the author, discussing B.T.'s vision of his own health, as did Ann Cunningham and Judy Balmain.

BIBLIOGRAPHY

Ackley, Michael. "Capt. Hook: Life of Party." *Sacramento Union*, December 5, 1990.

——"Collins Stays Our Hot Topic." *Sacramento Union*, March 24, 1993.

Advocate. University of Santa Clara Law School, "B.T. on the CCC, Medfly." November, 1981.

Ahrendes, Vern. "Politician's Rare Act of Courage Inspires Reporter." *Five Cities Times-Press-Recorder*, January 17, 1992.

Anderson, Mark. "B.T. Challenges Detractors: Sock It to Me." *Press-Tribune*, (CA), December 30, 1991.

Anderson, Peter. "And to Play the Part of Guv, How About . . . ?" *Sacramento Bee*, June 2, 1982.

Associated Press, Connecticut Post. "B.T. Collins, 52, War Hero Politico." March 22, 1993.

Atkinson, Rollie. "B.T. Only Sounds Like a Contradiction." *Heraldsburg Tribune*, January 25, 1989.

Auburn Journal (CA). Editorial, "B.T. He Was a Hot Media Attraction." March 21, 1993.

Balzar, John. "Ah, Yes, We Remember Him Well." *Los Angeles Times*, April 31, 1992.

——"Jerry's California: Best, Worst of Times." *Los Angeles Times*, April 5, 1992.

——"Brown Does His Duty for CCC." *San Francisco Chronicle*, March 28, 1980.

——"Brown's Most Conservative Aide." *San Francisco Chronicle*, December 17, 1977.

Barkas, Sherry. "B.T. Gets Serious About State Issues During town Meeting." *Orangevale News*, May 6, 1992.

Bass, Thomas A. "A Reborn CCC Shapes Young Lives With an Old Idea." *Smithsonian*, August 18, 1982.

Bird, Anita and Tim Prouty. *So Proudly He Served: The Sam Bird Story.* Wichita, Kansas: Okarche Books, 1993.

Blakeslee, Sandra. "Why a Long-Gone Limb Still Aches." *New York Times*, November 26, 1991.

Bonnivier, Carlene Sobrino. "Whatever Happened to Jerry Brown?" *Sacramento Magazine*, September, 1984.

Brazil, Eric. "Conservation Corps' New Director Gives It a New Life." *Stockton Record*, January 15, 1980.

Brinkley, David and Garrett Utley. "B.T. and the C's." *NBC News Magazine*, May 26, 1981.

Brown, Marc. "A Soldier's Second Battle." *Gannett Westchester Newspapers*, April 19, 1988.

Buckley, Jr., William F. *Gratitude: Reflections on What We Owe to Our Country.* New York: Random House, 1990, p. 92.

Caen, Herb. "Pull Cord to Stop Press." *San Francisco Chronicle*, February 22, 1978.

Calaveras (CA) Enterprise. "Democratic Central Committee Hears CCC Chief." March 14, 1979.

California Journal. "Advice from B.T. to New Chief of Staff." 1982.

——Editorial Page. "Fact Check of the Month." (complaints by opponent Barbara Alby re B.T.), May 1992.

Caltrux Newsletter. Obituary. Assemblyman B.T. Collins, March 1993.

Canfield, Roger. "Collins Candidacy an Inside Job." *Sacramento Union*, June 13, 1991.

——"Demos Don't Mind Collins One Bit." *Sacramento Union*, June 18, 1991.

Capa, Steven A. "In the Limelight: Swashbuckling Director of the State's CCC." *San Francisco Examiner*, June 1, 1981.

Carmichael Times. "In Memory of Assemblyman B.T. Collins." March 30, 1993.

Carroll, James R. "California Conservation Corps Volunteers Learn Early Just Who Is in Charge of the C's." *Orange Country Register*, March 1, 1981.

Carroll, Joe. "Political Bombshells Bursting in Air." *Auburn (CA) Sentinel*, June 14, 1991.

Carson, Daniel C. "Wilson Team Could Seize Solution for the Budget, But It's a Gamble." *Sacramento Union*, May 25, 1991.

Clifford, Jack. "Racing Room." *Quarter Horse of the Pacific Coast*, April 1978.

Cole, Carolyn. "Remembering a Class Act." *Sacramento Bee*, March 21, 1993.

Collins, B.T. "Another Payment on Freedom's Price Has Just Been Paid." *The Orange County Register*, Opinion, March 8, 1991.

——"Bring Back Work Ethic—Third Place Is Not OK." *Sacramento Bee*, August 10, 1981.

——"I Have No Quarrel with the Draft Dodgers." *USA Today*, March 26, 1992.

——"In Praise of a Comrade Back Home." *Wall Street Journal*, November 11, 1987. (Later reprinted in *Reader's Digest* as "My Friend in Need," April 1988.)

——"Johnny Gets a Second Chance to Show What He Can Do." *Sacramento Union*, November 25, 1980.

——"One Free Punch." (Invitation), December 11, 1991.

——"Raise Your Voice America, and Honor Them." *Highlander*, Guest Commentary, Highlands, NC, March 12, 1991.

——"Rekindle Respect for Human Dignity. Letter to Editor, *Sacramento Bee*, June, 1982.

——"Remembering How Vietnam Veterans Were Treated." *Daily Evening Item*, Lynn, MA, March 8, 1991.

——"Service to Country." *Southeast News*, (Downey, CA), May 1981.

——"The Courage of Sam Bird." © *Readers Digest*, May 1989.

——"The Shirkers in the Army Deserve Special Derision." *San Jose Mercury News*, April 9, 1992.

——"Treat Gulf's Vets Better than Vietnam's." *Standard Examiner*, Ogden, UT, March 10, 1991.

——"Vietnam Vet Has Answer to Hypocrisy." *Army Times*, June 1, 1992.

——"When They Come Home." © *Readers Digest*, April 1991. (Also printed in the *New York Times* and *USA Today*, March 7, 1991.)

Comstock, Winnie. Editorial. "B.T. Collins—One Man Can Make a Difference." *Comstock Publishing*, April, 1993.

Conner, Carolyn. "A Conversation with B.T. Collins." *Peacekeeper*, May, 1991.

Cook, Gale. "How the Prince Got a Free Lunch—The Secretaries Did It." *San Francisco Examiner*, October 31, 1977.

Cooper, Claire. "B.T. Urges Honesty, Candor in Handling Press." *Sacramento Bee*, November 20, 1981.

Creamer, Anita. "Goodbye, B.T.—A Community Returns Collins' Touch." *Sacramento Bee*, March 25, 1993.

Cruz, Many. "B.T. Collins Called to Run for Assembly." *San Diego Daily*, August 26, 1991.

Cunningham, Ann. "A Different Viewpoint on the Gulf Wars." *Sacramento Union*, January 28, 1991.

Daily Courier-Observer. "Collins: You Have No Right To Waste Your Life." Potsdam, NY, May 9, 1993.

Daily News (Woodland Hills, CA). Editorial, "Throwing the Book at Them." April 21, 1991.

Dean, Paul. "Quiet Battle Goes On for Vietnam Memorial." *Los Angeles Times*, May 26, 1986.

Dobbin, Muriel. "B.T. Does His Drinking and Listening for California's Governor." *Baltimore Sun*, February 3, 1978.

Dolan, Carrie. "Brash B.T. Collins Handles the People for the Brown Camp." *Wall Street Journal*, July 19, 1992

——"Burying Tradition, Forward-Looking People Opt for Fun Funerals." *Wall Street Journal*, May 20, 1993.

——"Private Citizen Jerry Brown Divides His Time Between Law Practice, Nonprofit Think Tanks." *Wall Street Journal*, February 19, 1985.

Domrose, Cathy. "Collins Scoffs at Liberty Without Responsibility." *Turlock Journal(CA)*, May 2, 1985.

Dru & Associates. "The Fire Season." Documentary, 1982.

Egan, Erin. "B.T. Talks, Kiwanis Listen." *Placer Herald* (CA), August 20, 1991.

Endicott, William. "Candidate B.T. Collins Says He Isn't an Atheist." and "Religious Right Misses on B.T." *Auburn Journal* (CA), July 17, 1991.

Fallon, D'Arcy. "Viet Vet Battles for a California Memorial." *San Francisco Examiner*, November 29, 1987.

Fleeman, Michael. "Advocate of Spraying Drank [M]alathion." *San Bernadino County Sun*, February 6, 1990.

——"B.T. Collins Says He's Living Proof [M]alathion poses no Health Threats." *Sacramento Record*, February 27, 1990.

Francis, Peter L. "Conservation Corps 'Father' Visits Family." *Stockton Record*, March 26, 1986.

Frein, Joe. "Corps Workers Bleed for State." *San Jose Mercury*, January 15, 1981.

Fremstad, Lee. "Anderson Visits Capitol and Courts Brown Aide." *Sacramento Bee*, June 12, 1989.

French, Barbara. "B.T. Collins: "Mover and Shaker for Brown." *San Jose Mercury*, April 19, 1978.

Furgurson, E.B. "Lake Tahoe—Playing for High Stakes." *National Geographic*, March 1992.

Gibson, Steve. "N.J. Group Gets Advice on Vietnam Memorial." *Sacramento Bee*, August 30, 1989.

——"Vietnam Veterans' Memorial Presented to the State." *Sacramento Bee*, May 29, 1989.

Gillam, Jerry and Carl Ingram. "Brash Legislator B.T. Collins Dies of a Heart Attack." *Los Angeles Times*, March 20, 1993.

Gillam, Jerry. "Collins Again Locked in Tough Fight with Alby." *Los Angeles Times*, May 19, 1992.

Green, Blake. "Brown's Outrageous Republican." *San Francisco Chronicle*, April 5, 1979.

Green, Stephen. "State Treasurer Hires Gadfly Collins." *Sacramento Bee*, January 18, 1989.

Greene, State Senator Leroy F. "And Who Will Weep for Me?" *Sacramento Union*, March 26, 1993.

Growald, R.H. "X-Rated Aide Will Simply Be Ex." *San Diego Union*, November 15, 1982.

Hartford Courant. "Brown—Man of Many Persuasions." September 5, 1977.

Hasemyer, David. "Wilson Mourns the Death of a Friend." *San Diego Union Tribune*, March 21, 1993.

Hirth, Diane. "Conservationist Group Is Hailing the Hard Life." *Fort Lauderdale News and Sun Sentinel*, April 24, 1983.

Holub, Kathy. "The Once and Future Brown." *San Jose Mercury News*, June 22, 1986.

Hull, Tupper. "Farewell to a Maverick." *San Francisco Examiner*, March 25 1993.

Jacobs, John. "The Genuine Political Article." Politics in Review: *Sacramento Bee*, March 25, 1993.

Johannsen, Betty. "B.T. Collins' Private War." *Sacramento Magazine*, June 1981.

Jones, Robert A. "The Bitter Season." *Los Angeles Times Magazine*, September 17, 1992.

Jones, Steven. "B.T. Remembered with Affection." *Auburn Journal (CA)*, March 21, 1993.

Joyce, Pat. "B.T. Collins Just Being Good Soldier." *Sacramento Union*, June 12, 1991.

KCRA TV, Sacramento. "Return to Vietnam." Videotape Series, June 1987.

King, Peter H. "Behind the Lines with B.T. Collins." *Los Angeles Times*, May 31, 1992.

Kinsella, Jim. "Athens on the Sacramento." *Sacramento Magazine*, December, 1985.

Krebs, Albin. "Notes on People." (Prince Charles California Visit) *New York Times*, September 28, 1977.

La Vally, Rebecca. "Conservation Corps Leader Tough on Himself." *San Jose Mercury News*, April 22, 1979.

LaPointe, Mary Anne. "CCC Chief Gives Rotary Sales Pitch." *San Luis Obispo Country Telegram Tribune*, January 15, 1980.

Leepson, Marc. "Larger Than Life." *WVA Veteran*, Washington, DC, March 1994.

Lopez, Valentin. "Helping the Medicine Go Down." *Sacramento Bee*, March 28, 1992.

Los Angeles Examiner. Editorial. "Our State CCC Is the Only Hero of the Medfly Farce." July 23, 1981.

Los Angeles Times. "Collins Takes Leave from CYA to Run for Assembly." June 12, 1991.

——"Reviving the American Work Ethic." August 24, 1990.

Mathews, Jay. "Hard Work, Low Pay, Miserable Conditions Popular in California Corps." *Washington Post*, March 26, 1982.

Matthews, Jon et al. "Collins Kept a Frantic Pace." *Sacramento Bee*, March 21, 1993.

——"B.T. Learns to Adjust to Life as State Assemblyman." *Sacramento Bee*, January 17, 1993.

McGrath, Dan. "B.T Had the Power to Make You Listen, Think." *Sacramento Bee*, March 22, 1993.

McKinley, Clark. "Reincarnated Conservation Corps Provides Outdoor Work for Youth." *Houston Post*, December 4, 1983.

McSwain, Christopher. "B.T. Collins Expresses Views on CA's Higher Education System." *State Hornet*, October 13, 1992.

Medved, Michael. "60's Generation Shouldn't Be So Smug." *Wall Street Journal*, April 28, 1986.

Mercury News Wire Service. "Political Holy War Targets Wilson Pal." July 23, 1991.

Minutes of The Memorial Commission meetings. November 9, 1984 . . . . May 9, 1988.

Mitchell, Larry. "The Bell Tolled for 5,822." *Butte County Notebook*, December 13, 1988.

Molnar, Alex. "If My Marine Son Is Killed . . ." *New York Times*, August 23, 1990.

Morse, Robert. "A Man Who Lived." *San Francisco Examiner*, March 25 1993.

Mountain Democrat and Placerville Times. "Memorial Dedication: A Time of Healing." December 12, 1988.

Neuman, A. Lin. "B.T. and the Big Guy, Cocktails with Rush." *Sacramento News and Review*, December 12, 1991.

New York Times. Obituary. "Brien T. Collins, 52, California Lawmaker." March 22, 1993.

Newman, Maria. "Behind Each Name a Young Man's Life." *Sacramento Bee*, December 10, 1988.

O'Toole, Patricia. "The Other Salvation Army." *Lears* magazine, December 11, 1991.

Oakland Tribune. "CCC Garners High Praise as Bill Passes." March 25, 1980.

——"Hippies in Woods' Program Matures Under Deukmejian." June 1, 1989.

——Editorial. "Teaching Youths How to Work." January 1, 1980.

Office of the Governor (CA). "Biography of Governor Pete Wilson," August, 1991.

Ontario Daily Report (CA). "CCC Director Challenges Recruits." January 14, 1980.

Otten, Michael. "Malathion Safe? B.T Would Drink to That." *Sacramento Union*, March 11, 1990.

——"Official Calls for End to Mass Hysteria." *Bakersfield Californian*, March 11, 1990.

Packer, Bill. "B.T. Collins: The Capitol's Wild and Crazy Guy." *Sun Valley News*, January 7, 1979.

Pasquet, Trinda. "The Man Behind the Mouth." *Sacramento Union*, June 4, 1989.

Patterson, Darby. "St. Peter Gave B.T. a 2nd Chance." *Sacramento Union*, March 21, 1993.

People and *International Herald Tribune*, "Prince Charles May Get Sandwiches in California." September 29, 1977.

People. "A Viet Vet Fights to Make Gov. Brown's Work Corps a Success." May 4, 1981.

Philadelphia Bulletin Sunday Magazine. "This War Has Been Hard on Legs." December 17, 1967.

Quintana, Joe. "Meet the Irreverent Irishman Running State's War on Crime." *Los Angeles Herald Examiner*, April 15, 1981.

Racquette, Potsdam College (Potsdam, NY) student newspaper, "B.T. Collins: Making a Difference." April 25, 1985.

Rafferty, Michael. "Fund Drive Report." *Mountain Democrat*, January 13, 1988.

Record (Stockton, CA). Editorial. "Vietnam Vets: Lest We Forget." December 10, 1988.

Reporter Dispatch (White Plains, NY). "Girls Give Show for Maimed Veteran." December 18, 1967.

Richardson, Senator H.L. "B.T. or Not B.T., That Is the Question!" *Sacramento Union*, June 19, 1991.

——*Richardson Special Report*. February 29, 1980.

Richie, David et al. "B.T. in Run-off Against Libertarian." *Press-Tribune* (CA), July 24, 1991.

Riley, Ellen. "B.T. Bids for Assembly Seat." *Lincoln New Messenger*, July 4, 1991.

Roach Ron. "CCC Rescued by Its Candid Director." *San Diego Tribune*, February 27, 1980.

——"B.T. Collins: The Mouth That Roared Once Too Often." *San Diego Tribune*, November 6 1981.

——"Governor's Conservation Corps Still Surrounded by Controversy." *San Diego Tribune*, March 30, 1979.

——"Tough New Director Saves CCC." *San Gabriel Valley Tribune*, March 9, 1980.

Roberts, Cynthia. "The Outrageous B.T.—Brown's Strong Left Arm." *California Journal*, December 1977.

Rood, W.B. "Brown Shifts Signals on Key Lobbyist Post." *Los Angeles Times*, January 14, 1979.

——"Assembly Panel Eliminates Conservation Corps Funds." *Los Angeles Times*, March 21, 1979.

Sacramento Bee. "Brown Appointments—Committee Accepts 1, Rejects 1." April 15, 1970.

——"CCC to the Rescue." February 28, 1980.

——"Inmates Challenge CYA Chief on Complaint Policy." April 19, 1991.

——"Jerry Brown Must Fix Ego, Ex-aide Says." October 7, 1987.

——"Senate Approves CCC Extension, Praises Members." March 1989.

——Capitol Bureau, "The . . . Uh, News . . . Still Drags On." October 30, 1977.

Sacramento News and Review. Editorial. "B.T. and Literacy." April 25, 1991.

——Editorial. "Farewell, B.T." March 25, 1993.

Sacramento Union. "Troops Get Loud Applause." May 26, 1991.

——Editorial. "A Fresh Beginning at Youth Authority." November 18, 1991.

——Editorial. "Collins' Corps." January 3, 1980.

——Editorial. "Has Jerry Brown Created a Political Monster?" June 1, 1981.

——Editorial. "Whirlwind B.T. Collins May Find Higher Niche." April 6, 1981.

——Opinion. "Three Cheers for B.T." April 24, 1991.

——Under the Dome. "Brown Outdraws Sheik." September 3, 1977.

San Diego Evening Tribune. "Candidate Collins: He's a Wilson Loyalist and He's Proud of It." August 23, 1991.

San Francisco Chronicle. "11th-Hour Candidacy Raises Some Hackles." June 15, 1991.

——"B.T. Collins Top Aide to Treasurer." January 18, 1989.

San Francisco Chronicle. "Court Ruling Puts B.T. Collins Back on Ballot for Assembly." June 18, 1991.

——"Plans to Punish Legislators If Budget Stalls Again." February 22, 1993.

——"The Face of Brown's CCC is Grimy and Proud." and "A Toast to Malathion." July 16, 1981.

——Editorial. "A True Friend for Kids in Need." June 11, 1991.

San Francisco Examiner. "In the CCC Hard Work Pays Off." March 10, 1980.

San Jose (CA) Post-Record. "He Raised His Right Hook and Was Admitted to Practice Law." June, 1994.

San Jose Mercury News. "6,000 Gather in Sacramento to Cheer on US Troops in Gulf." February 19, 1991.

——Editorial. "Correct That Complaint." April 22, 1991.

Saunders, Debra. "B.T.: All Hard Work and Spectacle." *San Francisco Examiner*, March 22, 1993.

Shields, Mark. "I Never Liked Any Politician More." *Washington Post*, April 3, 1993.

Shribman, David. "Political Overload: California Voters Must Sort Out a Host of Candidate Messages in Tuesday's Primary." *Wall Street Journal*, May 20, 1992.

Simon, Mark. "Embrace Those Gentle Heroes Left Behind." *Peninsula Times Tribune* (CA), October 2, 1989.

——"Leadership: The Essential Need to Establish Integrity." *Peninsula Times Tribune*, April 29, 1992.

Skelton, George. "B.T. Collins —A Gentle Side to the Bluster." *Los Angeles Times*, March 22, 1993.

Skelton, Nancy. "Conservation Corps Probe Stepped Up." *Los Angeles Times*, April 7, 1979.

Stammer, Larry. "Panel Votes Extension of Conservation Corps." *Los Angeles Times*, February 28, 1980.

Stanley, Alessandra. "Enigmatic Jacques Barzaghi, Brown's Man Behind the Scene." *New York Times*, April 18, 1992.

Stanton, Sam et al. "Heart Attack Kills B.T. Collins." *Sacramento Union* and *Sacramento Bee*, March 20, 1993.

Stanton, Sam. "Collins Decisively Wins 5th Assembly District." *Sacramento Bee*, September 18, 1991.

——"Alby, Collins Fire New Rounds In 5th District's 'Religion' War." *Sacramento Bee*, July 11, 1991.

——"B.T. Collins Gives Foes a Free Shot." *Sacramento Bee*, December 27, 1992.

——"Collins to Fight for Spot on Ballot." *Sacramento Bee*, June 14, 1991.

Steinke, D.L. "Chief of Staff B.T. Collins: Soldier of Good Fortune for California." *Timberline Times (CA)*, June 1982.

Stephans, Dan. "Fellow Vet Gives Finest Salute to B.T." Commentary in *Neighbors*, April 1, 1993.

Stephenson, Carolyn. *Friends for Folsom Today*, April 16, 1993.

Stockton Record. "Vietnam War Memorial Far Off Schedule." March 31, 1987.

——"Youth Corps Chief Names Objectives." March 1, 1979.

Stumbo, Bella. "Brown's New Staff Chief Has No Love for the Boss." *Los Angeles Times*, November 1, 1981.

Suttertown (CA) News. Editorial. "B.T.'s No Devil." August 1, 1991.

Tachibana, Judy. "Rally for Troops at Capitol." *Sacramento Bee*, February 19, 1991.

Taylor, Bob. "B.T. Collins at Its Helm Fighting for CCC's Life." *Sacramento Union*, May 7, 1979.

Tehaar, Joyce. "Vietnam Taught Collins to Manage By Example." *Sacramento Bee*, February 10, 1989.

Thomston, Gus. "Rabbi Criticizes Tactic by Supporters of Alby." *Auburn Journal* (CA), July 12, 1991.

Totaro, Michael J.L. "Remembering SCU Graduate and Board of Regents Member B.T. Collins." *Santa Clara University News.* April 18, 1993.

Tremblay, J.P. "Alby, Collins Trade Charges Over Funding." *Sacramento Union*, June 28, 1992.

——"Capitol's Farewell to B.T. Collins." *Sacramento Union*, March 25, 1993.

——"Collins Dies; Capitol Mourns Ex-Employee." *Sacramento Union*, March 29, 1993.

——"Collins Faces Alby—Familiar Ring?" *Sacramento Union*, April 26, 1992.

——"Insiders Rule Assembly Races." *Sacramento Union*, June 4, 1992.

——"Name Recheck Makes Collins an Ex-Candidate." *Sacramento Union*, June 13, 1991.

——"Saying B.T. Will be Missed an Understatement." *Sacramento Union*, March 21, 1993.

——"Showman Led a Colorful Life." *Sacramento Union*, March 20, 1993.

Trotter, Jim. "Collins Demands Literacy at CYA." *Sacramento Bee*, April 19, 1991.

——"To B.T. Collins, the Final Word Was Service." *San Jose Mercury News*," March 24, 1993.

Uelmen, Gerald, Dean School of Law. "B.T. Collins Dies March 19." *Law Alumni Newsletter*, Santa Clara University, April 1993.

University of Santa Clara School of Law Newsletter. "S.B.A. Board Tackles Budget." September 29, 1972.

USA Today. "Jail Lesson." April 19, 1991.

Valley Forge Hospital Newsletter. "Numbah One at VFGH: Good Example Set by Officer Patient Here." Winter, 1967.

Valley Veteran Newsletter. "Vietnam Veterans Say Good Bye to Their Best Friend." March/April 1993.

Wallis, Claudia. "Trying to Thwart the Fruit Fly." *Time*, July 27, 1981.

Walsh, Eleanor. Letter to the Editor. "B.T. Is a Respected Man." *Press-Tribune* (CA), September 21, 1990.

Walters, Dan, "Collins Will Be Sorely Missed." *Sacramento Bee*, March 25, 1993.

——"B.T. Strikes Again." *Sacramento Bee*, April 22, 1991.

Walther, Tony. "Challenger Vote Close in B.T. Race." *Press-Tribune* (CA), June 3, 1992.

Washington, Erwin. "Veterans' Call to Unity Month Law." *Southland News*, September 25, 1982.

Washburn, Patricia. "Can B.T. Collins Conserve the Conservation Corps?" *California Journal*, May 1979.

Water, Earl. "Conserve the Corps." *Napa Register*, January 24, 1980.

Wattenberg, Ben J. "Coaching from the Sidelines: A Conversation with Governor Jerry Brown and George Will." *Public Opinion*, June/July 1984.

WEAVE Annual Reports. 1990 . . . 1992.

WEAVE Newsletter. Winter 1990

Weir, Jeff. "California Dedicates Its Vietnam Monument." *Orange County Register*. December 11, 1988.

Werkman, Dirk. "Collins Holds Edge in Assembly Fight." *Sacramento Union*, June 3, 1992.

Wexler, Mark. "B.T. and the CCC." *National Wildlife*, February, 1982.

Willing, Richard. "I Will Not Be Silenced." *Associated Press*, Washington Bureau, February 5, 1992.

Willis, Doug. "Politicians, Veterans Honor Collins." *Auburn Journal (CA)*, March 25, 1993.

Wilson Weekly California Report. "A Veterans Day Message." November 9 1991.

Wilson, Theo. "Just What the Doctor Ordered for Vets." *New York Daily News*, December 1, 1967.

——"Troupers and Readers in Really Big Show." *New York Daily News*, December 18, 1967.

Wyman, Barbara. "B.T., A Touch of Wry." *Santa Clara Magazine*, Summer, 1989.

Yarborough, Lesley. "Former Director Speaks Out About California Conservation Corps." *California Journal*, date unknown.

Printed in the United States
120757LV00001B/4/P

9 780979 869747